Shamanic Healing
and Ritual Drama

Health/Medicine and the Faith Traditions

Edited by James P. Wind and Martin E. Marty

The series Health/Medicine and the Faith Traditions
explores the ways in which major religions
relate to the questions of human well-being.
It issues from Project Ten, an interfaith program
of The Park Ridge Center for the Study of
Health, Faith, and Ethics.

Barbara Hofmaier, Publications Coordinator

The Park Ridge Center
is a corporation of the Lutheran General Health System.

The Park Ridge Center
676 N. St. Clair, Suite 450
Chicago, Illinois 60611

Shamanic Healing and Ritual Drama

HEALTH AND MEDICINE IN NATIVE NORTH AMERICAN RELIGIOUS TRADITIONS

Åke Hultkrantz

A Crossroad Herder Book
The Crossroad Publishing Company
New York

1997

The Crossroad Publishing Company
370 Lexington Avenue, New York, NY 10017

Copyright © 1992 by Lutheran General Health System

Printed in the United States of America

Library of Congress Cataloging-in-Publication Data

Hultkrantz, Åke.
    Shamanic healing and ritual drama : health and medicine in native
North American religious traditions / Åke Hultkrantz.
      p. cm. — (Health/medicine and the faith traditions)
    Includes bibliographical references and index.
    ISBN 0-8245-1188-3 (cloth) ; 0-8245-1664-8 (pbk.)
    1. Indians of North America—Religion and mythology. 2. Indians
of North America— Medicine. 3. Indians of North America—Health and
hygiene. 4. Folk medicine—North America. 5. Shamanism—North
America. I. Title. II. Series.
E98.R3H825 1992
299 .75—dc20   92—18476
                                                       CIP

The map on page 7 has been adapted, with the permission of The University of Chicago Press, from the "Outline Map of Indian Tribes of North America" by Driver, Cooper, Kirchoff, Libby, Massey, and Spier, in *Indian Tribes of North America*, Supplement to *International Journal of American Linguistics* 19, no. 3 (July 1953). Indiana University Publications in Anthropology and Linguistics Memoir 9.

Contents

Foreword

Åke Hultkrantz's pioneering work on health, medicine, and religion in Native North American traditions appears against the context of controversies that began half a millennium ago.

Five hundred years after Christopher Columbus's first voyage across the Atlantic, the heirs of the Europeans (and, later, Africans and Asians) who came from one hemisphere were still debating how to think about the descendants of the people who were already living on the two continents. And vice versa.

The meaning of the voyage remained in dispute. Across all ideological boundaries people agreed that the old term, "the discovery of America," was useless—except to describe the naiveté of those who could not picture the worldview of people who did not feel their continents needed discovering. They could only agree positively that 1492 referred to that voyage of exploration after which Europeans began conquest and permanent settlement.

The naming of the people in the Americas also remained a source of confusion if not conflict. Columbus named them Indians, and this they were until decades ago when they and their friends began to assert the reasons for calling them what Hultkrantz does here and always: "Native Americans." Technically, they also were not native; ten or thirty thousand years ago, give or take a few thousand, their ancestors crossed the Bering Strait or a temporary landbridge, Beringia, to begin their claim on being what we today call Native Americans.

That quick recall of misperceptions, of misnamings of the Other, the stranger, helps provide a framework for this book. For most of the five hundred years of contact between the peoples, those of European descent paid little positive regard to the "health, medicine, and religion" of the natives.

Health? They may have been frightened by robust warriors, but they also saw the Native Americans, who lacked immunity to European diseases, die off without finding means to resist the invasion of threats to health. They saw people die young. In the nineteenth century, as part of policies of "reservating" and "civilizing" the people they called Indians, their would-be benefactors did establish some primitive clinics and found some people of goodwill to serve in them. But the transaction was one-way: the missionaries, educators, and government agents would bring health, not learn from the Native Americans on their reservations.

Medicine? That was worse. The explorers, conquerors, and displacers did get to see the dispensers of medicine in action. Key among them were the shamans—not thus named at the time—who were dismissed as "medicine men." Reports through the centuries wrote them off as magicians, appealers to superstition, tricksters and con artists who left their victims worse off than they had been. Whoever wants to study Native American religion has to take a drastically different view of these shamans—as Hultkrantz, with realism and sympathy alike, here does.

Religion? That was even less interesting and more repugnant to the Europeans. The Native Americans were seen as either having no religion, or having devilish, satanic, evil superstitions. By no means were all the missionaries mere chaplains to the conquerors. There is an often untold story of efforts by the Catholic brothers in the Southwest of today's United States, who fought their fellow Spaniards over whether the Indians dare be enslaved, and who spoke up for at least their limited rights. Many of them were genuinely sympathetic with the people who were drawn to or forced to be part of the missions. But even such sympathy was marked by condescension, by unwillingness to see that Native American religion had served the people and might be appraised with empathy.

What was most consistently overlooked is precisely the point of Hultkrantz's book: that health, medicine, and religion taken together made up a coherent and credible system. It enabled Native Americans to live in a relationship to the environment in a way that did not lead to exploitation or exhaustion of that natural setting. This system demanded that Native American healers draw resources from the natural elements of that ecology—herbs, and the like—while they offered solace and aid also in the context of the seasons, the beauty of the landscape, the contact with the "spirits" that inhabited that natural order.

Seeing how that system was integrated and employed is a major theme in this book. Curiosity about Native Americans has grown in recent years. First came the self-assertion movements by the peoples themselves. Concurrent with "Black Power" causes, with feminist and Hispanic and homosexual and other movements of self-assertion, the Native Americans began to speak up to their neighbors. In effect, the message was this: Don't do all the defining. You have killed off our ancestors or let them die or moved them to reservations. You have named us, dismissed us, made decisions about our destiny. We want to be taken, at last, on our own terms. The interaction of health, medicine, and religion was one part of their culture that attracted notice.

Next came response from various non–Native Americans: "hippies," environmentalists, advocates of holistic health movements. Perhaps often romantically and with a spirit that rejected technological medicine, they oversimplified the Native American heritage. To them, the wisdom of that heritage was easily accessible. Whoever wished could borrow from it, acquire its modes, and counter the modern clinic, laboratory, or hospital, where herbs and potions, rituals and incantations, were rejected. Åke Hultkrantz is not a romanticizer or an oversimplifier. The very organization of his book shows him to be attentive to the thickness, the diversity, the unclassifiability of so much Native American medicine and religion.

If patient attention to Native American ways reveals how difficult it is to borrow, why should there be a book on the subject by a scholar like Hultkrantz? Someone down the street is certain to publish do-it-yourself kits for those who would like to adopt the trappings and externals of Native American ways; they will have more appeal. Hultkrantz, like most scholars, is demanding of attention and capable of throwing up barriers against oversimplifiers. Why follow his way? How can one put anything on these pages to work?

Some of the volumes in this series are justified by the fact that they reveal beliefs, customs, practices, and laws which the medical system must understand in order to promote helpful policies and care. Thus if millions of Muslims or Asians make up the clientele of hospitals in North America, if thousands of citizens from their worlds staff clinics and serve as physicians and nurses, then it is urgent that "everyone else" learn about their complex of health, medicine, and religion. But very few, far too few, citizens of pluralist America staff the meager clinics on the reservations. The Native American population in urban America is too dispersed and often too demoralized to make up a cohort demanding attention when people plan how to promote medical care and measures of health. So why read on?

As a devoted reader of Professor Hultkrantz's earlier books and of this one in manuscript, I would have to say, first, for intrinsic reasons. Perhaps nine out of ten books any of us read are not designed to promote our professions or help us remake the world. We read for enjoyment, fascinated by the acts of imagination of authors or their subjects. We read for humanistic reasons: the texts help us enlarge our own imagination so we grow more fully human by being able to picture ourselves being someone else, somewhere else, in some other time. The book has to be of intrinsic interest: the subject and the style have to carry us along, even if no practical result is to come.

Second, by diagnosing the health-medicine-religion nexus, close as it is to the heart of personal and social existence, Hultkrantz promotes better understanding between present-day Native Americans and the rest of the citizenry. That goal may not be highest on governmental agenda, but it is critical if we are to deal with white guilt, Native American understandings and misunderstandings, unfinished business in general. The Native American still represents the misunderstood Other close to the home of 250 million to 300 million North Americans who cannot call themselves Native. Understanding those with whom the rest of us share a continent can make possible a change in us, so that we relate better to people who are also Other, on other continents.

Native Americans themselves have a third reason to read this book. Catholics find a Catholic book in this series of special interest, as do Muslim-Americans, Hindu-Americans, Jewish-Americans, Anglican-Americans, or other peoples whose life, creed, and practices have received attention here. The purpose behind these explorations of traditions includes making resources in each available to those who bear them. Native Americans, as Hultkrantz points out, are heirs of oral tradition, which means that they usually live by the norms that come with the stories of their peoples, their "tribes"—to use another term applied to their lives by others. But these Native Americans also read, and their traditions are being set down by themselves and patient, friendly informed observers like the Scandinavian Hultkrantz who is so at home with them.

I do not want to minimize one other feature of books in this series: they promote understanding and the possibility of borrowing. No author has set out to make a tradition easily available; good students of heritages know best how untransportable are many of their features. Hultkrantz knows that the dimensions of Native American healing processes are webbed in with other elements of Native American life that do not easily translate into other cultures.

But such borrowing goes on, and Hultkrantz performs a service by describing something of the terms that would be necessary if practices associated with it are to promote health. Never does he force the practices of one set of Native Americans into the patterns of another or, what would be worse, push them all into a mold. His book has to be organized as a kind of tour before it can come to elements of synthesis. But he succeeds in depicting ways of life that have their appeal. Some parts of those traditions can soften the hardness of technical medicine. From others readers can learn more about the communal context that bureaucratized medical networks in the rest of American culture often lack. Attitudes toward peoplehood, nature, the rhythms of life and the seasons of the year, the power of ritual— all these are displayed and exemplified on these pages.

The reader, then, does well to be prepared for visits to Ojibway and Tlingit people, to Shoshoni and Navajo; to the ways of the shaman and the keepers of shaking tents, sweat lodges, and holyways. All this en route to a conclusion that recognizes "a field of difficulties," but not of impossibilities. This book is thus one more contribution in a series that deals with possibilities offered others by those who are to them the Other. No one in the world could guide so effectively as Åke Hultkrantz. The rest of the book is his, and that of the Native Americans he knows and describes so well.

Martin E. Marty

Preface

Although several works on tribal medicine among Native North Americans have been published, none has integrated the rich materials in a meaningful way. That is the task I have undertaken in this book. The underlying theme is that Native American medical beliefs and practices can be assessed only in relation to their religious ideas. Health, disease, and death are woven into a pattern that is understandable only if we see it from the point of view of religion.

I have selected different cultural achievements from several tribal areas in North America to discuss such issues as health, illness, madness, suffering, caring, ethics, healing practices, the treatment of the aged, death, and dying—in short, the themes delineated for treatment in the Health/Medicine and the Faith Traditions series. In addition, this study offers vivid portraits of medical scenes and dramatic descriptions of shamanic performances. It all amounts to proving that Native American healers have paid their greatest attention to a psychosomatic medicine that is directly related to religion—a medicinal dimension largely absent among Western doctors.

Introduction

Anyone familiar with Native North Americans knows the crucial role of the medicine man in their hunting societies. A medicine man—sometimes a medicine woman[1]—is more than a doctor, or physician. The medicine man gives evidence of powers that exceed the bounds of a normal individual. He is, in other words, a person with supernatural gifts, and he has relations with supernatural powers. Indeed, his curing capacities are a gift of higher powers. In this respect the American healer deviates basically from his colleague within the Euroamerican medical tradition. In aboriginal North America, medicine and religion are two sides of the same coin.

This is the underlying assumption in the following effort to demonstrate the interaction of health, medicine, and religion in Native North American cultures. We need not seek the particular common features between medical philosophy and practice and religious beliefs and practices—the bonds are always there. From a wider perspective we perceive how all concern with health and curing is a religious transaction. If a person suffers from bad health, if he or she falls critically ill, it is all provided for by his or her relations with the supernatural world. Of course, smaller wounds and inflictions may be seen as independent of immediate religious motivation (or as so insignificant that this motivation falls away for the moment). The general rule, however, is that all disease has its origin in a disturbed relationship with the supernatural.[2]

This aboriginal conviction gives a most fascinating flavor to the understanding and treatment of bad health in Native North America. Of course, we are dealing here with a whole continent, and medical systems and activi-

1

ties vary a great deal among Native groups. In some societies the medicine man is a mystic, a shaman; in others he is supplanted by simpler "wise men" (and women) with no obvious relations to the supernatural, or even by fraternities of doctors who are learned in their subject but who work without the medicine man's charisma and insights into the other world. In some societies guardian spirits direct the medical operations; in others the curers scrupulously follow rules laid down by tradition. Such differences—and differences in ideas of illness, morality, sexuality, and life after death—make it necessary for us to observe various Indian cultures and traditions. Our road will take us over large parts of North America and into many changing milieus and situations. We shall find worlds that are sometimes poor and dull, at least in their outer aspects, but other times sparkling and exciting. And we shall find rich and splendid cultural traditions with fairly indifferent medical programs. We cannot forget that we are dealing with many tribes over an entire continent.

Native American medicine is strongly traditional. Even those healers who receive their medical instructions in visionary experiences of spirits act according to traditional patterns, for such experiences and such inspiratory instructions conform with old rules in the tribe. Although there is great diversity in the individual cases, the overall pattern remains the same. If, therefore, aboriginal medicine basically retains a conservative stamp, this is mostly due to its sacred, religious character, for religion is a conservative factor in culture. This is particularly true of enacted religion, the ritual expressions of religious beliefs. Anybody who has attended a Lutheran, Roman Catholic, or Greek Orthodox church service can attest to that. Native American rituals are no exception. They may sometimes change according to inspirational visions, but basically they keep their old structures. Since so much of medicine rituals among these peoples is linked to religious rituals, or may be identified as religious ritual, medical cures have a conservative emphasis.

Even when newer religions have broken this solid pattern—usually as a consequence of changed cultural situations brought about by the presence of white people—traditionalism enshrouds the new ways. A good example is furnished by the diffusion of peyotism, the ritual around the small cactus peyote which spread over areas of North America at the end of the last and during the first half of the present century. It made its way into the reservations where to some extent the traditional religion was receding under the pressure of Christian missionary activity. With peyotism a mixture of Catholic and Mexican rituals took over much of the scene. More and more, however, attitudes and ritual forms were adjusted to the Native North American patterns. Since peyote was regarded as a medical herb, besides having general supernatural qualities, the medical practice that was predominant in the area of adoption largely influenced its ceremonial setting.

All this means that even if we are looking into the use of Native American medicine today, we are facing an old tradition. The general contours of medical treatment are the same today as they were yesterday. Of course, some of the more extreme curing practices are no longer extant because they clash too much with modern life: the soul excursions in trance, for instance, have disappeared or are on the wane. Likewise, some modern practices borrowed from Western medicine may occasionally be observed in Native American medical routine. When medicine men work together with white doctors at hospitals, as happens both in Africa and North America, the psychic cure is possibly more in focus than it is in their original milieu. The medicine man is basically a psychotherapist.[3]

The traditionalism of Native American medical practice has been emphasized here because, in describing and analyzing this practice, we are often forced to return to sources from some decades ago, or even earlier. In these sources we find a fuller description of Native American medicine than we can gain by present-day observations. Traditional medical practices are today sometimes hidden to the outsider, much more so than in earlier days—a general consequence of Native discontent with anthropological observers. Yet in some cases Native Americans have pursued an aggressive medical program, challenging the supremacy of white medicine.

The persistence of Native American medical ideas has impressed many observers and, as we know, inspired forms of the new Euroamerican "alternative medicine." This is an interesting subject, but it cannot be dealt with in this volume.

Although old patterns remain, the contents are slowly changing in Native American medicine—a natural phenomenon in a set of cultures that are, as we shall see, so often reformed by inspirational visions. In our day pan-American ideas help to reshape the Native medicine. For some years recently the Stoney (Assiniboin) of Alberta arranged rendezvous for medicine men at which practitioners from tribes as different as the Aztecs, Navajo, Lakota, Iroquois, and Slave came together to exchange ideas and ritual procedures. Such trends point to an outgoing dynamic process in which many old customs will probably be discarded and new medical ways take form within the tribal context. It is not possible here to record all these changes, many of which are little known to the outside world, in a general treatise on traditional Native American health, medicine, and religion. In a very wide sense they are traditional, that is, Native American. On the other hand, their pan-American direction may in the long run erase old tribal traits and ideological boundaries and thus create a new picture—a more unitary but also less colorful picture, perhaps.

It is my endeavour in this book to present Native American medicine as it has been, and still is, within the tribal setting. The chapters follow a road over the North American continent from north to south, which is also a journey in time from old hunting patterns to more recent cultural outlooks, as we shall find. The two final chapters touch upon the new medicinal developments that have been prefigured in the preceding text.

The following account should give an overview of the richness of Native American traditions in medicine. It also aims at giving a vivid impression of the role that religion plays today and has played in this traditional medicine. Our sources are very uneven, and they do not always deal with all particulars about health and medicine. There is little information on health care, but more on such topics as healers, healing techniques, passages of life, dying, and the states of the dead. In Native American ideology all these items form a chain of beliefs and rituals, or a religious complex (belief complex, ritual complex) which stands apart from other religious complexes, sometimes conflicting with them. A study of North American religions reveals that the more loosely integrated a society is, the more profiled and independent are the belief complexes, and the more they tend to conflict with each other; the hunting religions are an example of this.[4] On the other hand, the more integrated and consolidated a society is, the better organized and integrated with each other are the belief complexes. Most agricultural religions give evidence of this. The health-medicine complex is very pronounced among hunters like the Plains Indians, among whom the demands of physical fitness are very high.

In the long run many North American religions have come to focus on health and disease. Navajo religion demonstrates this development beautifully, but we also find it among, for instance, the Plains and Great Basin groups. Concern about food and war gradually faded out during reservation times, whereas concern for health and family happiness became dominant issues. This was a natural process when white authorities had taken over the necessary external needs, providing nourishment and safety. After all, health and long life, shared with the ones we love, are the deepest desires of humankind.

It is my sincere hope that the outcome of this book will be an awareness in the mind of the reader that Native Americans are very much concerned about human health and that they see health problems in a religious perspective. This seems logical—after all, is not human life an existential issue, and are not all existential issues basically religious? They certainly are among Native Americans.

We shall begin our odyssey with a survey of the ethnographical map of North America and a general presentation of the medical ideas that have ruled Native medicine men and their clients.

INDIAN TRIBES OF NORTH AMERICA

(discussed in this book)

1   Ojibway (and Saulteaux)
2   Chippewa (branch of Ojibway)
3   Cree
4   Montagnais
5   Plains Cree
6   Iroquois
7   Tlingit
8   Haida
9   Tsimshian
10 Kwakiutl
11 Nootka
12 Coast Salish: Puyallup-Nisqually, Twana etc.
13 Washo
14 Paiute
15 Sheepeaters
16 Eastern or Plains Shoshoni
17 Comanche
18 Crow
19 Lakota (Oglala Lakota)
20 Arapaho
21 Kiowa
22 Pawnee
23 Cherokee
24 Natchez
25 Creek
26 Yuma, Mohave
27 Taos
28 Hopi
29 Zuni
30 Navajo
31 Apache
32 Pima
33 Papago

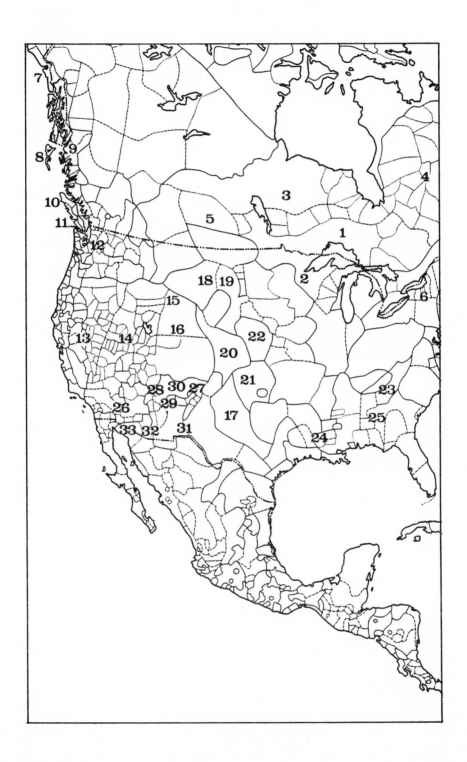

·1·

The Cultural and Religious Setting

Some time very long ago, perhaps about 30,000 years before the present time, the first ancestors of today's Native Americans arrived in North America.[1] At that time ice still covered enormous stretches of the northern parts of the Eurasian and North American continents, leaving here and there narrow corridors of ground with tundra grass vegetation where human and beast could roam. Periodically the Bering Sea bottom constituted a land bridge between northeastern Asia and Alaska. The proto-Mongoloid groups that lived in northern China and northeast Asia made their way over this bridge in pursuit of reindeer, mammoths, and bears. Little did they know that they had discovered a new, unsettled continent, thousands of years before Columbus thought that he had done the same thing.

The small hunting groups that filtered into the New World spread over the plateaus and valleys. As climatic conditions improved, and as the immigrants pushed further south, their ways of living became more settled, and they adjusted to divergent cultural and historical tradition, social preferences, and ecological possibilities. The immigrants—whom we may now call Native Americans, or even *Indians*, (the erroneous designation that Columbus and the conquistadors used)—were still hunters, but their cultures began to diversify as they adapted to new conditions. Many of their ancient cultural traits have survived right into our own century, such as some dwelling types (earth lodges, conical tents or tipis, birchbark lodges or wigwams, wickiups of grass and brush), feathered ornaments (including feathered crowns or "war bonnets"), a democratic political organization (relative lack of chiefly authority, predominance of tribal or group councils), hunting ceremonialism, and a deeply spiritual religion.

Moreover, some of the early regional hunting cultures remained the same in pattern and essence until recently. Thus, the Arctic and Subarctic hunting

9

cultures that for thousands of years had characterized the interior of Alaska and Canada were still functioning at the beginning of the nineteenth century, when they were increasingly changed through the influx of Euroamerican fur trade and industrial civilization. The interior Alaskan-Canadian cultures—with their use of snowshoes to hunt fur animals, their sledges (toboggans) and birchbark canoes, practice of shamanism, animal ceremonialism, and beliefs in supernatural animal masters, governing animal species— clearly represent a late continuation of Eurasian and American Paleolithic hunting culture. They may thus at least in part carry some of the cultural materials and ideas that once characterized the first immigrant groups in America.

Other hunting cultures display a change from the original patterns. The Eskimo have a distinct way of living on the Arctic coast, perhaps representing a specialized development of an old fishing culture around the shores of the Northern Pacific. Their material and spiritual culture is thoroughly adapted to their precarious existence in a world of ice and snow: their kayaks, harpoons, clothing, igloos, shamanism, hunting customs, and spirit beliefs testify to this close adaptation. Another branch of the expansive fishing culture is found on the North Pacific Coast. Tribes from the interior have created a strange but esthetically attractive culture, characterized by its rank structures, complex ceremonialism and symbolism, and exquisite wooden art. Experts have long wondered if this striking, seemingly non-American culture came about autochtoneously, without inspiration from outside. It is certain that Euroamerican stimulation produced its more exaggerated forms, such as the well-known large totem poles, which almost all belonged to the nineteenth century; however, direct connections over the Pacific Ocean have also been posited—these Indians had large, seaworthy wooden boats. There are reasons to suppose that American hunting and fishing cultures did not take form in splendid isolation, as many still think.

Behind the Northwest Coast and the coast range is the Plateau area, inhabited by people who are partly akin to the tribes of the coast but generally represent an inland hunting culture. They are best known for their guardian-spirit beliefs and winter dances.

South of the Northwest Coast culture proper, fishing played a major role along the coast down to Northern California (or even farther south: indeed, the Indians of the Santa Barbara region were probably the last outpost of the North Pacific fishing culture). In Central California, where oak groves covered the hills in the old days and climatic conditions were pleasant, the Indians collected acorns, fruits, berries, and wild seeds and supplemented this diet by hunting deer. Like the Indians on the Northwest Coast, where fish, berries, and some game could supply rich food resources, the Central Californians had proficient means of existence. Later observers have asked why these Indians never developed horticulture, since during the last thousand years they were familiar with agricultural Indians further south. Whether the Mohave Desert was an insurmountable barrier or not, it seems that the affluence of food products available precluded any initiatives to more work than necessary. And who could blame them?

The Californian Indians retained many of the cultural elements and customs of the hunters but developed within this pattern several institutions of their own: a shamanism built on spontaneous calling, puberty ceremonies, secret societies, and a lofty concept of the high god are the most conspicuous features in their religion. A multitude of cultural directions and influences have made Indian culture in California richly variegated.

As we go east from California, deserts and semideserts take over, in aboriginal times leaving few other animals for food than rabbits and, occasionally, antelopes, and not much of vegetational food either: some pine cones, seeds, and nuts. It is therefore not surprising that the scarce human inhabitants of the Great Basin were among the most destitute human beings on earth, suffering an extremely inhospitable environment and periodic starvation. Indeed, some of these Indians were reduced to a snake diet. In very early days this wide, monotonous area probably had a higher precipitation, more animals (such as bighorn sheep), and a better climate than today; however, increasing desiccation forced the Indians to adjust themselves drastically, to abandon large game hunting, and to adopt a limited vegetative diet. Rudimentary food ceremonies and visionary experiences characterized their religion.

This kind of living, nomadizing between groves of trees and bushes and spending the nights in primitive bush shelters, was once common over the so-called Greater Southwest, the enormous area taking in all land between the Mexican highlands in the south and the Plateau lakeland in the north, and between the Southern California coast ranges in the west and the Rockies and high plains in the east. What a great transformation in life-style this meant for a people originally adapted to the rich hunting life of the north!

Yet there were still greater changes to come, not least within this sterile area. About 5,000 B.C. the whole of North America was still settled by hunters and their descendants, fishermen and collectors. Then, suddenly, a new era was born in Mexico: humankind learned not only to consume but to produce. From the refuse heaps of the seeds gathered by women there grew plants that the women could put into the ground, sow, and harvest. Maize, beans, and squash became staple foods, which facilitated relatively fixed settlements and a greater population density. Rituals centered around the growth of vegetation became more important than the old annual hunting ceremonies or were amalgamated with the latter. As time passed, shrines and cultic centers developed into large establishments. Cultic servants or priests took over some of the tasks administered before by medicine men, and they achieved a high social standing. Collective priestly organizations and hierarchical systems diffused over wide areas of North America. Power through office slowly tended to supplant power through inspiration. It was a great revolution.

The agricultural perspective, with its well-integrated interpretation of a spiritual cosmic harmony, dispersed over the southern and eastern parts of North America during the first centuries of the Common Era. In the Southwest, hitherto a part of the desert cultures of the Greater Southwest, the well-known Pueblo culture slowly took form. In many aspects it represents an incipient phase of agricultural civilization, since it is heavily collectivistically oriented, with egalitarian ideals and people living together in multistoried adobe houses. All ceremonies are directed to secure rain and fertility, and they are performed by intricately tied ceremonial organizations. In the southeastern United States, more developed forms of Mexican high civilization found their ways along the coast and inland paths. The sacred kings, plazas, and temple mounds are long since gone, but the ways in which ceremonies and therapeutic procedures are conducted among latter-day Indians reveal their origins in a complex social and ceremonial setting.

General, less subtle influences of the horticultural wave found their ways into the Northeast, where maize cultivation partly reshaped local cultures. The Iroquois of New York stand out as the great agriculturists of the area. Their semimatriarchal social structure, with the living in longhouses ruled by matrons, seems to reflect an early agricultural horizon. In the whole Northeast, however, hunting remained an important subsidiary means of livelihood, and the informed observer can see how old hunting rituals are hidden behind the forms of horticultural ceremonies.

Further west, on the tall-grass prairies, many tribes, among others the Pawnee, made an existence that oscillated between maize cultivation on the riverbanks and hunting expeditions in the interior. Their most elaborate ceremonialism reminds us of Mexican prototypes. Indeed, the Pawnee and their Caddoan kinspeople constitute the best examples of tribes that in their cultural and religious composition have united the two main strands of Native American traditions: the hunting heritage and the agricultural heritage. Some Siouan groups along the Upper Missouri could also be included in this picture.

This was the situation when Euroamericans appeared on the scene. The immediate consequences of their appearance were a retreat of the eastern tribes into the interior of the country—typified by the removals of the Shawnee and Delaware Indians from their homelands in the eastern woods and coastland to the periphery of the woodlands in the west, and to the prairies and plains—and the spread of epidemics that reduced the aboriginal population from perhaps twelve million to under half a million individuals at the turn of the last century. We can imagine what these devastating diseases meant to the existential, social, and political concerns of the Indians, and to their ideas of medicine and health. Other factors associated with the Euroamericans that contributed to the destruction of the Native peoples were the military assault, the introduction of alcohol, the expansion of the fur companies, the spreading white settlements, the Christian missionary activities (as they were conducted in many places), and the devastation of land and animals. In at least one respect, however, the whites provided the Natives with a valuable gift: they gave them the horse.

The horse fundamentally changed Native life in most areas south of the Canadian woodlands—particularly on the prairies and plains, but also in parts of the Southwest, the Basin, and the Plateau. The invasion of northern and eastern tribes into the prairies and plains as a consequence of white oppression, and the acquisition by the Indians of guns and horses, created the prerequisites for the emergence of the colorful Plains Indian culture. The latter became a hybrid where old hunting patterns, ceremonial organizations, and cosmological perspectives derived from horticultural groups mixed with material instruments and means of communication taken over from the white culture. We all know how the Cheyenne, Crow, Lakota (Sioux), and Blackfoot a little more than a hundred years ago spent their days hunting buffalo on the wide open plains, participating in war organizations, and dancing the yearly thanksgiving dance, the Sun Dance. The mounted Indian with a warbonnet, living in a tipi is only thinkable in the Plains culture.

Other cultures were also partly refashioned through Euroamerican impact. In the Southwest the roving Navajo, Athapascan intruders from the far north, learned some ways of the Pueblo Indians during the Pueblo uprising in the 1690s, when these Indians settled with the Navajo. Later the Navajo became weavers, silversmiths, and shepherds, branches of art that they ultimately borrowed from the Spaniards. We shall later see how they adapted Pueblo Indian ceremonialism in ways that expressed their own concerns about health and welfare.

After 1825 the United States worked to create reservations for the Indian

populations. Policymakers believed that the relatively few Indians constituted an irritation to the flood of immigrants from the east, that they did
not utilize their enormous land areas in an efficient way, and that their
passage to modern agricultural techniques, which was desired, could best
be achieved within smaller reservation boundaries. Most reservations are
situated on lands once used by the respective Native American tribes. In
the late nineteenth century the decimation of the buffaloes and the end of
the cruel Indian wars made a quick resettlement on reservations necessary.
The white administrators' goals—a quick assimilation of the Natives to the
white religion and way of life—were not realized. Up to the present day
Indians have guarded their spiritual life and, to some extent, their ways of
living. It is not so much acculturation to the life values of white people as
tribal revivalism and pan-Indianism that today characterize the growing Native American populations.

This short summary of the development of Native American culture in
North America provides a glimpse of the many and complicated historical,
social, and ecological turns in the forming of regional ways of living and the
variety of local cultures. Any overview of Native healing systems in their
relation to religion has to take this multiple pattern into consideration: we
are concerned not with one healing tradition but with a whole continent of
healing traditions that vary from people to people. Each healing tradition is
grounded in the particular outlook that every culture offers (consider, for
example, Ruth Benedict's classic *Patterns of Culture*),[2] and it works with
the particular means of expression that the culture has brought forth. This
complicates the task of writing a "Native American version" of health, medicine, and religion.

Some might argue that our focal interest should be Native medicine as it
is performed today, in the less and less Native-looking reservation areas, but
we must not delude ourselves in believing that modern wooden houses,
Western dress, and salaried jobs also mean a Westernization of the mind.
At heart and in his thoughts the average Native American living on a reservation is still a Native American, rooted in ancient spiritual traditions that
compete with those of the West. The modern relativization of values and
new spiritual inroads find an eager and positive answer in Native American
traditions. There is, among Native Americans, an awareness of the immense
value of the collected experiences through history. There is also a strong
feeling for the values of one's own tribal traditions. This means that while a
Cherokee can appreciate the white person's heritage, he is much more in-
fatuated with the religious expressions of the Native North American, and
even more so with his own tribal spiritual heritage. In other words, even in

modernized reservational settings old tribal medical beliefs and practices live on. They have certainly been modified by the change of time and contacts over the tribal borders, but basically they follow the trodden historical paths. That is why it is so important to see Native healing systems against their diversified culture-historical background.

At the same time there are certain principles of Native American medicine that transgress ethnic and cultural limits. They will be our next concern.

As I stated in the introduction, in Native American thought health and medicine are part of the religious interpretation of the human situation. Health is the natural human condition for humans were created healthy, and health signifies a harmony and balance between the human and the supernatural world.[3] As we shall see, some tribes emphasize the latter point more energetically than do others. All Native Americans agree that a weakness of health, manifested in an injury or a disease, means a potential introduction to death. It sets a person off on a course that may lead to his or her transition to another state of being, an appearance as a spirit of the dead. In many tribes there is a linguistic means to express this continuity from living to dead: the same term is used for the human soul, or one of the human souls (the free-soul, the double), and the dead person. In other tribes it is rather the disruption between the living and the dead that is emphasied: the soul has one name, the dead person another. Sometimes the soul that reaches the final abode in the beyond is no more, but the individual reappears, covered by the name for ghost. In some Athapascan tribes, however, the name of the ghost is better not pronounced. Such cases indicate that death here means a transformation of the individual to something different or even unspeakable and dangerous.

The Native American has not been afraid to die—far from it. His warlike history in the past and his stoic appearance in the face of death by starvation give ample evidence of this; however, he appreciates life, for himself and his dear ones, and he is, like most humans, insecure in his perception of the vague and contradictory notions of a postmortal existence. Many old-time warriors have paid more attention to their behavior when threatened by sudden death than to their hopes for a future on the other side. The uncertainty of the other realm is reflected in the fact that most tribes set the land of the dead off from the world of the gods: at most we hear that the country of the dead is ruled over by a divine or spiritual personality, who may be the brother of the mythic culture hero or the first man. Only in some specific cases do the dead and the gods share the existence in the beyond: the Pueblo dead become *kachina,* spiritual beings who may live in the clouds and give rain and fertility, and the ancient sacred rulers of the Gulf Coast kingdoms joined the realm of the Sun.

The disruption between the worlds of the living and the dead is also expressed in the plentitude of horrifying ghost stories that are spread all over North America, particularly among hunting peoples. Sometimes the land of the dead is a place not far from the living, filled with whistling ghosts and ragged tents, as among the Blackfoot. Ideas of this kind are connected with the deficiency of ancestor cults in North America. An investigation of the available material tells us that only among Central Algonkians and Pueblo, and especially among the latter, are there tendencies toward a cult of the dead. In Africa where the ancestor cult is much developed among most Bantu tribes there is not such a gap between the living and the dead; the dead are, it has been said, part of the collectivity of the living.

Not fear of death, but avoidance of death—this has been the natural behavior among Native Americans. As some observers have noted, many Natives of western North America have avoided the "death stuff," even rushed out in fear from a lodge where a person has just died and abandoned it for good, but they have been prepared to die. Among the migratory tribes many people of old age were abandoned with some food and a fire against wild animals, for they were too decrepit to follow their kinfolk on their tiresome wanderings. Their fate was certain, but they did not fear it. They had had their time, and that was it.

They knew that death had been ordered into this world by the command of a divine person at the beginning of time—the Creator, or a clumsy assistant, or by a divination game between two primordial beings. They also knew that many dangers in life may promote disease and dying. The world is infested with dangerous spirits; even the helping spirits that are sought in visions may be of an evil kind. There are evil-minded witches, mostly former medicine men who now are intent on damaging their people, and who to this end use supernatural means. There are tabooed places and actions whose transgression may result in loss of medicine, paralysis, and even death. Or a person may be struck by lightning or drown because he has aroused the anger of the gods. Whatever the cause, death is never natural; it expresses the will of supernatural powers.

There is, therefore, no ultimate protection against death. It is true that the right way of living (according to tribal ideals), the care of one's family, and the participation in life-giving rituals like the *midewiwin* of the Ojibway, or the acquisition of many life-saving guardian spirits, could supposedly postpone the final exit from life. In the long run, however, such measures do not succeed.

The most common causes of death were disease and accidents in the old days, and they still are. Suicides and homicides occurred, but less frequently than they do now. Death in battle was formerly an honorable way of ending one's life; remember the battle cry, "today is a good day to die!" With the exception of the historical warfare between Natives and whites, however, few people died in battle in the old times; it was generally customary to interrupt an intertribal skirmish when a leader or a few men had been killed. Besides, even in the fiercest fights a warrior tried to save his life, although it might not have seemed so to an outsider who saw, for exmaple, a daring warrior riding in front of a large hostile force, relying solely on his guardian spirit or his ghost shirt.

Life, then, has always represented a supreme value to Native North Americans. Death is a vague dream; life is palpable reality, the subject of all care and all hopes. Threats to life have to be counteracted by one's own deliberate actions and by the help of others, friends and kinfolk, but primarily by knowledgeable specialists. Their task is to relieve the individual from diseases, the major threat to life. If we remember the dual origins of Native American cultures, the horizons of the hunter and the horticulturist, we may divide the therapeutic methods according to this same scheme.

The hunters, we recall, are individualists. Each man relies on his own skill and power. His capacity is strengthened by the supernatural power that he has achieved through spontaneous dreaming, a vision quest, or even inheritance or purchase. This supernatural power, the individual guardian spirit, is the foremost religious expression among Native North American hunters. We should of course not overlook the importance of the Supreme Being, the atmospheric divinities, the tribal ceremonies, and so forth in aboriginal religious beliefs, but what may be called the "vision complex" usually integrates these forces and rituals or constitutes a primary pattern of religious belief and behavior. It plays the same dominant role in North America as shamanism in Siberia, ancestor worship in Africa, and initiation rites in Australia. All beliefs and thoughts are oriented from the vision complex; all actions are placed in relation to their output of supernatural power.

The specialists able to handle diseases are judged according to the same value scale. There are the experienced old men and women who have little or no supernatural powers but who, on account of their wisdom and experiences, occasionally function as healers. There are the medicine men who derive their medical abilities from their guardian spirits. And there are in some tribes the shamans, whose very actions demonstrate their closeness to the supernatural powers who can save people.

Let us look a little closer into these three classes of healers among Native American hunting tribes—the wise men and women who will here simply be called herbalists, the ordinary medicine men, and the shamans who actually represent a certain sort of medicine men, the ecstatics.

The herbalist is a noninspirational person who deals with simple wounds, aches, and bone conditions because he knows through experience and tradition how to cure these afflictions. There are plenty of such individuals around. They are sometimes labeled medicine men or women, which may be confusing, for they usually do not share the medicine man's inspirational equipment. Their main resources are herbal medicines and magic formulas and movements, as well as cleaning medicines like incense and emetics. These wise folks do not always appear as herbalists, for instance, when they straighten broken bones or remove pus or practice bloodletting. Even in such cases, however, herbal medicines may sometimes be used as supplementary remedies. On the whole, *herbalist* seems to be a term that may be used for such healers.

It should be noted that with the exception of magic procedures the ambition of these herbalists is to work through natural means. The use of magic is a reminder of the fact that diseases ultimately may stem from supernatural causes.

By *medicine man* is here meant a doctor who has supernatural sanction to make a person well and who follows supernatural dictates in his curing activitis. Yet a medicine man may not be restricted to curing the sick. When the first French colonizers arrived in New France—roughly the area around the Great Lakes—they noticed that *les hommes-médécine* were not just curers but jugglers who could achieve many assertedly supernatural things. However, as their main feats were medical they were called medicine men. Native American languages do not usually single out the medical aspect but tend to use terms like *power men* or *mysterious men*. The effect of this was that *medicine* came to mean "supernatural power." It is from this usage that we have "good medicine," "medicine bag," and Medicine Bow (mountains). The import of all this is that a medicine man is not only a doctor but a man credited with handling supernatural power; there is no particular Native word to designate him as a doctor.

Sometimes the Siberian (Tungus) term *shaman* has been used to cover our word for doctor, but this is even less accurate. Although in careless linguistic usage any medicine man is called a shaman by some anthropologists, this term should better be limited to persons who manifest such powers and abilities that are typical for Siberian shamans. The shamanic ability *par préférence* is to fall into a deep trance or ecstasy (the two words will be used alternatingly, for they refer to the same state of mind, although the first one is medical, the other theological). In his trance the shaman may journey in spirit to far-off places or summon the spirits to give him counsel. The former technique has been called soul journeys or soul excursions. It is very typical for true shamanism, but the summoning of spirits is another genuine shamanic experience that must not be overlooked (as Mircea Eliade has done).[4]

While in a trance the shaman may find out the cause of a disease or even cure the diseased person. The ordinary medicine man may certainly heal the sick while in a light trance, but he does not sink down into the deep trance that is necessary for making contact with the supernatural world. Only at the moment of his calling into office may the ordinary medicine man have experienced such meeting with the powers.

The ways of the medicine men, including those medicine men who might be called shamans by us, will be richly demonstrated in the following chapters. The common denominator of the cure by shamans and medicine men is the fact that, since the origin of a disease is supernatural, it has to be removed or done away with in a supernatural way. The medicine man, or shaman, is primarily a religious—or, if we want to be precise, a religio-magic—officer. He is a religious man, insofar as he has supernatural sanction to perform his work, and his curing is undertaken with the help of spirits. He is at the same time a magician in his way of manipulating power. The word *magic*, however, is rather unfortunate and not a little ambiguous. It seems more important to underline that the medicine man or shaman is in the service of religion.

Besides using an outside therapist, the hunter who suffers from a disease may also resort to what may superficially seem to be a kind of self-healing in a religious context. He may get well by seeking a vision from a comforting spirit, by undergoing self-torture in order to evoke a spirit's compassion, or by going through rituals that may bring a reward of blessings. Often an individual performs these tasks to help out a sick family member or friend. The medicine man may be present, but his role is less personal, more ritualized.

Some persons may recover automatically, by confessing some taboo infringements (as has been common among the Eskimo and Lakota). As mentioned above, taboo transgressions may be punished by diseases, wounds, and paralysis. In most cases charismatic leaders supervise the confessions that are supposed to annihilate the scourge.

This model of medical treatment among North America's many hunting peoples is of course a very general one, and it should be checked against the specific cases in the following. It should also be observed that particular developments due to influences from other quarters, such as agricultural tribes, cannot be ruled out, particularly not in the Plains area and the Southwest. The following chapters will bear this piont out.

At the same time, it is clear that agricultural tribes often refer to healers like medicine men and even shamans, which are not very typical for these societies. In fact, here we have to deal with survivals or relics from the old hunting societies. As was noted above, it is sometimes easy to discover the hunting pattern beneath agricultural rituals; the same observation may be applied to the medical ideological pattern.

The essential feature of the agricultural ideology is, as we saw, the interpretation of existence in terms of fertility process and collective ritualism. Man's fate is likened to that of the plant, which is coming out of earth, growing, maturing, and finally being harvested. Ritualism has become more important than inspiration by spiritual powers (although the number of spirits has certainly not declined). Collective organizations and priest hierarchies have taken over many of the concerns that among hunting peoples fall upon the individual and his guardian spirits. These developments have, of course, had repercussions on medical service.

It is thus characteristic that the individual professionals retreat before the corporations, learned guilds of ritual undertakers and singers. Inspiration is replaced by erudition, the authority from spirits by hierarchical authority, the wisdom from the spirits by the learned knowledge of formulas, songs, and medical herbs. Mostly, however, there is a coexistence between inspired and noninspired doctors or doctoral organizations, sometimes in the form that some diseases are treated by the former, others by the latter. Or the inspired doctors divine the roots of the disease through their particular techniques, whereupon the ritualists take care of the curing process in their particular ways. Or the official circles use the medical service of the ritualists, whereas on the family level an inspired medicine man is called in. There are many possible combinations.

Seen in a larger perspective, there is a solid grounding of the medicine of the hunting pattern all over North America. In some nuclear areas, primarily in the south, agriculturists have introduced a more ritualistic medical cure. It is anchored in a more systematic worldview where the will of supernatural spirits has ceded to the more impersonal idea of the balance of the universe. This idea is largely a product of the horticultural tribes, brought to North America from Mexico, we presume, and first of all realized in the Pueblo culture of the Southwest and the Mississippian temple-mound culture of the Southeast. As outlined earlier, influences from these cultures spread to marginal groups in the Southwest and California, and to the Prairie and Plains Indians. Through the pan-Indian movements of the last seventy years the ideas of cosmic harmony have become synonymous with North American religious perspectives in general.

According to these ideas, sometimes labeled "cosmotheistic" (Hartmann), sometimes "cosmo-magical" (Wheatley),[5] disease and pain represent disruptions in the harmonious cosmic pattern that involves gods and spirits, people and animals, and all of nature. The medical performances aid at reestablishing the disturbed pattern, placing humans again inside the cosmic order. In some tribes this restoration of health is theoretically implied in the ritual performances, whatever their character; in other tribes it is plastically mirrored in the dramatic sequences of the ritual. We shall see examples of both alternatives.

The final stage of Native American therapy is manifested by the health and cure programs that are at least partly inspired by Euroamerican sources, partly by pan-Indian remedies. Chapters at the end of the book will deal with the broad range of these phenomena.

·2·

Traditional Medicine in the Northeast

Our journey across North America will start in the boreal regions, among the northern woodland peoples whose cultures in so many ways continue the Paleolithic traditions in northern Eurasia. It is no caprice that we begin here. As we have seen, this was the area where the first Indians, and the first medicine men, arrived from the Old World. The very fact that there is a cultural continuum between Canadian Indians and North Siberian cultures—scholars usually speak of a Circumpolar or Circumboreal culture—indicates the ancient character of this stratum. Naturally, we cannot today expect to find a Paleolithic cultural program realized in Canadian Indian life. Yet there are patterns and relics that remind us of the past continuum. Climatic conditions and ecological adaptations have contributed to their retention. The ideology produced around health and medicine pertains in many respects to this old and vast horizon.

Alaska and Canada are mainly populated by two large Indian linguistic families, the Athapascans and the Algonkians. The former dominate Alaska and Western Canada, the latter Eastern Canada and parts of the northeastern United States. The Athapascans are fairly recent immigrants, perhaps from the seventh to the second millenium B.C.E. Their cultures are not so well known, however, since they were much changed by the fur trade when the first source writers appeared. From the evidence we have it would seem that the Athapascans have been only weakly integrated with the Circumpolar culture, probably because they had received decided influences from the emerging East Asian cultures before the time of their immigration.

The Algonkians are in comparison more interesting for our purposes. Although they, too, were influenced by the fur trade they have kept many of their old customs until recent times, customs which often have a clearly Circumpolar stamp. Their religious features are also better known than those of their Athapascan neighbors. There are excellent descriptions from two Algonkian divisions, the Cree and the Ojibway. These Indians inhabit the northwestern and southern areas of the so-called Canadian (or Precambrian) Shield, an enormous area of woodland, lakes, and bogs (and, in the far north, tundra) that includes Manitoba, Ontario, part of Minnesota, Michigan, and Wisconsin, and the southern part of Quebec. The Cree are found in the north of this area, the Ojibway in the south. Culturally there is no great difference between the Cree and Northern Ojibway, whereas the Ojibway of the western Great Lakes and Minnesota and Michigan may be said to have developed more complex cultural forms. The Cree, once roving through the woods far north of Lake Superior, live today further northwest but mingle with the Ojibway. The latter, coming from the border lands of the Great Lakes, have taken over areas left by the Cree in their westward expansion. In many cases it is the matter of an "ojibwayization" of the vast Cree population.

The Ojibway and Cree have been big-game hunters, following the moose and the woodland caribou on their wanderings, and also killing bear, beaver, and geese. They are still hunters today, but their ways have been changed by the fur trade and modern urbanization. Snowshoes, toboggans, and canoes make the passage through the wilderness possible. Formerly people lived in birchbark-covered tents, conical or dome-shaped ("wigwams"), during the summer, and in ridgepole lodges covered by skins during the winter. Today these lodges have been substituted by modern habitations, but the Shaking Tent ritual (see below) is still performed in a tent. For most of the year the Indians in the northern districts live in small groups, unless they belong to larger urban settlements. In the southern part of the area fishing, gathering of wild foods, and, in some places, even a little corn cultivation have constituted the staple economy besides the products of hunting (moose, deer, bear).

The social organization varies according to natural and cultural conditions. In the north, the group structure does not exceed the family unit or task group size except during the summer months when various groups come together in bands. In these communities the shaman is often more respected than the hunting chief. In Minnesota and Wisconsin there are larger units with clan totemism: each individual belongs to a clan named after an animal, bird, or fish. These clans are patrilineal and exogamous. One, two, or more clans make up a phratry. Thus, the Fish phratry consists of clans named after different fish species, while the Loon phratry includes the Loon, Goose, and Cormorant clans. The clan and phratry organization is not common among the technologically simple peoples but presupposes a more complex organizational level.

The religious picture also varies with the cultural levels. The Cree in the northwestern woods believe in *manitous* (spirits) everywhere in nature, in the sacred treatment of food animals (animal ceremonialism, in particular bear ceremonialism), in animal masters, and frightful cannibal spirits. Like all other Algonkians they venerate a Supreme Being, called Manitou or Kitche Manitou, Great Spirit. (This is the Great Spirit that we know from the general literature on Native Americans.) Hunting luck is secured through guardian spirits, which are achieved during vision quests in adolescent years. As a gift from the spirit every hunter carries his own medicine bag, which helps him in the chase. Hunters also receive spontaneous dreams, inspired by the manitous. Shamanism is common.

The Southern Ojibway offer in some respects a more complex picture, mirroring their contacts with more advanced semiagricultural societies (perhaps also a heritage from the prehistoric Hopewell civilization). The world of spirits is the same as among the more northerly groups, although cannibal spirits are practically absent, and there is the idea of a cosmic fight between thunderbirds and monster snakes. The vision quest is a ritual for young boys and is much regulated, with fasting, blackening of the face, four days' isolation in a distant hut in the woods, partly under the supervision of an elder, and festive rituals on the successful return of the visionary. The single most important ceremony is the *midewiwin*, the annual celebration of the Great Medicine Society. The latter consists of men and women who have been initiated into one or several of the degrees of this secret organization. Through their secret knowledge they appear as healers. This organization shows us a partial collectivization of the medical profession. True shamans may certainly be members of this society, but they also operate independently.

As will be understood from this short survey, the issues of health and medicine have a prominent place in the Cree-Ojibway world. Genuine shamanism flourishes in the north but is also found in the southern areas. Here, however, we also meet a ceremonial organization of doctors, including both shamans and sucking medicine men, that indeed has become the apex of ritual activities. In its strong appearance it is a counterpart to other American complex ceremonies, such as the Sun Dance among the Plains Indians or the kachina dances among the Pueblo Indians. This demonstrates clearly the importance of health and disease ideology among the northern tribes.

THE CARE OF THE SICK: A SEVENTEENTH-CENTURY DOCUMENT

All writers agree on the strong feelings of solidarity, generosity, and helpfulness that characterize the small Cree and Ojibway groups. Kindness, not least to the children, distinguishes people's emotions within the group. Only uncooperative tribal members and those who break the tribal moral code are excluded from the solidarity. They are also looked down upon and ridiculed.

Their care and kindness, and the limitations of this behavior, are also reflected in the treatment of sick persons. In order to illuminate how the conditions were in the first days of encounter between Native Americans and Europeans I should like to quote passages from the well-known Jesuit missionary, Paul Le Jeune.[1] He visied the Montagnais of southern Labrador in the 1630s. The Montagnais are a Cree-speaking population who today have lost most of their old customs. They are not, strictly speaking, counted among the Cree, but the customs and religions of the two peoples were in the past nearly identical.

Father Le Jeune reports that sick children were treated with utmost endearment; even a father would fondle and comfort his sick baby in the way a mother did. On the other hand, sick grown-ups were not particularly attended to when they asked for food:

> As to the food, they divide with a sick man just as with the others; if they have fresh meat they give him his share, if he wants it, but if he does not eat it then, no one will take the trouble to keep a little piece for him to eat when he wants it; they will give him some of what they happen to have at the time in the cabin, namely, smoked meat, and nothing better, for they keep the best for their feasts.

Elsewhere Le Jeune states that the Indians were never keen on coaxing a sick person to eat; we may add, a more urging attitude would not be in line with their general ideas of interpersonal behavior. When once on a journey the good Father suffered from a stomach ailment and he asked his Indian hosts for a little water, they offered him some melted snow.

> As this drink was bad for my disease, I made my host understand that I had seen a lake not far from there, and that I would like very much to have some of that water. He pretended not to hear, because the road was somewhat bad, and it happened thus not only this time, but at any place where the river or brook was a little distance from our cabin. We had to drink this snow melted in a kettle.

Another lesson Le Jeune learned was to endure suffering and hardship when there was no food during the winter. The Indians warned him not to become sad; they exhorted him to laugh in face of all adversities. During a period of sickness they admonished him, "Do not be sad; if thou art sad, thou wilt become still worse; if thy sickness increases, thou wilt die. See what a beautiful country this is; love it; if thou lovest it, thou wilt take pleasure in it, and if thou takest pleasure in it thou wilt become cheerful, and if thou art cheerful thou wilt recover."

The trying climate was difficult for the sick. Le Jeune states that as long as they could eat they were carried on sleds when the group moved. Those who did not want food any more were abandoned, or even killed—according to Le Jeune, a deed of compassion. The sick were also done away with when people were starving, and aged people who were too feeble to follow their kinfolk on their wanderings shared the same fate. Up to our own days travelers have found remains of camp fires where abandoned sick or old people have spent their last hours, finally falling victim to beasts of prey. Such abandonments have been common in the northern parts of the world, where hunting peoples in search of game have been forced to extended wanderings, particularly in wintertime. There is plenty of evidence from Canada, the Plateau, the Basin, and the Plains. The killing of the sick and aged was everywhere thought of as a good deed for their own good. There are instances from all over North America, from the Eskimo in the north to the Seri in the south. Occasionally the infirm asked their relatives to kill them, or they committed suicide.

Belief in a postmortal existence facilitated such actions. It is true that among the Ojibway and Cree, as among other North American aborigines, beliefs in life after death have been vague and contradictory. Only a few have managed to visit the beyond—medicine men, some visionaries, sick persons in a coma. For them this other life has been a palpable reality. Like other Native Americans, however, the common Ojibway and Cree only believes in what he has himself experienced or what a reputed visionary has experienced. There is always a doubt in his mind as long as he has not had a visionary glimpse of the world of the dead. When Le Jeune asked for the conditions of the killed beaver in the land of souls his informant angrily retorted, "Be silent, thou hast no sense: thou askest things which thou dost not know thyself: if I had ever been in yonder country, I would answer thee."

Still, there is an old tradition among these peoples about what the fate of the dead is like, and the subjective experiences are spun on this tradition. Le Jeune tells us that the Montagnais dead depart for a large village where the sun sets. They spend their time there hunting, apparently in a happy mood. Practically everybody comes to this place (we may make exceptions for wrongdoers), that is, at least every Montagnais. There is the notion that the dead travel to the beyond over the Milky Way, and this may indicate that the land of the dead is situated in the sky, an opinion held by the Montagnais of this century.

Information from the Cree proper is much later than the Jesuit documents, but the picture that is suggested by our sources makes it probable that the Cree have embraced the same afterlife conceptions as the Montagnais'. In our own days, Christian ideas of heaven and hell have mostly taken over.

The conclusion we can draw from all this is that the relative consolation of a happy existence after death (reflecting the order of life on earth) constituted a rationale for the abandonment or killing of diseased and aged persons right up to our own time. The individuals might have disputed the exact contours of the other-world existence, but they were positive that they should live on in a happy realm. Since this was the case weak and sick people would fare better in that other world than in this miserable existence, full of daily toil, cold and famine, and other suffering.

The appearance of Christian eschatological ideas may have changed this certainty, at least in part. It is true that to some extent Christian doctrine was a supplementary force, strengthening many old values. Mostly, however, it formed a separate segment of religious beliefs, activated intermittently. Christianity introduced the concepts of hell and damnation, and thereby reduced the Algonkians' certainty of a safe postmortal existence. Since the seventeenth and eighteenth centuries, Christian eschatological dualism has been grafted on traditional Cree and Ojibway ideas of the future state. Unfortunately, we do not know how this change affected the custom of abandoning the aged and infirm. It seems reasonable to assume that a son who had to expose his mother did so in the belief that she was a person worthy of entering the happy hunting grounds.[2]

HEALTH, WELL-BEING, AND THE CAUSES OF DISEASE

The Cree and Ojibway have always been concerned about their health. Hunting luck and health are indeed their major concerns. If we except the epidemics of smallpox introduced by the whites and the sufferings of starvation during severe winters, particularly among the Cree, theirs is a history of relative well-being and, in the case of the Ojibway at least, of a good life. A missionary to the southern Ojibway, Rev. J. A. Gilfillan, testified that he rarely saw a crippled, diseased, or mentally retarded Ojibway.[3] The situation could be different among the Cree, where hunger and hunger hallucinations produced an identity crisis: the suffering person believed, and others believed, that he had turned into a *witiko*, a mysterious cannibal being. He was reputed to have eaten human flesh. Whether or not actual cannibalism occurred will not be discussed here. We know that there have been cases of cannibalism in hard times, and we may expect that the beliefs about cannibalism have functioned as determinants of behavior, as Morton Teicher has pointed out.[4]

The rule is, then, that an average Ojibway has good health. All kinds of precautions are taken to uphold and improve health. Sources tell us that in the past individuals frequently bathed in a lake or a river, and their hair was thoroughhly washed; in wintertime one's face and hands were washed with snow (but the whole body was never immersed in the icy cold water). On journeys travelers dared not drink the cold water if they were uncertain about its purity; instead they boiled it, mixed in twigs and leaves from a supposedly healthful vegetation, and then drank it (hot or cold). Today sweat baths are common to prevent illness (among the Western and Plains Cree they are extremely common). Other measures are also taken to safeguard life and health: the individual relies on his charms and offerings to the spirits (of food and, more important, tobacco), and at least older people turn to their guardian spirits for protection. It is considered important to pay attention to the right ritual observances and to avoid all people that may turn out to be witches. Finally, an ethically correct behavior, according to tribal norms, is supposed to improve one's chances to escape ill health.

In spite of all precautions, illness cannot always be avoided. According to a mythic story, deteriorated relations between animals and human beings brought disease on the humans at the beginning of time. The humans wanted to eat the animals, but they killed more animals than necessary. The animals then decided in a council to send diseases to the humans through mosquitoes. The defenseless people were aided by the culture hero Nanabozho, who taught them herbal cures he had learned from the chipmunk. This was the introduction of diseases and medicines into the world. And, as Christopher Vecsey has pointed out in his work on traditional Ojibway religion, although the Ojibway consider many ailments to be natural, they consider none normal: they are all introduced, not original.[5]

The Ojibway only discriminate loosely between different sorts of disease etiologies. On the basis of the material available to us we may, however, establish two explanatory types.

1. Ultimate causes. These are basically supernatural in kind, and they often presuppose the commission of a crime or negligence concerning the supernaturally established order. The spirits, manitous, guard this order. They react if humans behave unethically—for instance, if they recklessly kill other people, or, almost more condemnable in this hunting culture, if they are cruel to animals or kill them wantonly without needing them for food.

In the latter case the supernatural masters of the game punish the violator by depriving him of hunting luck, thus causing hunger in his family, or by making him sick. If a man lies in claiming that he has a certain spirit for his guardian spirit, the spirit punishes him in a similar way. Failure to make the right offerings to the powers can also enrage them and result in their inflicting diseases on the delinquents.

A particular set of transgressions are the violations of taboos, prohibitions with religious or social sanction whose infringement unleashes an unfortunate, mysterious, and practically automatic effect. The Ojibway have many ritual rules that are dangerous to break: there is the prohibition against incest, the prescribed treatment of the dead, and the correct treatment of the killed game animal (for instance, the displacement of its bones and the elevation of the skull in a tree). Some authors have called transgressions of these rules "sins," and in their consequences they obviously are: the violator feels himself a culprit and misdoer. Sometimes, certainly, the individual is not aware of having committed a crime; however, he falls mysteriously ill, and he is then called to the Shaking Tent rite where he is informed by the spirits about his sin and has to confess it.

A more subtle form of the transgression of a taboo arises when a person through no fault of his own is contaminated by dangerous influences. They may be of two kinds. One sort of contamination derives from unclean elements, like menstrual blood. Exposed to such influences a man becomes sick, a sacred place will be desecrated, and spirits abandon the polluted area. The other kind of danger springs from contact with supernatural power. Whoever has without sanction walked on sacred ground, or unawares been exposed to spirits or medicine power, risks his health. It is characteristic that the taboo situation holds both these aspects, pollution and sacred power; the common denominator is that both are dangerous, forbidden, and both may cause disease and injury.

In all these cases the spirits, manitous, control and supervise the infringements of the sacred order and their consequences, the diseases. In the actual occasions, however it is not always spelled out that it is the will of the spirits or their supreme master, Kitche Manitou, that is carried into effect. Rather, the transgression as such seems to release a whole machinery of related effects, as if one were dealing with an impersonal mechanism. The two interpretations, personal and impersonal, exist side by side, the latter resorted to at the moment of the acute experience, the former as the theoretically conceived ultimate cause.

The spirits are not alone in provoking disease situations. Other factors are the wizards and witches. As almost everywhere in aboriginal North America they emerge from the ranks of the medicine men. It may be that the medicine men have become more interested in using their powers for their own good than for the benefit of others, or they have been diverted from their former tasks as healers, or they have become mentally distorted by having evil guardian spirits. Among the Ojibway these witches turn upon people, making them suffer from starvation or disease. The infliction of hunger is less frequent—it is accomplished by magically destroying the hunting luck. More often the magicians cause disease. They do this by drawing an outline of the image of their victim on the ground, placing poison over the organ that should be hurt. Or they tie a carved wooden image of the person they want to destroy to a tree, and when the thread breaks he will die. This is regular homeopathic magic, known also from other continents. We furthermore hear of medicine men dressed up as bears and thought to be bears, who harm their personal enemies. Finally, these sorcerers may use intruding objects or soul-stealing procedures to destroy their victims.

A third category of disease producers are the dead. They may revenge themselves upon the living, envious of their living, or they may be angry because of some injustice, such as wrong ritual behavior at their funeral. It is, however, more common that they long for their living kinspeople, wanting them in their close company.

Beings with supernatural power and cosmic forces may thus lie behind a person's falling ill. Direct acting by the spirits, witches, or ghosts is not excluded, as we have seen above, but usually the manifest causes of diseases are occurrences on a lower level, involving the intrusion into the body of a pathogenic object or some spiritual disease agent, or the loss of a person's soul, or one of his souls. Sometimes there is not enough information on the disease, the main observation being that the patient is plagued by a sickness of some kind, which can be removed through the right ritual means. This is often the case when the Grand Medicine Lodge, midewiwin, is appealed to.

2. Instrumental or immediate causes, or manifest causes. They include intrusion, soul loss, and witchcraft.

Most curing aims at the removal of the disease. Where the nature of the disease is indicated (which is not very often), it is said to be matter of some kind, or a living thing like a worm or an insect. There is substantial evidence from the Plains Cree, of southern Saskatchewan, that the disease, displayed by the medicine man, is "a yellowish, foul smelling substance." When examined, "it might have the shape of some strange insect, or it might resemble a piece of flint, or perhaps be only a bit of a twig."[6] More central to our area, the Chippewa (Ojibway) of a Wisconsin reservation told an observer not so long ago that, when the doctor sucks out the disease, "sometimes worms or whatever causes the sickness, appear."[7] An old manuscript on the Ottawa (southern Ojibway) mentions as disease agents "a bone or the screw of a musket, a thorn, or a fishbone or some hair, or something of the kind."[8] It is thus obvious that the agent is sometimes animate, sometimes inanimate— perhaps the distinction is vague, as it is between personal and impersonal power.

Soul loss generally presupposes a belief in soul dualism. That is, a person has two opposed souls, or two opposed soul systems, one representing the forces that keep the body vital and active, another representing the person himself in his extracorporeal form, as he experiences himself in dreams or as others experience him in their dreams. The former soul, the "body soul," keeps the body alive while the "free-soul" or "dream soul" makes its dream wanderings. The Ojibway certainly have two souls, but the relations between them are not quite clear.

Diagnoses of soul loss are less common, but they are well known. Diamond Jenness, the eminent expert on the Ojibway Indians, reports that the soul that is located in the heart is capable of traveling outside the body, but if it is gone too long, the person will die. Apparently, a short separation of the soul from the body occurs in dreams, while a longer absence of the soul due to its inability to return brings disease and ultimate death, or—in some cases—insanity. Since the soul is also the force of intelligence and under-standing in human beings, an absence of the soul means that the person has no reason. "A drunken man," Jenness continues, "or a man just recovering from a bout of drunkenness, is temporarily in the same condition; his soul moves at a distance from him, so that he consists of body and shadow only and remembers nothing of what occurred during his drunkenness." Most interestingly, the alcoholic tendencies have a repercussion in the next gen-eration. "In his son this disharmony between soul and body may take the form of stuttering, especially if the father lay torpid and memoryless for a day or two after each bout." This is one of the rare references to the conse-quences of alcoholism in our source material.[9]

So far we have found that an individual could be himself responsible for the separation between body and soul; however, as we have noticed, danger-ous powers are just as frequently active in carrying the soul away. For in-stance, the shaman of a Shaking Tent has the power to take a person's soul while asleep to his own lodge many miles away. If the soul does not return to its body the victim will be found dead. The dead in the other world may also fetch a person's soul, or entice it over to their realm. Performers of witchcraft have similar powers.[10]

The Parry Island Ojibway describe how through witchcraft a person's shadow, which really is a soul, may become divided and thus cause disease. One part of it may wish to be in harmony with soul and body, while the other one wants to travel or go hunting. The person thus becomes a center of conflicting desires—or, as Jenness remarks, he is the victim of neurosis in psychopathological terms. This is an interesting example of Ojibway psychology.[11]

DOCTORS AND DIVINERS

When, in spite of all precautions, a person falls ill, several actions are taken. First, if the patient is seriously ill, as far as his close relatives can judge, preparations are taken to diminish the dangers. To cleanse the air in his lodge cedar boughs are burned there. If the disease is thought to be contagious the relatives throw sage on the fire.[12]

The next important task is to call on a doctor. This may be difficult, for there are several classes of doctors, and it is important to know whether the disease situation suits this or that doctor. Fortunately, doctors who are not experts in a certain type of disease refer to colleagues who are more expert. Another difficulty is that some doctors, although they are considered good, do not make diagnoses. Instead they urge the patient or his relatives to invite a skilled diviner, that is, a shaman who has the supernatural gift to discover the cause of disease or who through his contact with the spirits may be able to receive information from them on the disease.

The Ojibway recognize the following categories of doctors:

1. Herbalists, who have a reputation for curing diseases by the use of herbal medicines. They are no medicine men, but they draw on knowledge of medicinal plants and their effects.[13] Most herbalists are members of the midewiwin, for the secret knowledge of plant medicines is transmitted in this society. If a disease seems to be caused in a "natural" way, a herbalist is usually summoned; if he is unable to relieve the pains, a real medicine man—that is, a supernaturally inspired healer—is called.

Besides the herbalists there are experts on tattooing and bloodletting, both professions in the service of medicine but with no immediate reference to the supernatural sphere. Tattooing was formerly resorted to in cases of muscular pains such as rheumatism, dislocated joints, and backaches. It was done on the affected part. The profession of bloodletting follows a hereditary succession; the knowledge is transmitted from father to son. Bloodletters are required to have a good knowledge of the circulatory system.[14]

2. Regular medicine men who are, primarily, seers.[15] They have received their extraordinary powers during their puberty fasting visions. As noted above, a young boy is expected to withdraw for some time, usually four nights and days, to an isolated hut that his father or grandfather has prepared for him in the thickness of the woods. His face is darkened by charcoal to invoke the pity of the spirits. He is now prepared to fast and wait until a spirit shows itself in a vision. Some visions are very forceful, sweeping the dreamer away on a tour to the sky where he receives the supernatural powers connected with a mighty spirit. Sometimes this spirit confers medical powers on the visionary, and in such cases he becomes a medicine man when he has reached a mature age. Medicine men may be relatively young, but most people prefer older doctors, men in their fifties and sixties.

A medicine man has usually received his medicine power from the thunder. When called upon by the relatives of a sick man he comes to the patient's bed with his rattle and some hollow bird-bone pipes. First he makes the diagnosis. He kneels on the ground, sings his medicine song—the song that his guardian spirit taught him in the vision—and shakes his rattle. He says that he hears the spirit or spirits that gave him powers, perhaps the thunder, but in at least one account hummingbirds and kingfishers. Everybody around hears a dull thud, indicating that one to four spirits have entered the rattle. The helping spirits open the doctor's eyes so that he beholds the disease object.

Next the curing sets in. The medicine man swallows the hollow bones in such a way that the last one protrudes from his mouth. Through this bone he tries to suck the disease object out. He vomits all the tubes out into a basin of water. There, visible to all bystanders, the bones float around together with a small feather or other object, such as a worm, which represents the disease.

There are many variations of the medical procedure, including the medicine man's blowing on the sick spot through a hollow bone, his beating a drum and singing, his imitating the guardian spirit ("he would cock his head on one side exactly like a robin does before he sinks his bill into the ground after a worm"),[16] his drinking the contents of the water basin, and so forth. Sometimes the medicine man makes a tobacco offering before he starts the séance.

3. Shamans *(jessakid)*, commonly called jugglers or conjurers.[17] They are the performers of the Shaking Tent ritual. Primarily diagnosticians, they are also engaged in active curing. Like the ordinary medicine man the shaman derives his powers from spiritual blessings obtained in visions. Because the power is conferred in his early youth, the shaman has to wait until full manhood before he can start his career. The séances are exhausting, and we are told that they cannot be performed more than two or three times during a summer. When the conjurer is very old he has to give up his demanding profession entirely. His physical strength is no more sufficient.

The jessakid usually operates in a Shaking Tent (see further below) to find out the nature of the disease and, sometimes, to cure the patient. He often seemingly plays a passive role once his spirits have appeared on the scene. One Parry Island Ojibway relates, "We heard the *manidos* [spirits] say to one another inside the lodge 'We cannot do anything. The child will have to die.' The child died."[18] The shaman is here completely dependent on his spirits. He can call them forth, but he is left to their precognition, medical knowledge, and assistance.

Outside the Shaking Tent ritual the shaman is sometimes (but not very often, at least not in later times) engaged in rescuing a lost soul. We hear of a shaman in northern Michigan who faced the task of freeing a sick person's soul that had been captured by a witch in raven disguise. In his trance the shaman—that is, his soul—turned into a hawk and traveled to search for the soul. He found it in time, before the patient died, and returned with it. Finally, he blew the soul into the man's mouth.[19] A Saulteaux shaman (Lake Winnipeg area) by the name of Northern Barred Owl was sent for to cure a girl who was very ill. She died shortly after the shaman's arrival. Nevertheless, he did not give up. He lay down beside her, tying a piece of red yarn around the girl's wrist. Then he went into a trance so deep that he did not move at all. His soul now followed the girl on her way to the realm of the dead. There he found her, with the help of the red yarn, in the crowd of the dead, and he then brought her back to the land of the living. The spectators saw him move a little. As he moved, so did the girl. He moved more, and the girl did the same. Finally he raised himself up into a sitting posture, and the girl did the same. She was restored to life. (We might say that this was a case of apparent death.) Only very powerful shamans can attempt such things. Northern Barred Owl was notable for his powers.[20]

Mostly the shaman serves as a diagnostician and leaves the actual curing treatment to the "doctors." The latter may call on a conjurer to make the diagnosis before they begin their treatment.

4. The *wabeno* is reputedly the strongest doctor, although it is difficult to see why this should be so.[21] Like the regular medicine man and the shaman he receives his blessings from a spirit during a vision. Thereafter he becomes an apprentice with an older wabeno who is willing to share his knowledge as herbalist. In spite of their spiritual calling the wabeno are namely first of all experts on plant medicine. It is said that this knowledge once came down through a vision but was then transmitted as a tradition from generation to generation. A good wabeno has often had many good teachers whom he has paid well for their services.

The candidate cannot function as a doctor until he has proved his powers at a feast. The occasion includes general drumming, dancing, and singing, with special performances by the candidate: he takes burning coals in his hands, he dips his hands in cooking water, and he swallows knives.

The wabeno combines the roles of herbalist and sucking doctor in his medical performances. It is said that at the curing he first locates the place of the disease and thereafter covers this place with a piece of birchbark or a leaf that has been smeared with herbal remedies. He drums and sings, and then he draws away the leaf. Thereby he also removes a stick or bone that is the cause of the disease, which has been shot into the patient's body by a sorcerer.

There is evidence that originally the wabeno constituted a society of magicians. It had been formed around 1800 to counteract the depletion of game animals. It seems that the wabeno at that time used a secret language. To the present generation, however, they are known as doctors.

Medicine men, conjurers, and wabeno are all recruited among persons who have undergone the vision-quest probation. The healers of the midewiwin, however, are not necessarily visionaries. They may be medicine men or (rarely) conjurers, or just common herbalists, but their competence as members of the midewiwin lodge lies in their knowledge of traditional teachings in the lodge.[22] Now, besides receiving instruction in the composition of the universe, from myths and legends pertaining to the lodge, and in the lodge's own sacred ritual and symbolism, the candidates for the *mide* order have to learn to cure disease by means of a death and revival ceremony. We shall soon look more closely at this ceremony; the important thing here is that doctoring is a part of the midewiwin ceremonial complex, and that not supernatural inspiration but initiation into the lore and traditions of the society constitutes the basis of medical knowledge. Indeed, like the herbalists and the wabeno the mide "priests" give greatest importance to the knowledge of medicinal plants. It is therefore not surprising to find that the herbalists, practically all healers, are members of the mide order. The wabeno, however, seem to constitute a competing order and therefore do not belong.

The members of the midewiwin seem not to have particularly high prestige as doctors. Although we find statements to the effect that their healing (in the midewiwin context) represents the last resort of a sick person, most people turn to free-standing curers. What is so important in the midewiwin is the initiation rites with their death and resurrection symbolism. These rites guarantee health and prosperity to a sick individual and a good existence in the world beyond the grave. The midewiwin is thus more than a doctor's clinic. It is, as will be discussed later, a converted annual ritual.

As such it is probably not so ancient. Its beginning as a medical lodge goes back to a time when most Ojibway were concentrated in the southern part of their present area, south of Lake Superior. It is therefore no surprise to learn that the more migratory Cree of the north do not know the midewiwin. (Actually, the term *mitewiwin* stands for the Shaking Tent ritual among the Northwestern Cree.) Nor do wabeno exist among the Cree. Both the midewiwin and the wabeno societies mirror a more complex social structure. Cree doctors are thus common herbalists, sucking medicine men, and Shaking Tent conjurers.

Let us now take a closer look at the two most spectacular curing institutions of these Algonkians, the Shaking Tent and the midewiwin.

THE SHAKING TENT PERFORMANCE

The Shaking Tent is a shamanic séance that is diffused from western Siberia, over the Eskimo groups to northern North America where it is particularly frequent among Algonkians like the Cree, Montagnais-Naskapi, and Ojibway. In slightly changed forms it occurs among Plateau and Plains tribes (see below, the Arapaho Spirit Lodge), and even in South America and Southeast Asia. It is thus a most constitutive shamanic ritual.[23] It may have been the model for modern spiritualistic séances in the occidental world, although the role played in this connection by the American Shaking Tent has been denied by some ethnologists, I believe on erroneous grounds. The Shaking Tent rite is really a classic example of a shamanic rite when the latter is not primarily concerned with the shaman's soul journey. Here, the shaman sends out his auxiliary spirit, less frequently his soul. (The Eskimo séances, in contrast, offer good examples of soul flights.) The shaman's ecstasy is not always so deep, but it is there; it is a mistake to think, like some investigators do, that trance states are absent. The Algonkian performances of the Shaking Tent give us good examples of the shaman's place in this cultural context.[24]

When a conjurer or shaman has been called in to divine a patient's disease or even to heal him through the Shaking Tent, the next step taken is to construct such a tent—a task that rests with the sick person's family and friends, not with the shaman. Strong poles from a variety of trees are thrust into the ground to a depth of about two or three feet, forming a narrow circle. The tips of the poles are bent toward each other and lashed together. The structure is finally covered with canvas. The construction thus has the form of a cylindrical or hemispherical, barrel-like miniature hut, fit to house one seated man, the medicine man. Onlookers place themselves outside the booth, watching the train of events.

The shaman enters the conjuring hut, practically naked. He chants and shakes his rattle. He is then bound up with strong thongs. In this condition he is still capable of calling on his spirits—the spirits of the air, the spirits of the animals. Those outside sing to the rhythmic beats of a drum. The singing becomes more excited and reaches a high pitch when the shaman's main helping spirit, usually Mikenak, the turtle, arrives. The public hears a range of strange noises. A witness thus mentions "the sound of snowshoes in the snow; the thud of an axe biting into wood; the rasp and scraping of a paddle along the gunwales of a canoe, and the splash as it dips into the water."[25]

Apparently the main spirit in his turn calls in a lot of smaller spirits of a partly more comic character—humor and piety get along well in Native American religion. A Mistassini (East Cree) says that one can see the paws of a bear, the head of a beaver, and a wriggling fish protrude from the canvas wall of the spirit tent. The spectators see it clearly with their own eyes and are breathtaken. Faith is really rewarded here.

During these events, and all through the séance, the little tent is mysteriously swaying. The constructors of the tent know this is not natural, for the man inside could not have the physical powers to do it. Scholars who have seen the strong poles are of different opinions. An Ojibway conjurer who had turned Christian told the German explorer J. G. Kohl that the phenomenon of shaking is perfectly mysterious, due to no operation on the part of the shaman.[26] Of course, cases of unconscious simulation are certainly not uncommon among shamans. How it would work in this connection (and how the popping animals should be explained) remains an enigma. Whatever the answer, the performance of shaking strengthens the faith among the spectators.

Questions are now directed to the spirit master, who answers through the shaman. Some witnesses state that it is the spirit that speaks; but this should probably be understood as the shaman retelling what the spirit has told him. On the other hand, some investigators report that there is a dialogue between the shaman and the spirit, the shaman speaking from the ground, the spirit—talking with the shaman's twisted voice—speaking from the top of the conjuring booth. Most of the questions and conversation concern the divination of lost persons and articles, things that have passed and things due to come. Diseases, their origins and future development, are themes forming part of the divination procedure. Curing may also figure conspicuously in the séance.

Thus, in the Ojibway Shaking Tent the spirits that are present discuss among themselves a sick man's condition. If they decide that he has been bewitched, one of them departs, with a violent rocking of the hut, and summons the soul or shadow of the culprit for trial. As the spirit brings in the soul, the lodge shakes again. The spirits now threaten to kill the soul. It cannot flee, for the mighty thunder keeps guard at the top of the booth. The owner of the soul, being present among the spectators, shamefully appears. He is forced to pay a sum of money to the spirits and to take away the disease in order to have his soul released.

The spirits leave. The tent becomes stable again, and the shaman crawls out, mysteriously liberated from his fetters. Some say the fetters will be found hanging in the top of the hut. How the shaman was freed from them nobody can tell. He is completely exhausted and must be assisted back to his wigwam. On the next day he will be paid for his services. The goal is achieved: the sick man will now slowly become better. Or so it is expected.

The Shaking Tent is also the scene of confessions of sins or taboo transgressions that are supposed to have caused diseases. When this etiology is thought to be correct, no other remedy is sought: sucking operations or herbal applications, for instance, would be to no avail. The shaman calls on his guardian spirits, and the patient is admonished to appear and confess his misdoings. It may soon be obvious, however, that the real wrongdoers are the patient's parents. In such a case they are asked to make confessions. If they are dead, it is the task of the shaman's guardian spirits to bring them back from the other world to testify. As A. I. Hallowell points out, such performances strengthen the society's morality. People are shown the right behavior and are trained into the ethical code.[27]

MIDEWIWIN AS A DOCTORS' ORGANIZATION

The midewiwin or "Grand Medicine Society" is best characterized as a fraternal order where individuals buy the right to membership. They also (likewise through payment) pass through the four grades of the society, each one of these grades marked by visible changes in the individual's appearance, such as a particular facial painting and a special type of medicine bag. It is obvious that only well-situated Ojibway are members of this society.

It is difficult to label the midewiwin a medicine society, if medicine here refers to curing. It is indeed a rather complex phenomenon. Many ethnologists think that it originated in an acculturative situation some three hundred years ago when culture contact with more southerly Central Algonkians, Northern Plains people, and white immigrants occurred. This is possible, but it seems preferable to say that about this time, and through cultural contact, the existing society changed to its present organization and aims. Its cosmic symbolism, creation mythology, and rituals reveal that originally it may have been a kind of annual ceremonial lodge, perpetuating life on earth. In its present form it is a lodge instituted by the Great Spirit or the culture hero to grant the initiated members a good and long life. In this connection the healing program has become of major importance—perhaps as an answer to devastating epidemics spread by the whites. The mide members are experts on herbal medicine, the sacred wisdom of which is transferred within the lodge. Furthermore, outsiders who are sick may regain health by being initiated into the society. Healing is thus part of the process toward a good and long life. Outside the lodge, however, the mide members are not necessarily considered medical specialists themselves. Furthermore, midewiwin is an inclusive institution—it is, according to what the Ojibway themselves explain, their religion.

Much more could be said about the nature of this complex and enigmatic institution. The ritual procedures have been described by many investigators (Hoffman, Densmore, Jenness, Kinietz, Hilger, Landes, and others).[28] The drawings on bark scrolls that have served as mnemonic devices for the participants in the ritual have been investigated by some students (Kohl, Dewdney).[29] Midewiwin has today almost fallen into oblivion, although there has been renewal of the tradition in secret and remote places.

Our concern here is with the medicine lodge as a doctors' organization. As they have in the Plains Indian Sun Dance (see below), therapeutic interests have taken over with time, as is easily recognizable in the initiation of new candidates. According to Diamond Jenness, a young man or woman (yes, women have the same rights to enter the lodge as men) who is interested in joining the society asks a member to introduce him or her at a feast. The candidate is then assigned a preceptor from whom he or she receives instruction for several months. The information is given by day in the solitude of the woods, by night in an empty wigwam. Each lesson is begun with a smoke offering to the spirits. The tobacco is, like the expenses for the instruction, provided by the candidate's family.

The annual ceremony of the Grand Medicine Society takes place in midsummer. The lodge for the rituals is a large rectangular enclosure built of poles and boughs, without a roof. There are an eastern and a western opening at the short sides, and a mat is placed inside in the center for the candidates and their preceptors. Right outside the eastern entrance is a domed sweat house where the candidate takes a vapor bath on each of the four evenings prior to the initiation. Sweat bathing is a common purifying procedure before a ritual, making the performer ritually clean.

The candidates and mide members come with their families to the initiation lodge. Relatives who are not initiated are not allowed to enter the sacred lodge, but they still meet in numbers, for these are great festive occasions, and the whole community usually enjoys them. The day of initiation has to be a fine, clear day, or the whole ceremony is postponed. The mide members enter in their regalia, beaded bags suspended from beaded bandoliers. After some time candidates and their ritual grandfathers form a procession, circling four times outside the lodge in a sunwise direction. Then they enter and make the same circuit four times inside, whereupon they take their seats—the old members along the walls, the candidates and mentors on the central mat.

The head priest begins the ceremony by beating a water-drum and chanting a song. The candidate kneels in front of him, and one of the priests cries *hwa, hwa, hwa, hwa, hwa,* at the same time that he takes hold of his otterskin medicine bag with both hands and pretends to throw it into the initiate's breast. The candidate shakes violently, held by the preceptor and an assistant. The same reactions take place as a second and a third priest "shoot" the candidate. Finally the head priest shoots him, and he falls down as if dead. Some mide priests then place their medicine bags on his back. The candidate now lets a sacred shell, a *migi*, drop from his mouth, and he shows signs of life. The head priest dances round the lodge with the migi and shows it to all the members, whereupon he brings it back into the candidate's mouth so that the latter again falls down as if dead. Once more the priests touch him with their medicine bags. He comes to life and stands up. He is now a member of the society, with a new, healthy life. Singing and smoke offerings to the spirits of the six directions (the cardinal points, sky and earth) complete the initiation ceremony. In the continuation of the program, the new mide is presented with a medicine bag for his sacred shell, and he shoots one or several of his mide brothers.

As mentioned, this initiation can function as a medical treatment. There are examples of mide members who have carried a sick man inside the medicine lodge and initiated him, thereby making him healthy. We hear of cases where the disease was so bad that there was no other cure. The mide "consulted over him exactly as would a group of European doctors. Then they administered whatever medicine they had agreed upon and immediately initiated the patient into their order."[30]

We have seen how the mide members specialize in the use of plants for curing sickness. We also notice that the small white shell, the migi—a saltwater species, *Cypraea moneta* ("money cowrie")—is both a disease sender and a remedy. We find a similar concept in northern California where the disease object, the "pain," is also the medicine man's guardian spirit. In the midewiwin the migi planted in the candidate's chest stands for power. It all conveys the impression that the spirit that makes disease also has the capacity to avert disease and to serve the individual positively. This is not so farfetched: the same spirit that is a guardian spirit to a medicine man can be used by him for witchcraft purposes. The Ojibway provide many examples of that.

With its collectivistic medical treatment and its authority in handed-down tradition rather than inspirational visions the midewiwin is a characteristic feature in a complex civilization on the boundary between two cultural trends, hunting life and agriculture. In this respect it differs basically from the Shaking Tent, which is a typical exponent of the old hunting culture of the northern woodlands. We have here a neat example of how medicine and medical cure are steeped in cultural forms. From the points of view of this study it is even more rewarding to find that the two major ritual performances of the Cree and Ojibway are directly related to medical treatment. This is convincing proof of the import of health in its relation to religion in these two societies.

·3·

Traditional Medicine on the Northwest Coast

On the fringe of the massive Canadian woodland, along the misty North Pacific Coast with its breathtaking mountains and deep fiords, its archipelago of islands wrapped in a lavish verdure of bush and grass, pines and cedar trees, and its rainy climate of mild winters and warm summers, live the Northwest Coast tribes. They differ in several ways from their relatives in the woodlands. First, their culture is extremely colorful and has an exquisite profile in wooden art. Second, there is reason to suspect an impact from Asian and South Sea sources in their cultural makeup. Third, the basic cultural resource is fishing rather than hunting. Fourth, the social differentiation is remarkable considering the underlying fishing culture. Thus, in distinction from the inland hunting culture with its rather uniform and monotonous Circumboreal pattern we have here one of the great and profiled cultural traditions in aboriginal North America.

The Northwest Coast is populated by Native Americans from different linguistic families. Far in the north, from Yakutat Bay to the Dixon Entrance, live the Tlingit. They probably have some linguistic affinity to the Athapascans of the interior. Their neighbors in the south, on the Queen Charlotte Islands, are the Haida, who may also be related to the Athapascans (but less probably so). On the mainland south of the Tlingit live the Tsimshian. Together the Tlingit-Haida-Tsimshian form the northern group of Northwest Coast tribes who share an organization in matrilinear exogamic clans.

The central maritime group consists of several tribes, among them the Bella Coola who verge on the inland and belong to the Salishan family, and the well-known Wakashan-speaking Kwakiutl and Nootka on the Vancouver Island and adjoining mainland. East and south of the Vancouver Island live a good many smaller groups primarily belonging to the Salish language

43

family. It should be observed that the corresponding inland, displaying the Plateau cultural area, is inhabited by Salishan groups.

Little is known of the prehistory of the Northwest Coast. It seems, however, that about 7,000 B.C.E. there appeared a fishing culture around the beaches of the North Pacific, from the Amur River in the west to the Columbia River in the east. A particular trait of this culture was sea hunting with harpoons. This basic culture was in America differentiated into Eskimo-Aleut and Northwest Coast cultures. In its southern part the Northwest Coast fishing culture was less pronounced in the area of the Salishan and other smaller tribes. The three northern tribes—the Tlingit, Haida, and Tsimshian—initiated a development of their own. Into this mosaic of tribes and cultures, overseas elements penetrated—most certainly things rescued from stranded Japanese vessels, but possibly also elements brought from other quarters: witness the coolie fashion of South Chinese hats used on the Northwest Coast, or the South-Sea-like arrangement of carved pictures of spirits on the totem poles. Here, however, we have to be cautious. What is quite certain is that totem poles in their classic forms did not come about until after the 1770s when, according to Captain Cook, European iron tools had been introduced to the Northwest Coast.

There are certainly wide differences in life styles among Northwest Coast tribes. Still, there is a dominant cultural profile, qualitatively outstanding, which is common along the northern and central coast, whereas the southern Canadian coast culture is more simple. I have selected two groupings for a closer ethnomedical description here, the Tlingit and the Coast Salish. The former inhabit the northernmost part of the coast. (As a consequence of the nineteenth-century fur trade, part of the Tlingit also took up their abode east of the Cordillera as fur hunters, but they will not be considered here.) The Tlingit are one of the classic Northwest tribes, famous for their warlike behavior in ancient times and their developed shamanism. The Coast Salish in the south are interesting because their shamanic and medical practices preserve traits that can be traced back to the first American immigrants. Many of these traits have been developed in a unique fashion by the Coast Salish, forming a pattern that deviates in many respects from the common Northwest Coast shamanic pattern. Furthermore, the Tlingit material that will be used is mostly historical, although there are today efforts to revive the old shamanism, whereas the Coast Salish therapeutic procedures are still used.

Basic to the Northwest Coast culture, as it was still seen in the last decades of the nineteenth century, was the easy access to food—the harvest of the sea, the meat from an assortment of land animals, and many kinds of berries contributed to a rich and varied diet. All kinds of fish, but particularly salmon, were caught. Equipped with large wooden plank canoes, tribes like the Nootka and Kwakiutl set out to sea to hunt seals and whales with harpoons in an Eskimo manner. (The Tlingit, however, despised whale meat.) Land animals like deer, bears, and mountain goats were also hunted, but not to the same extent. Berries were picked by the women.

As we might expect, these Indians built wooden plank houses, which were often placed in a row with their gables facing the beach. Many houses were painted with totem symbols, and in front of them totem poles were erected. These totem poles usually depicted an ancestor and the spirit that had given him his privileges and clan names. Other spirits, acquired later or connected with the primeval vision of a guardian, were also symbolically represented on the pole. These spirits were thought to show themselves as animals, and some of their characteristic animal features were designed on the pole. The cedar canoes drawn up on the beach were also decorated with these totemic emblems.

Each village or collection of houses constituted a political unit where the dominant lineage or clan was the owner. Hunting grounds, fishing waters, and berry picking localities were also owned by the lineage. (In the south the lineage was replaced by the kin group.) The totem animal symbolized the lineage. Each lineage had a series of titles ("names") and ceremonies, all controlled by the hereditary chief. The northern tribes, among them the Tlingit, applied a hereditary system of matrilinear descent, that is, a person inherited his titles and privileges from his kin on his mother's side. The southern tribes, among them the Salish, were organized in extended family systems, whereas the northern tribes had sibs (clans), that is, lineages joined together in larger units with an imagined common ancestor; or they were divided into two moieties, among the Tlingit eagles (or sometimes wolves) and ravens. A man married a wife of the opposite moiety, and moieties served each other in the carving of sib emblems and on ceremonial occasions, such as funerals. The Tlingit think that people belonging to clans of the Raven moiety are wise and cautious and that people belonging to clans of the Wolf moiety are quick-tempered and warlike—just like the animals in question. Each settlement usually counted people from both moieties.

In addition to the complicated social system of kinship ties there was a ranking system, a division of people into nobles (that is, chiefs and their closest families), commoners, and slaves. Even today members of the highest rank receive a certain courtesy from "commoners." Slaves were originally prisoners of war. In the old days slaves or their descendants could be given away or killed as their lord pleased. A person rich in names, wealth, and slaves was accorded a high prestige. This social structure strikes us as rather un-Indian. Its ranking system has provoked scholars to imply dissemination of ideas from non-American sources; however, the system may very well have grown from indigenous beginnings.

The conferring of titles and property on a person took place at the potlatch, a giving-away ceremony which validated the transaction. Members of the opposite moiety were invited as guests to witness the occasion and to perform their dances, whereupon they received a great number of gifts. The gift-giving sometimes achieved grotesque expressions—the owner destroyed parts of his property and killed some slave—and it secured the authority of the host and enhanced his social reputation. More recent research shows that the potlatch probably had its origin in memorial festivals over deceased persons. Among the Tlingit, for instance, the potlatch was often part of the mourning ritual for a dead chief. Totem poles were raised on these occasions as memorial posts over the dead chiefs and their totems (that is, guardian spirits). Sometimes these poles contained boxes with the remains of the chiefs.

The Northwest Coast Indian world is even today permeated with religion. Spirits are everywhere—in the sea, in the woods, among the mountains. Most spirits have something to do with animals, and some may be the very spirits of animals. This is the background of the whale cult, which follows here the same pattern as the bear cult among the northern woodland tribes. The Coast Salish practiced the vision quest of the Plateau Salish and the woodland tribes; however, among other tribes the guardian spirit quest so common in the rest of North America has been reduced to a dramatic ritual performance in which a person displays his acquisition of a clan spirit. These dramatic rites have taken place primarily among more southern peoples, for instance, the Kwakiutl. In the north, on the other hand, common men seem to have been without personal guardian spirits. Among the Tlingit, for instance, such spirits have been reserved for medicine people.

These differences tell us a good deal of the medicine men. Among the Coast Salish they are hardly distinguishable from other visionaries, but they still evoke respect because of their medical abilities. Among the Kwakiutl, medicine men have a certain standing: they belong to a particular society and compete with each other to be the most clever in their profession. The Tlingit, again, have the medicine men set off as a separate category. Only medicine men engage in vision quests; only medicine men are visited in trance by spirits. Whereas a Kwakiutl medicine man is more or less "owned" by the chief of the village, the Tlingit medicine man has a free position and reminds us most of all of the Siberian shaman. Indeed, the insightful anthropologist John R. Swanton argued that Tlingit medicine men or shamans have had more power than their colleagues all along the Pacific Coast.[1]

It is possible to see Tlingit medical practices, concentrated around the figure of the medicine man, as a continuation of Siberian shamanism. This conforms with other cultural traits that link the Tlingit and other northern tribes with Siberia.

HEALTH, GOOD LIVING, AND PASSAGES OF LIFE AMONG THE TLINGIT

The Tlingit have been described as one of the most warlike tribes on the Northwest Coast, which may be a wrong judgment. In their dealings with the Russians who occupied their country until 1867, when all of Alaska was sold to the United States, the Tlingit were forced to guard their independence, often in violent ways. They managed to keep their culture intact for a long time. When their country was passed over to the Americans they were only superficially touched by Greek Orthodox Christianity. Moreover, they kept their shamans in times when the shamanism of their southern neighbors, the Haida and Tsimshian, in many ways was a thing of the past. There is no doubt that the rather impressive size of the Tlingit population has contributed to the success of their resistance. It is also evident that the Tlingit from childhood onward was trained to withstand difficulties and oppression.

This evidence is historical. The Tlingit culture as it once existed is a thing of the past, but it is not forgotten by the people. Many Tlingit are trying to revive it, particularly in the spheres of wooden arts and social ceremonies, and the shadow of the old shamanism still remains and leads to ecstatic outbursts here and there. The old ways of preparing the individual for living are certainly gone. Nevertheless, they deserve to be mentioned here, for the whole attitude to health and living still partly recognized among the Tlingit was grounded in these customs.

The birth of a baby was an ordeal, at least for the mother. An early observer, Heinrich Johan Holmberg, relates that on a cold December day in 1850 when he was about to sail from Sitka to California he heard women howling in agony in the forested hills above the settlement. According to some Tlingit serving on board, these women were about to go into labor. There were many of them in the woods, and their outcries testified to their torments.[2] We may dismiss the information Holmberg received that nobody assisted these women since they were considered unclean—this information is not trustworthy, for an even earlier writer, the Russian ecclesiastic Venia minov, tells us of the existence of midwives.[3] It seems possible, however, that the birth occurred out in the wilderness. In 1882 two other observers, the brothers Aurel and Arthur Krause from Berlin, inspected a Tlingit birth hut of snow in which a mother with her newborn child was found. Apparently a mother spent some five days with her baby in a simple hut made from snow or twigs.[4] Among the Tlingit as all over North America it was thought that a woman in that condition was an unclean being and had to be separated from the living quarters of other people. Her sojourn in that cold hut in wintery Alaska must have been a time of both suffering and hardening.

Her newborn child was then cared for by midwives, who washed it in cold sweetwater and bedded it down in a cradle of moss. The child was not nursed until it had been made to vomit, the idea being that in this way it got rid of all inward impurity that could bring about illnesses in the future. In other words, it was supposed that a child was born with an inherent quality that stood for disease, an idea which may have to do with the current belief in reincarnation. It is reported that a young girl just reaching maturity after a dear relative's death fasted and prayed that the dead person would be born again from her. If, according to their beliefs, a child was found to reincarnate a dead person, it might contain the matter that made that person die. That situation had to be remedied.

Basic to this belief was the idea that the disease clung to the individual after death. A corpse that was carried out through an opening in the back wall of the house where the death had taken place was followed by a live dog, a scapegoat that had to take upon itself every trace of the death-carrying disease; however, nobody could be quite certain that the obliteration of the deadly stuff was complete. To make sure, the reincarnated man or woman in the guise of the newborn child had to vomit any remaining uncleanliness.

There were indeed all kinds of precautions taken to strengthen the child. Its first breath was caught in a bag that was placed on a path where many people would tread on it; this prevented the child from crying when it grew older. Red paint was put on its nose to make it strong. A boy's umbilical cord was placed under an eagle's nest to make him brave.

As soon as the child was able to walk it was daily bathed in the sea, irrespective of the time of the year. Ethnologists have presumed that this custom explains why so few children survived their first years. On the other hand, it also explains why those few who survived became so hardened. The Tlingit are known to bathe daily in the sea even in coldest wintertime. If a little boy refused to dip himself in the cold water, he was flogged with a cane by his uncle; the flogging, we are told, was not really a punishment but a means of hardening the body.

The same exercise was performed among adults. The brothers Krause watched men with naked abdomens whipping each other with rods of elder-trees on the seashore. This was done, they write, "in order to become strong and hardened."[5] Another observer, Veniaminov, reports that this morning custom was repeated indoors in the evening. The same author also mentions that some young men cut the flesh of their chests and hands with sharp stones until the blood flowed and then went down into the sea, where they stayed until they were almost numb.[6]

It is important to stress that the seemingly harsh treatment of small boys was supposed to be for their own good. Aurel Krause writes that "small children are cared for in a kindly even a tender, way. Nowhere did we see them receive blows and only seldom were they spoken to harshly as a matter of correction."[7] Krause's observation agrees with what we know from other Native American tribes. Certainly, this parental kindness did not bring about any laxness in discipline and obedience to the elders, in particular the parents and the maternal uncle from whom they were supposed to inherit in this matrilinear society. What, then, was the aim of hardening the children and youths? Was it to make them indifferent to affection on public occasions, as we can witness in so many Native American societies? Actually, such an emotional indifference in certain situations is well attested to in our sources. The real cause, however, was another one, which the Tlingit shared with the Iroquois, the Sioux, and many other tribes.

It was the conviction that in order to live the good life—a life according to tradition, a life which gave meaning to existence—the Tlingit had to be prepared for war. Their warlike spirit is recounted in our sources, and it is further underlined by their big war canoes and armors (of a Northeast Siberian and Japanese type), which can be seen in some museums. This predilection for war may be related to their social structure. It seems that the Tlingit society, with its chiefs, nobles, commoners, and slaves, built up an intratribal aggression that was partly channeled through ceremonial competition—as in the potlatch—but partly found an outlet in murder and even open war. In war "they do not withhold cruelties," asserts an old-time witness, Holmberg.[8] In this kind of cultural and social climate the hardening of the individual was a necessary educational task. The demands were not on work for food gathering—the resources at hand were rich, and the slaves taken on the warpath could assist in the procuration.

It in this light that the importance of health should be seen. The physician Eduard Blaschke, who in the 1830s was working in Sitka, writes that because of their outdoor living and daily bathing in the sea, even in winter, the Tlingit had become hardened and seldom susceptible to illness. Those who as babies survived the icy winter baths were remarkably healthy and often attained old age. Dr. Blaschke complained, however, about their indulgence in alcohol, a liquid introduced by the whites that here as always among Native Americans had devastating effects. Add to this the ravaging epidemics noticeble from the 1780s, and we perceive that after this date the curse of disease and failing health was common, notwithstanding the Tlingit concern about building up healthful conditions.[9]

Perhaps we should remark here that the means of promoting health were scarcely of modern standards. Dipping babies in icy water led to illness and sometimes death. Only slowly did soap replace the use of urine for washing (a similar custom existed among the Eskimoes). Aurel Krause points out that the Tlingit devoted little time to personal cleanliness. He mentions, however, the steam baths that the Tlingit had, in particular, sweat lodges constructed of poles covered by woolen blankets. As always in North America, the steam was produced by pouring water over heated stones in the lodge. After a sweat bath the Tlingit plunged into the cold sea water.[10]

If we disregard the precarious bathing of infants, the Tlingit showed great care for their children, who were nursed up to their fourth year. At the time of puberty the girl was confined in a small, dark hut of branches where she had to spend some months until everybody was satisfied that her uncleanliness had ceased. She wore a brimmed hat so that her unclean eyes should not fall upon the sky, rendering it unclean. Her face was smeared with soot and charcoal. As long as the girl remained unclean, her look might destroy the luck of a hunter, a fisherman, or a gambler and turn objects into stone.

Taboos of this sort have been common in North America, and at some places still are. The custom has been particularly deep-rooted among the Athapascans of Alaska and Western Canada, and among their descendants in the Southwest, the Apache. The Tlingit are, as noted above, possibly related to the Athapascans, and one may wonder whether that is the reason they have taken girls' puberty rites so seriously. There were no corresponding rites for boys. The vision quest is reserved for those who will become shamans. A marked degree of attention given to girls' ceremonies seems to be connected with a high social position of women. This was so among the Tlingit, among whom women were very influential, unless, of course, they were slaves—slaves had no human rights whatsoever, and they could be killed on any occasion.

Many old-time Tlingit lived to a high age, and some of them, chiefs and nobles, could enjoy a high reputation, many name titles, land privileges, and rights to ceremonies and myths. At death most people were cremated, except for shamans, who were enclosed in small funeral houses, and slaves, who were simply thrown into the water. It has been mentioned that reincarnation beliefs were common; indeed, one of an individual's names was taken from a dead ancestor. Parallel with this belief in reincarnation runs another belief in the departed person's continued existence in a supernatural realm. Most people went to a happy country high up in the sky, sometimes said to be the realm of the sun, the moon, and the stars. Somewhere even higher up is a place, called "way up," whither went persons who had had violent deaths. Drowned people lived somewhere in the underworld, in the country of the land otters.

Such a differentiation of final destinations, determined by the way of dying, is rather common among Native Americans. There is no theory of retribution. We hear of murdered people who have not made revenge of their killers and therefore are unable to enter the land "way up." They drift away with the clouds because they have not fulfilled their obligations.

The Tlingit's eschatological notions thus do not introduce any questions of morality in a deeper sense. We may ask, what happened to those who violated social norms—what was their fate after death? On this point our sources are mute. The usual fate of such people in other North American cultures is exclusion from the social community in the next life, and this was also probably the case among the Tlingit.

Crimes against society were otherwise punished in this life. A thief had to return what he had stolen or repay its value. Murder was expiated by murder. Unfaithfulness in marriage, which characteristically only referred to actions on the part of the wife, received no other consequences than divorce and the husband's demand for a return of the gifts he had sent to his father-in-law. On the whole modesty and marital faithfulness distinguished Tlingit women as long as they were unaffected by European prospectors and adventurers.

Although we cannot expect a democratic sharing spirit among a rank and class society like the Tlingit, the solidarity between individuals within the same village group was great, albeit very much enforced. Krause emphasizes that even in his relationship with friends and close relatives the Tlingit evinced great selfishness. "For every service he renders, for every gift he gives, he expects a return." This is, of course, the psychological background of the competitive potlatch feasts. Krause recounted how one morning a shaman went from house to house, calling on the members of the bear clan to help him build a new house. The effect was that all these men helped him out, and when the house was ready they were entertained by the shaman and given gifts. [11]

Social stratification rules and mutual obligations regulated life. The value of life was relative, and slaves were not accorded much attention, although there were slave owners who cared for and even set free their slaves. We must keep these relative life values in mind when now we turn to the medical beliefs and practices among the Tlingit.

THE NATURE OF DISEASE

Our sources do not directly disclose how the ancient Tlingit understood the nature of diseases, but we may gather some insights into the complex natural/supernatural causes of diseases from the implications of the material at hand. One entrance to the subject is to study the function of medicine in Tlingit society.

Like other Native American tribes the Tlingit used many medicines that impress modern observers as being empirically sound. For instance, for coughs a warm effusion of sweet cicely *(Osmorhyza brevistyla)* was used. Pleurisy was cured with an effusion of wormwood *(Artemisia vulgaris)*, which was taken in sweat baths. For colic an extract of the roots of locoweed *(Oxytropis)* was used. Skin ailments were healed by washing in an effusion of the American laurel *(Kalmia glauca)*. Sores were treated with several herbs, among them devil's club *(Panax horridum)*. And so on. Such medicines could apparently be handled both by medicine men and common people who knew the recipes.[12]

This of course does not exclude the possibility that natural diseases may be supposed to originate with supernatural powers. Moreover, we know that some apparently natural remedies were thought to have a supernatural rather than an empirical effect. Many herbs that were used to treat a cold or relieve a person from pain are still considered to have supernatural rather than profane medicinal properties. For instance, "smelling medicine," a herb that grows on the mountain tops and has a strong odor, "is rubbed on the body for any kind of sickness or blown upon the traps to make them successful."[13] The effect of this medicine lies certainly not in its medicinal qualities but in its supernatural power. To take another example, there is a "medicine-that-makes-things-humble," a medicine taken to make animals and men humble before the owner of the medicine. "To make this medicine efficacious," writes anthropologist John Swanton, "the possessor spits some of it out in front of himself as he goes along."[14] It is obvious that some medicines are magical means in general, and not specialized medical remedies.

We may presume that the Natives around Sitka, for instance, recognized the value of bathing in the nearby hot springs impregnated with sulfur, salt, and magnesia. We do not know, however, whether the healthy influences of these baths were ascribed to their intrinsic qualities or to the intervention of spiritual forces. It seems probable that the latter alternative was operative. Reference could be made to the sweat baths, which were hygienic and health-protecting (if not indulged in too often) but involved supernatural action.

Dangerous diseases, according to Tlingit beliefs, were caused by witchcraft. So far the evidence tells us that witchcraft in any case meant more than disease-initiating spiritual agents. Witchcraft has been strong all over North America, and the Native Americans traced many diseases to the activities of witches. Among the Tlingit practically all severe diseases were believed to have their origin in witchcraft. The most important task of the shamans was to reveal the witches.

Witches were driven to hurt some persons.[15] The Tlingit say that witches learned their devious art from the ambivalent culture hero Raven when he once lived on earth. The witch tries to obtain an object connected with the person he wants to harm, such as his hair, nails, or spittle. Then he goes to a burial place and puts the object into a grave where there is a body, or the ashes of a body, and curses it. Or he makes an effigy of his victim's body and treats it as badly as he wants the victim to be treated, for instance, making it as thin as a skeleton or deforming the hands. After some time the targeted person becomes ill, suffering in that part of his body from which his property was taken. If he believes that he is bewitched, the shaman is called upon. Possibly the strength of the pain, or the weakening of the victim's consciousness, decides the issue; however, we do not know for sure.

In many parts of North America witches are simply shamans or medicine men and women who misuse their powers to gratify their own egotistical interests. Among the Tlingit the shaman has been a much feared person because he is potentially dangerous, a possible witch. Holmberg mentions that a shaman who is in a powerful mood may throw his helping spirits into other people who distrust him and his shamanic art. This seems to be an action tantamount to witchcraft.[16] There is a report about a shaman in Sitka whose advances had been refused by a girl. He retaliated by accusing her of having caused the illness of the chief. The girl was saved by the Russians, but the shaman had to leave his community for a time when the truth of the matter came out.

Witchcraft was a very dangerous activity and, at least until the middle of the nineteenth century, punished by death. The witch's own relatives could kill him as soon as the shaman had pointed him out. It is characteristic of this culture, however, that witches of a high social rank were not attacked because of their position. They were simply asked in secret to heal the person they had bewitched. We are not told how, if they consented, they would do this.

THE TLINGIT SHAMAN AND HIS HEALING PRACTICES

According to our foremost expert on the Tlingit, Frederica de Laguna, their shaman

> is the intermediary between men and the forces of nature. He cures the sick, controls the weather, brings success in war and on the hunt, foretells the future, communicates with colleagues at a distance, receives news about those who are far away, finds and restores to their families those who are lost and captured by the Land Otter Men, reveals and overthrows the fiendish machinations of witches, and makes public demonstrations of his powers in many awe-inspiring ways. He is the most powerful figure in his own lineage, or sometimes even in his sib.[17]

It is true that women could also become shamans, particularly after their menopause, although in some cases we learn about female shamans who are quite young. But there were not many female shamans, and they were considered to have less power than their male colleagues.

The shamans are now generally a thing of the past (although I have heard of individuals who have tried to become shamans in recent years). The great shamans have been gone since the turn of the century.

The Tlingit shaman held a high rank; he was respected and, as we have seen, dreaded. His sheer appearance was dreadful. Aurel Krause writes that "the shaman, called ichta, is recognized by his wild, dirty appearance, with hair loosely hanging in strands, or bound in a knot at the back of his head, but never touched by a scissors or comb."[18] From other descriptions we know that the shaman's long hair reached down to his feet. It was all twisted round and was said to move when spirits arrived. Since it was believed to contain the shaman's life it could not be cut, for then the shaman died. The shaman wore clothes of tanned skin or woven basketry, and necklaces of animal bones, for instance, bones of brown bears to represent his guardian spirits. He also had a little whetstone hanging about his neck, which he used as a head scratcher.[19] Add to this rattles and drums and masks, and it is understandable that even in Tlingit surroundings the shaman made a very strange impression.

A shaman inherited his profession from his maternal uncle (since the Tlingit had maternal descent) or, occasionally, his father, but not everyone who was in filial line was chosen by the spirits to become a shaman. There is a report of a shaman with two sons, one of whom wanted to become a shaman but never saw a spirit, while the other seemed always to be persecuted by the spirits though he did not want to receive their calling. Finally he gave in to them and became one of the famous shamans at Yakutat Bay.

Although the office of shaman was hereditary, the shaman did not as a rule inherit his ancestors as guardian spirits. It is uncertain whether the guardian spirits of his calling were also identical with the helping spirits of his séances, although this seems possible. It was through these spirits that the shaman could experience the unseen, mysterious world; it was through them that he could perform his wonderful deeds, including the curing of the sick. A mastering of several spirits was necessary for the shaman. He had to be able to "produce" them when it was necessary and to direct them. Compared to the shamans of other tribes like the Haida and Tsimshian, the Tlingit shaman disposed of several spirits, perhaps seven or eight main spirits and a number of lesser spirits. We are informed of three classes: the sky spirits that appear in the northern lights, the spirits of the land that live in the north, and the spirits of the sea. The two last groups of spirits appear as land animals and sea animals, respectively. The sky spirits are supposed to be courageous men who have fallen in war. There is also information that the land spirits are really the souls of all people who have died a natural death; it is difficult to reconcile this with the other information. It is also mentioned that some animal spirits were more closely attached to a shaman than others. Thus, whenever an animal spirit was the totem of a sib it appears to have come primarily to shamans of that sib.[20] The animals—or rather, supernatural spirits in animal forms—were the masters of the animals.

On the death of a shaman his guardian spirits tried to find a successor among his near kin. His nephews who came close to his grave would especially run the risk of spirit visits. These were manifested as diseases that did not disappear until the chosen person had accepted his calling to become the new shaman. Very often the sick man became dizzy, fell unconscious, and foamed at the mouth. It was meaningless to try to avoid the spiritual choice. There is an account of a young man who received the calling and fell down, with white foam coming from his mouth. He refused to give in to the spirits and seemed to get well again. One year later, however, he succumbed to tuberculosis.[21]

Sometimes the guardian spirits of the deceased shaman appeared uninvited to a dreaming kinsman. The latter then could tell the spirits what specific powers he wanted—for instance, the power to heal wounds. Other people could deliberately seek shamanic powers out in the woods. Like those who had been chosen by the spirits, they dwelt for a time in isolation in the wilderness, suffering thirst and hunger, purging and ritual abstinence. It was most important that the supplicant did not comb his hair, the seat of power. The candidate stayed in the woods from one week to a month, depending upon the time it took for the spirits to appear. All this time he lived on roots. The chief of spirits sent out a land otter whose tongue was supposed to contain all secrets regarding shamanism. When man and animal met, the former said "oh" four times and killed the animal. The otter fell upon its back, stretching out its tongue. The candidate cut out the tongue and hid it carefully so nobody else could find it (he would lose his mind if someone found the tongue). The tongue was now his talisman, or "medicine." The shaman's power was increased by obtaining many (usually eight) tongues from different sorts of animals. Unless they were hidden in the woods these tongues were carefully kept together with eagle claws and other objects in what may be termed medicine bags.

We do not know how the candidate experienced the meeting with the spirits. All that can be said is that he learned four songs from his principal spirit. When the novice returned home from the woods he sang these songs for his sib so that they could learn them. Later on, when a spirit visited the shaman in a vision, and the latter saw it arrive in a canoe, he donned his fine apparel: a large hat with a high crown, a dancing blanket, leggings, and a Chilcat blanket. He also painted red stripes across his face.

If the shaman candidate could not call forth the spirits, *yek*, while in isolation he sought the grave of a deceased shaman and spent the night there with the corpse. He took a tooth or a finger of the dead shaman in his mouth. This made it easier for him to conjure forth the spirits and through them get hold of the mysterious land otter (land otters are supposed to be transformed persons with dangerous powers). Keeping company with corpses reminds us of the witches who, it is said, in the early dawn gather at the graveyard associating with the dead. It is obvious that among the Tlingit the dead possess the wisdom of the other world in which both doctors and witches want to share.

The shaman had to acquire as many spirits as he could, because his power was dependent upon the number of spirits he owned. Spirits were supposed to strengthen different capacities in the shaman. Once he has "collected" a crowd of guardian spirits he has to be careful in his relationship to them, for they may kill him. Each spirit brings its name and its song, and the shaman may take his name from the principal guardian spirit—a custom that points to his mysterious identity with this spirit. With drum and rattles the novice shaman learns to call the spirits; in order to succeed he may have to practice for three to twelve months. The spirits appear when the shaman is in a frenzy. As he perceives them one after another, he dons a wooden mask of each spirit as it comes along. He does not know which spirits will appear or in what order. He changes his mask and ornaments according to the attire of the spirits. When he puts on the mask representing a spirit, not only is he supposed to resemble the spirit in outward appearance, but he becomes actually inspired or even possessed by the spirit and speaks, dances, and acts as the spirit.[22]

Sometimes the ancestor ghosts of the shaman appear as well. On such occasions the shaman is so powerful that he can throw his spirits into persons around him who do not believe in his performances. These persons lose consciousness and suffer from a terrible cramp.

At the initiation of a new shaman all the people came together in the deceased shaman's house, and ceremonial dances were executed in the light of the fire in the middle of the room, accompanied by drumming. The brothers Krause, who took part in such a ceremonial evening in 1882, testify that on a rack behind the leader of the ceremonial hung "all the regalia of the shamans, heavy with teeth, beaks and other kinds of rattles, which they wore around the neck, their headgear with its ermine which cascaded down the back, the dance aprons woven of mountain goat wool, various masks and many other things."[23] The Krauses add that two old shamans, who were recognized by their long, untidy hair and fantastic headgears, were also present. A box with some of the late shaman's ceremonial regalia was lowered into the room through the smoke hole in the roof.

During the singing and drumming a young man who had been hidden among the others suddenly plunged toward the wooden drum through the fire. He fell to the ground and after some convulsive jerks he lost consciousness. One of the deceased shaman's necklaces was thrown over his head. After regaining consciousness he retired into the crowd. The same dramatic occurrences were repeated during the remaining days of the ceremony. The young man was, of course, the new shaman to be initiated. It is obvious that his behavior symbolized a ritual of death and rebirth. Perhaps it should be interpreted as a return of the old shaman in his successor.

The shaman now had to let his hair grow long, for his power, like Samson's, resided in his hair, and its was dangerous for him to have it molested. Curiously enough, we are told that witches also tried to save their hair. Could this mean that such witches were shamans, evil shamans?

The new shaman had many tasks to perform, the foremost among them being to function as a ritualist on the days of new and full moon in wintertime. It was then his duty to save the village from diseases and bad luck. He was also a magician in many respects, such as producing good weather (by bathing), invoking rain (by wetting his hair), and summoning seals and fish (by diving to the bottom of the sea with all his paraphernalia), but our focus here will be his healing activities, which certainly were the most important and numerous of the shaman's tasks. He appeared as diviner and doctor whenever somebody was seriously sick.

The winter ceremony, which recalls the winter dances of the Salish peoples (see below), has a wider purpose than being a healing ritual. It is intended to promote health and luck for the whole social group during the year to come—a sort of annual tribal ceremony, we could say, and as such related to other annual rituals like the Sun Dance of the Plains Indians. Nevertheless, our focus here is the performances of the shaman, who acts as diviner and doctor. In order to do so he has to fall into ecstasy. At sundown participants of the ceremony enter a special house, which has been cleaned. Men and women start singing and beating a drum. Dressed in his ceremonial regalia the shaman runs in a sunwise direction around the fire, all the time looking up toward the smoke hole, his hair flying wildly, his face covered by an animal mask. Swinging their daggers some of the singers pretend to pursue him. At some performances the shaman is caught in a net, and the whole procedure repeated three times, whereby the shaman each time turns up with a different mask, that is, a spirit. Then, behind a curtain, the shaman makes his diagnosis of a disease, for example, in a staccato voice. At other performances the shaman suddenly stands still and screams loudly, which is a sign that a spirit has entered him. All noise stops and the spirit gives its verdict.

In the cases described here the shaman's task is that of a diagnostician: thanks to his ecstatic possession he is able to state (or his spirit is able to state) the cause of the disease. It is not often that we meet possession by spirits in a true psychological sense in Native American shamanic trance. There are, however, several instances from the Northwest Coast—a testimony perhaps that we are here not far from Asiatic shamanism where possessional states occur. That the Tlingit shaman really was possessed seems certain. We have seen how the shaman when he has put on a mask of a spirit behaves like that spirit. A modern scholar, Frederica de Laguna, stresses that the shaman "was possessed by one or another of his spirits in turn, speaking in its voice and language, and wearing the mask, forehead mask, or special facepaint appropriate to each one."[24] We may of course suspect a role play, but parallels of similar situations among the Haida, where shamanic possession is well established, seem to rule out this alternative.

There are some descriptions of curing séances in which states of shamanic possession most probably have occurred. In these accounts the shaman cooperates with his assistants, often his nephews, one of whom will become his successor in due time. We are informed that one of the assistants watches over his master, another beats the shaman's drum, a big tambourine about a yard in diameter with a sealskin head. The shaman himself shook a rattle, which could have the form of a bird and was ornamented with designs probably symbolizing guardian spirits. As they handled the shaman's paraphernalia the assistants sang the shaman's songs. The principal assistant was responsible for the choice of the right song, for each of the shaman's spirits had its own song, and if a wrong song was chosen the spirit that was called upon might stay away. When the spirit arrived it sounded as if it were inside the shaman. The shaman sounded like his spirit animal. "They claim he doesn't talk—just his spirit animal. "They claim he doesn't talk—just the spirit talks. But it sounds funny. They can't understand it. It sounds like animals." The assistant tried to translate the spirit's words. After the departure of the spirit the shaman told the public what he had seen and heard.[25]

In his state of possession the Tlingit shaman, or his spirit, gave information concerning the remote source of the disease. According to our literary testimony, it seems that witches and bad spirits have been responsible.[26] The shaman might stop at this, but he might also engage himself in curing the ailing person.

If the culprit was a witch the shaman pronounced the name of the offender. Usually he then put on his headdress, a crown made from the horns of the mountain goat or the claws of the bear. These crowns were particularly worn when the shaman was dealing with cases of illness caused by witchcraft. The shaman then pretended to draw out an object with the likeness of a spear from the affected part of the patient's body, making a noise with his lips. Sometimes the guilty witch was another shaman who, it was said, had put a spirit into the spearlike inanimate object. When the healing shaman had extracted the "spear" he thrust it into water and then blew eagle down over it. If the witch was present in the assembly around the curing scene he was forced to confess his guilt; otherwise there ensued a witch-hunt in which the community at large took part. When the witch had been caught and had confessed, his or her powerful hair was cut off, and, according to some sources, after severe torment the poor sinner was put to death. Other reports, however, indicate that the culprit could escape death after a confession.[27] It would in any case appear that the confession dissolved the bewitchment, and the sick person was thereby healed. If this interpretation is correct the "spear" was only a symptom of the disease, not its origin.

If, on the other hand, some spirits were held responsible for the disease there were other possible remedies. Aurel Krause tells us of a séance where the patient, a boy of five years, was seated on a mat beside the fire, with an old shaman beside him whose gray hair reached his knees. The shaman wore a crown of wooden sticks, which had been bent to resemble the horns of the mountain goat, and he was otherwise naked to the waist. He moved the upper part of his body with convulsive violence, sweating tremendously. He sang, now and then interrupting his song with a wild groaning, and gesticulated with a wooden rattle in the figure of a crane. (There is much evidence that the animal-formed rattles represented the shaman's helping spirits.) Suddenly he grasped the boy's hands, laid them on his hips and thereafter on his abdomen, and called out the names of various animals—perhaps the disease agents themselves. Then the shaman led the little boy around the fire, in both directions, several times, while his assistants, singing monotonously, beat time on a board with small sticks. Finally she shaman declared that the spell of the spirits was broken and that the boy was cured.[28]

In this case the shaman had to break the powers of the bad spirits, driving them away. Such an exorcism could also be accomplished by other means. W. S. Libbey observed in 1886 how in a curing séance one of the shaman's attendants blew eagles' or swans' down into the sick man's face and over his hair to drive away bad spirits, and how the medicine man made motions with his arms as if shooing away the same spirits.[29]

In other cases the shaman felt compelled to remove a foreign object that had intruded into a person. He did this by blowing and sucking or by passing carved objects over ailing parts of the body. We hear that a shaman could pull a "spear" from a wound, throw it into water, and then blow eagle down over it; in other words, the procedure was the same as in healing a person from disease due to witchcraft. It is not always easy to determine whether such an operation was based on a diagnosis of witchcraft or intrusion caused by spirits.

There is, finally, the type of spiritual aggression whose result is usually labeled "soul loss." In other words, the soul (free-soul) of an individual goes astray or is stolen by spirits, with the consequence that he falls ill. We know that such cases occurred among the Tlingit, but there are no close observer's descriptions, not even accounts by Tlingit informants. From the data that can be gathered it seems that the lost or captured soul may lurk in the vicinity or steer its course to the realm of the dead. The Haida, a related tribe south of the Tlingit, had shamans who after some fasting went out into the woods to catch the forlorn soul. We have reasons to suspect that Tlingit shamans did the same. Both the Haida and the Tlingit shamans had small bone instruments, "soul-catchers," with which they captured the lost soul. The soul was then brought back to the patient and blown into his body.

We do not hear, however, of shamanic soul journeys to fetch a patient's fugitive soul on its way to the other world among the Tlingit. It seems that such shamanic excursions were not the rule. If a person's soul had been stolen while he or she was bathing in the sea or walking in the woods by a land otter man (which was not uncommon) the shaman could send his guardian spirit to locate the person and guide the searchers, but he could do no more.

On the other hand, he could send out his spirits to gather news about people, and he could for that purpose even send out his own soul. On such occasions the shaman fell in a deep trance and lay lifeless on the ground.

Shamanic treatment of the sick usually took place at night, in the main room of the wooden house. Native remedies administered by women were always tried first, but the shaman was called upon in cases of violent or difficult diseases that could not be healed by ordinary medicines. Shamans handed health talismans over to their clients. They had medical and surgical skills. Shamans could, for instance, let out pus from the patient's body, and they directed women to sew up wounds.

THE HEALED HEALER AMONG THE COAST SALISH

If the Tlingit manifest the culture, religion, and therapeutical measures of the northern and most "typical" Northwest Coast tribes (excluding the Kwakiutl of Vancouver Island and neighboring areas), the Coast Salish of the middle and southern Northwest Coast present a simpler and more "normal" Native culture. To be sure, theirs was in the old days a hierarchical social structure with hereditary slaves and differences in wealth, but the ranking of individuals was less palpable, and the standing of a chieftain less exclusive. In many respects we get the impression that the Coast Salish once offered the foundations, as it were, on which the northern tribes, including the Tlingit, built their splendid cultures. The archaeological material suggests, however, that the Coast Salish originally represented a more southern tradition that was basically independent from the northern (more circumpolar) culture.

Characteristic of Salish villages has been the conglomeration of simple plankhouses with shed-roofs, instead of the saddle-roof houses with gables so typical for the Wakashan and northern wooden houses. The house posts lack the clan crests of the northern tribes, and the wood carving is simpler and less frequent than among other coastal tribes. Residence has been patrilocal, that is, new families are gathered in the husband's community. Descent is bilateral, but we find that some families inherit privileges on the

father's or mother's side. Potlatches occurred formerly, but at least south of
Puget Sound they were not instruments for claiming prestige as has been
the case among more northern tribes. On the whole, the Coast Salish have
had a less formal ceremonial structure than other northwestern groups.

Whereas clan spirits have been nonexistent or without much importance,
much confidence was put in individual spirits (which could be patrons of
societies to which individuals belonged). Guardian spirits existed for both
sexes. As we shall see, this religious complex has been invigorated through
a conscious renascence in modern days. The performance of dances cele-
brating the guardian spirits at a winter ceremony is again becoming more
frequent. The combination of initiation rites into societies and the guardian-
spirit quest has resulted in intersting ritual forms, where spiritual experiences have been sanctioned by ritual performances of a type well known
from the Kwakiutl.

It is interesting to compare now mainly historical Tlingit medical practices
and health programs with corresponding Coast Salish practices still in existence. We shall find that the Coast Salish display more variegated forms of
concern about health and medicine, thereby representing a transition to the
Interior Salish of the Plateau with their more continental medical patterns
(of the type described in the preceding chapter).

Since the guardian spirit quest has been general among Coast Salish people the difference between a common visionary and a candidate for the
position of a medicine man is rather slight. One sharp-sighted observer to
whom we owe much clarification on this topic, Dr. Wolfgang Jilek, makes
the following distinctions: The medicine man, or shaman, undergoes a long,
rigorous quest and receives in his vision, or dream, a specific power to heal
the sick, whereas a common person sometimes receives a vision without
quest, and this vision confers only the ability to sing and dance.[30] The
Puyallup-Nisqually at southeastern Puget Sound take it for granted that
every person has "power" and that this power is expressed by his or her
personal nature. Marvelous abilities are due to affiliations with powers, and
they imitate the particular abilities of the spirit animals. Where the vision
quest for laymen occurs it is shorter and weaker than the vision quest for
medicine men, and the vision itself lacks the force and intensity of that of
the medicine men. Among the northern Coast Salish the guardian spirits
are the same for ordinary visionaries and medicine specialists, but the latter
are blessed by several spirits with particular sorts of curing powers. The
Coast Salish of Puget Sound have distinct classes of helping spirits for medicine specialists and laymen.

Among some groups, known collectively as the Stalo of the Fraser River, usually only novice medicine men, warriors, and gamblers have undergone a vision quest. Other people have been satisfied to be blessed by sudden visions that confer a song and dance ritual, not curing powers. There are reports that some medicine women have lived among the Stalo. The same guardian spirits appear to all individuals, including novice medicine men.

It is difficult to tell to what extent these vision patterns are extant today. It is probable that in many places they continue or have been revived, for since the 1960s the entire ritual program for the demonstration of spiritual acquisitions has been resumed after decades of apparent oblivion. Such ritual confirmations presuppose spiritual revelations. And there is now good evidence that such revelations occur according to old visionary patterns in some places.

The future medicine man or shaman pursues his quest by going out into the woods or to the mountaintops and staying there for some time, enduring all kinds of hardships. He may be a young boy, only about ten years of age, at the time of his first vision. Thereafter his supernatural gift may lie dormant for years and then become actualized by a new visit of the supernatural being. Otherwise the candidate for shamanhood who has just acquired a spirit power keeps secret about it until the following winter. He is then forced by the spirit to reveal his power, for it makes him sick.

It has been characteristic of shamanic power from northern California and Oregon (as among the Yurok and Klamath) to the Bute Inlet in British Columbia that it makes itself known as a disease inside the candidate, a "pain." Indian opinion is divided whether this pain should be removed by a shaman or not. It is not a common disease, they point out; it is a sign of the appearance of the guardian spirit. With some tribes the shaman has tried to oust the spirit and then called upon it again to empower the candidate. In other tribes the candidate asks his friends to help him sing the songs the spirit has taught him, which relieves him from pain.

The condition of the shaman candidate has been described by many scholars as a state of possession. There is no doubt that the spiritual power is supposed to reside within the individual. This in itself is no sure token of true possession, that is, possession in a psychological sense; however, sudden noises, other persons' singing, a general feeling of weakness and pain, and fits of fainting or frenzy may call forth a state of what could be called partial possession: the individual seemingly makes no movements of his own—he acts because it is the spirit that acts with him, but he retains his consciousness.

The harmonizing between the candidate and the spirit power is effectuated by dancing and singing at the winter dances. Spirit dances are known among the Plateau tribes as well, and they are probably a common Salish heritage, but their placing at wintertime concurs with the winter ceremonies of the southern Northwest Coast. It is the candidate who has to sponsor a dance in the longhouse, the big meetinghouse where invited guests sit along the walls and three fireplaces are situated in the middle of the hall. He is not alone in dancing. All persons who have been blessed with spiritual power during the past year have to stand up to dance if they want peace from their spirits. Among the Twana (a Salishan group southwest of Seattle), a shaman calls on the guardian spirit which then possesses the dancer. The latter dances and sings, but it is really the spirit that is supposed to animate him. By manifesting the spirit presence in this way the candidate wards off his malady. If in the long run he resists the manifestation of power he runs the risk of dying.

The spirit dancing is often combined with the candidate's loss of con-sciousness. As many authors have remarked, this is the "initiatory sickness" that the well-known investigator of shamanism, Mircea Eliade, has identified as a characteristic feature in the career of the shaman.[31] He dies from his old condition and returns to life as a new inspired being—a true transition rite, or ritual of passage, as the technical term runs. It is far-fetched, however, to say that the candidate's experiences, his psychic weakness and loss of consciousness, brand him as a truly sick person, mentally retarded and unbalanced, as some American and Russian writers have insisted is the case among shamans in the North and everywhere. This could not be correct. Shamans are usually forceful personalities who control both themselves and, in their practice, the spirits that help them. They have, however, an extreme sensitivity, and at initiatory programs they adapt their sensitivity to the ritual scheme. This is apparently what happens at the spirit dance. There is no basic shamanic disease, but there is the ritual idea of disease, death, and resurrection. And this ideological complex forms the personal experiences through its strong (collective) suggestion. Thus the shaman becomes the healed healer.

One new shaman told Dr. Jilek, "You call a new dancer a baby because he is starting out his life again. . . . You have a funny feeling, that's the way they treated you like a newborn. The way they explain this is that you die and wake up to a new life."[32] This rebirth is not just the case of empathy into a dramatic pantomime. It is true that the ritual leader "kills" the candi-date by clubbing him with a hammer or a ceremonial staff in an imitative act. The reaction of the candidate may be extreme: he falls into motionless rigidity and is lifted up "stiff as a board." As soon as he wakes up, after some minutes or a couple of hours, he starts singing and dancing.

This twilight state of the shamanic neophyte closely corresponds to inner experiences of a tradition-bound content. As he is, as it seems, killed by a stroke of the club he travels—in his free-soul—to the land of shades. He goes downriver, toward the west, for it is there that this land is situated. He has to be careful there, for the dead try to entice him to eat their food, and that is dangerous: once you have tasted their abominable dishes you are bound to stay in their country forever. Thanks to his new, although still vulnerable, shamanic power the candidate is able to return home. (There is some indication that sometimes he receives his medicine song, and thereby his supernatural power, in the realm of the dead.) He slowly regains consciousness, making movements with his new power as if he were "paddling upstream" in a canoe. He travels back to the land of the living, and takes up the spirit dance.

This trip is proof that the new shaman is able to visit the dead and to return from them. This also means that he will be able to restore the souls that because of disease have lost their anchorings in the body and gone to the land of the dead.

THE SPIRIT CANOE CURING CEREMONY

Coast Salish therapy proceeds from two presumptions concerning the origins of disease: that malevolent shamans (witches) have shot pathogenic objects into a person; and that ghosts have stolen the soul or supernatural power of the person (or that it has gone astray for other reasons). The measures taken to restore the person's health correspond to the diagnoses, but in a very liberal way. For instance, it is considered—at least today—that spirit dancing has curative effects on all participants, on family members and other observers as well as the particular individual who has been diagnosed. This import of the spirit winter dance may be connected with the fact that at present the spirit dance is ranked as more important than the vision quest.

The shaman, or medicine man, can be either male or female in the northern Salish areas; however, particularly at Puget Sound (and perhaps elsewhere) female shamans are rare, and their powers are inferior to those of male shamans. The sources at hand give the impression that female healers in the past concerned themselves more often with the curing of diseases due to intrusion, whereas male shamans undertook perilous journeys to the land of the dead to bring back a soul or a spiritual power to its owner.

Diseases due to intrusion are mostly caused by a malignant doctor (witch) shooting into the patient an object into which he or she had put his or her power—a typical case of Native American witchcraft. We do not hear emphatically that intrusion of spirits occurs, as among other tribes; however, several reports show that this intruding object may occasionally appear as an animate being. The object has to be removed by a competent medicine man or woman, but usually not by a shaman. These doctors enjoy mostly a high reputation.

The therapist removes the disease object by sucking through a hollow bone or putting the mouth directly on the affected part of the patient's body. He or she may also pull out the sickness with his or her hands, or just by touching the sore part, or by rubbing it. In some cases the medicine person resorts to bleeding; with the "bad blood" the disease disappears. In other cases the patient is ordered to bathe. The methods that doctors prefer are those taught them by their guardian spirits.

Sometimes the curing method and the way of making a diagnosis are almost the same. About a certain medicine man it is reported that "he sat with his eyes closed, singing and drumming [on a cedar board]. As soon as an Indian doctor starts to sing, his power comes close to him, and the power is right there with him while he's doctoring."[33] Such a séance could last half an hour. We notice how close the connection is between the sacred song and the spirit. But the same applies to the diagnosis made by the Puyallup-Nisqually medicine man:

> The diagnosis was accomplished by power singing which he engaged in with his eyes shut. His right arm was bent so that the hand almost touched the left shoulder, the elbow before him horizontal to shoulder level, and his head lowered so that the arm covered his eyes. The singing included dancing.[34]

This performance continued for half an hour. When the doctor has "seen" the trouble he informs the patient quietly about it and tells him what could be done. Apparently, the same medical behavior could be used for several aims.

Whereas the intrusion diagnosis refers to cases of bodily afflictions—wounds, aches, sore spots, and similar things—the soul or spirit-loss diagnosis focuses mental disturbances of some sort. This is where the shaman comes in as doctor; he is the curer for all diseases applying to the soul.

What separates this diagnosis from other similar diagnoses in Native North America is that the entity lost is so often the guardian spirit. In the Puget Sound area it is nearly always this spirit that has been lost. This situation certainly represents a local patterning of beliefs, but it has its roots in the fact that the free-soul and the guardian spirit may come very close to each other; the former may through dream wanderings, trance experiences, and the like temporarily withdraw from the body and thereby achieve some independence like a spirit; the latter may become intimately associated with the person and thereby take on some "soulish" qualities. One can observe here how self-evident and universal the belief in guardian spirits must be among Puget Sound tribes.

Now, as was pointed out above, the Natives of this area make a sharp distinction between the guardian spirits of common individuals and the guardian spirits of shamans. Only the guardian spirit of a shaman is able to bring its client to the other world and back again. (In this connection it is interesting to note that the Puyallup-Nisqually use the same word for the shaman and his guardian spirit—they are obviously next to identical.) Furthermore, only a shaman's spirit can rescue the spirit of an ordinary individual.

A spirit power may leave its client as a result of a psychic shock or activities of the dead. In the latter case it is a ghost from the hereafter, and particularly a dead relative who longs for his living kin, who is the thief. The theft may be extended over a long time: the dead relative removes piecemeal property belonging to his living kinsman; the loss of a great number of these personal things is the sign that the person has lost his spirit and will die. If, on the other hand, a person is sick without the interference of ghosts, but the power is lost—according to the diagnosis of the shaman—the destination of the lost power is not necessarily the realm of the dead. The power could linger somewhere in the neighborhood.

Medical methods therefore change with the diagnosis.

When the power or free-soul looms in the vicinity of the village the shaman need not go on an expedition to fetch it. There is a report of a woman who could not be cured by white doctors. A Native doctor then came to her assistance. He told her husband that her guardian spirit had left her and was now stuck in the mud of the river. The shaman's guardian spirit then listened for the song of the woman's guardian spirit. He caught it up and started to sing it. Then the woman rose and sang it together with him. Her guardian spirit returned, and she was cured. Only a shaman is able to sing a foreign spirit's song.

The therapy is different when the patient's guardian spirit has passed over the river bounding the realm of the dead. Then the lone shaman's power is not sufficient. In the old days a ceremony was performed which has become classic in the history of shamanism and therefore should be mentioned here: the Spirit Canoe ceremony. It has been described by the anthropologist Hermann Haeberlin in the following way.[35]

If a person's guardian spirit had been carried off to the land of the dead, he or she was struck by an ailment that was psychic rather than physical and consisted in a general feeling of indisposition. The sick person would die if the spirit were not regained. It was therefore necessary to arrange a shamanic ceremony of a major order, a ceremony in which many shamans had to participate actively. Since at least eight and often more shamans were required it was necessary to call some of them from neighboring groups, for the small Coast Salish tribelets did not each possess so many shamans. There were two conditions, however. First, the shaman should have the kind of guardian spirit that could work in this kind of ceremony. Second, the shaman coming from another Coast Salish group should have the same belief in the realm of the dead and the same conception of the way to this realm as the arrangers of the ceremony. This information shows how ideas of the afterworld could deviate between small neighboring tribes of the same language and general culture.

It was the task of all these shamans to cooperate in a canoeing expedition to the spirit land. The traveling had to take place in midwinter and always at nighttime. The Coast Salish believe that everything in that land of the dead is opposite to conditions in the land of the living. Thus, the dead have their summer in the middle of the winter, and their days are nights to us. We even hear that the trail to the land of ghosts is only passable at midwinter time. (It is said that only at that time can the spirit of a sick man leave him for this region.) Only the dead can travel that trail by foot; other visitors have to come in canoes. They will follow the river in a westerly direction. Somewhere over there the ghosts have their homes.

The shamanistic séance took place in the patient's house, or any other house, provided it was situated east to west. The shamans placed themselves in two parallel rows along the axis east-west, facing west. Beside each of them was an upright board, which represents the shamanic guardian spirit (or, according to some informants, the shaman's visionary experiences). The room was transformed, as it were, into a big canoe steering downriver. The shamans used magical poles as paddles, making paddling movements. In turn they sang their spiritual songs, which were echoed by the onlookers who had crept up on the sleeping platforms along the walls. A shaman at the rear of the "canoe" was supposed to steer it.

First they arrived at a river crossing that the dead had to pass over on a tree trunk (a favorite motif in Native American tales about the journey to the land of the dead). The shamans made an imitated crossing by walking on their sticks, which they had laid out in front of them. Then they continued their voyage in a new imaginary canoe and arrived at the land of the dead.

Everything there looked like it does here on earth, but the dead walked with crossed legs. The shamans met a ghost who was out picking berries— a ghost which was impersonated by an Indian who walked with crossed legs, making strange grimaces. Well arrived in the village of the dead the shamans found that the inhabitants refused to give up the patient's guardian spirit. There was a fight, which was dramatized by boys shooting off burning cedar splints toward the roof. The shamans grabbed hold of the lost guardian spirit and rushed to the canoe.

The shamanic crew returned, this time facing east in their canoe. They landed in the world of the living and brought the guardian spirit back to its client in their closed hands. They sang the song of this spirit. This made the patient rise and join the same song. The ailment was over, and it remained for the recovered individual to pay the healers (a considerable amount of money) and give presents to the spectators, who had also been singing the shamanic songs.

If only one night was used for the ceremony the first part of this night was spent traveling to the dead; midnight was the time of arriving there and fighting the dead, and the late night was occupied by paddling homeward. Based on the statement of one of his informants, Haeberlin suggests there is a solar symbolism in this scheme, which parallels the course of the sun during the night. This is quite possible, considering all rituals the world over that are dependent on the position of the sun and its movements.

What is difficult for us to understand is how this so-called "imitative shamanism" could be accepted as a true medicine cure. It is less surprising perhaps that a patient after such a cure stands up and feels sound—here is the suggestion of belief at work. But how could all the partakers believe in a rite that so obviously was grounded in prearranged theatrical action? Probably we have to explain the outer activities as demonstrations of an interior psychic experience—we face a psychodrama, in other words. Presumably the shamans have been in a sort of trance while they acted out their mysterious experiences.

Parenthetically it should be noticed that these transcendent voyages have stimulated the growth of eschatological conceptions. A specialist on the Puyallup-Nisqually, Marian W. Smith, points out that her informants postulated the existence of the realm of the dead from the fact that souls were brought back from there by shamans.[36] This is perhaps to go too far, but the details of the realm have certainly been supplied by these shamans.

The Spirit Canoe ceremony has in our days been thinned down to a Power Board ceremony. The latter is performed in connection with the annual winter spirit dance. On this occasion the medicine man prepares himself while two power boards of the kind described above are carried by the doctor's assistants. The boards are heated at the fire in order to gain more power. The doctor asks the public to help the patient by mentally concentrating on him or her. We are informed by Jilek that "the patient is surrounded by relatives and friends, who support him affectionately and accompany him home."[37]

As the séance starts there is a fast beating on the drums, the medicine man sings, women throw food into the fire as an offering, and the two boards are carried around. Or rather, these mysterious beings decide their own course: like magnets they are drawn together—to be separated only by the medicine man—and then seek their way through the room. Finally they reach the patient. They stroke his or her head and body. A patient of Dr. Jilek's who underwent this treatment afterward declared, "I really felt the power, a great big load taken off my shoulders."[38]

Dr. Jilek informs us that this fellow had been treated by many white physicians; he had spent a long time in hospital for severe neurotic and psychosomatic derangements and had made three suicide attempts. The Power Board ceremony made him recover. Jilek has supplied a list of other patients who became healthy after spirit dancing, and the high percentage of successful cases is impressive. Evidently, recovery through faith is an important medical alternative in situations of psychic or psychosomatic disease.

·4·

Traditional Medicine on the Plains

As we leave the North Pacific Coast and move inland, over the Plateau lands around the rivers Fraser and Columbia and over the mighty Rocky Mountains, we arrive at the geographical heart of North America, the wide, open grasslands that in Canada are called the Prairies, in the United States the Plains (the Prairies of the United States are the tall-grass plains with interspersed woods that stretch along the eastern border of the Plains). The undulating Plains country was, until the end of the nineteenth century, the home of innumerable buffaloes, antelopes, and other quadrupeds and thus an ideal country for hunters who could move quickly. The colorful and warlike Plains Indians had the means to do this in the horse, an animal they adopted from the whites, just as they equipped themselves with another white treasure, the gun. We can say that the horse and the gun facilitated the Indian conquest of the Great Plains.

This historical glance tells us that the Plains culture as it existed in the nineteenth century, the most "Indian" of Native cultures in the eyes of the world, was a very recent culture, a product of culture contact ("acculturation"). Before the 1700s, some of the tribes later to constitute the true Plains Indians roamed primarily the peripheries of the Plains country—moving about on foot, hunting and gathering. Only eastward, in the Prairie lands, had some tribes of different linguistic affiliations (Caddoan like the Pawnee, Siouan like the Omaha) established settlements, alternating between hunting and agricultural pursuits. Toward the end of the eighteenth century the great Plains tribes invaded the Plains, many of them—tribes like the Algonkian Blackfeet, Cheyenne and Arapaho, the Siouan Lakota, Assiniboin and Crow, the Shoshonean Comanche, and many more—reacting to indirect pressure from the whites. Arriving from the north, northeast, east, and west they developed the culture that during the last century typified the North American Indian.

THE EASTERN SHOSHONI

The westernmost part of the Plains area where the grass changes into sagebrush-covered foothills and wooded Rocky Mountain country had been held by Shoshoni Indians for many centuries. We still find them today in some of their ancient heartlands, the Wind River Basin. The Shoshoni are in fact the easternmost offshoot of the Numic tribes that in the old days foraged over the Great Basin area: ethnic groups like the Paiute, Ute, Gosiute, and Shoshoni. Shoshonean culture in the Plains therefore has many reminiscences of an existence in the arid Great Basin; however, it also has references to the Plateau Indian fishing culture. Indeed, one Shoshoni group, the Sheepeaters of the mountainous regions in Wyoming and Idaho, lived the lives of woodland hunters. Wyoming members of this group are now integrated with the Eastern Shoshoni.

During the nineteenth century the Eastern Shoshoni were mounted buffalo hunters like other Plains Indians, and their culture was generally a Plains culture. Thus, the Shoshoni had a strong military organization under a head chief (Washakie, chief from 1843 to 1900), warrior societies, and a system of war honors. The tribe was dispersed in small bands during the winter and came together for spring and autumn hunts and for ceremonies and feasting during the summer. Most famous during this time was the Sun Dance, a great ceremony at which, under the leadership of medicine men, the Indians danced in honor of the Supreme Being, *Tam Apö* ("Our Father").[1] The Sun Dance, which lasted for three days and nights, was basically a thanksgiving ceremony to praise Tam Apö for the year that had passed and to ask a blessing for the coming year, for this was also the time for the new year that arrived with lush grass and thriving animals. During the Sun Dance the bands formed a large circle with the dance lodge in the center. The lodge represented the universe, and its center pole was a replica of the world pole and the sacred means of communication between God and mankind (the tribe).[2]

Add to this scene the characteristic Plains Indian tent, or tipi, the war bonnets and Plains Indian garments, scalp dancing and war dancing, and magnificently decorated horses, often pulling sleds ("travoises"), and we have the typical ingredients of the Plains culture.

Behind this glittering façade however, there remained many vestiges of the poor Basin culture that had once been the common Shoshonean heritage. The whole mythology, with the tricky Coyote as central character, belongs here. So do the menstruation rules for women, the institution of "antelope shamans" particularly endowed to lure the shy but curious antelopes, and the idea that medicine men could receive their mysterious capacities through spontaneous dreams. The general rule on the Plains was otherwise that medicine men, and in some cases medicine women, received their powers through deliberate vision quests.

Vision quests existed among the Shoshoni as well, possibly as an addition to their original pattern: men of all ages sought their visions of guardian spirits who could bless them with their powers up in the foothills. There the spirits were supposed to have left their mark in the rock drawings that one can find there. The spirits were portrayed as animals whose powers they represented to a miraculous degree. The supplicant had to wait for the spirit to arrive in a vision and hand over its powers, medicine song, and various medicine symbols (medicine bag, particular facial painting, arrangement of feathers, and so forth). Whereas the spontaneous dream primarily favored what we would call a medicine man, the vision quest was open to any man, and to women after their menopause.

The Basin background has been so conspicuous in many respects that some anthropologists have ruled the Eastern Shoshoni out as a true Plains tribe. This is, I believe, an incorrect conclusion. All Plains tribes have vestiges of their earlier existence as Woodland, Plateau, Desert, or agricultural Indians. It is also strange to exclude the Plains Shoshoni as Plains Indians whilst their offshoot the Comanche (from whom they did not effectively separate until the 1840s) are regarded as one of the "typical" Plains tribes. Indeed, I have not seen any commendation of Plains Indian military drill and fortitude equal to what General Crooke's aide-de-camp, Major John Bourke, bestowed upon the Washakie Shoshoni during Sitting Bull's war.[3] We certainly do not receive any impression from the Eastern Shoshoni of the rather infrequent, anarchical, and informal warfare that characterized the Great Basin area.

After the end of the Plains Indian independence in the 1880s and 1890s, Shoshoni culture resumed some of its older customs of Basin origin. Thus, the atomistic spirit was strengthened as wars and warrior societies faded out. Medicine men no longer used the vision quest as frequently as before but were blessed by spirits and powers during their dreams, not least in the Sun Dance. On the other hand, some of the dance traditions from Basin days died away, and the Sun Dance became more and more the center of religious activities. Today the most important medical rituals take place within the frame of the Sun Dance. Of course, the impact of Christian notions has lately been considerable, but in the main Christianity and traditional religion have appeared as two parallel, and alternating, systems.

The following sketch of medicine and health among the Plains Shoshoni is based upon my own fieldwork among this tribe in the 1940s and 1950s. A return to the Wind River Reservation in the 1980s has convinced me that medicine ceremonies are more hidden today than they were before. Pan-Indian medical ideas (that is, American Indian ideas picked up from other tribes) are very common and have been substituted for some older traditions that apparently have fallen into disuse or oblivion.

SHOSHONI PASSAGES OF LIFE

At the beginning of time, so the Shoshoni relate, there was one world and one people. At that time men and women lacked mouths. When they needed sustenance they cooked elkmeat, smelled it, and then threw it away. They could only communicate by signs. A mythical being—some say, Coyote—cut their mouths open when they asked for it (!), and thus human life as we knew it began.

Stories of this kind are popular among the Shoshoni and are part of their mythological tales. They are probably very ancient (and remind us of medieval tales of mouthless inhabitants at the Ganges whose food was the smell of flowers). With few exceptions, however, the true philosophy of life for the Shoshoni is not preserved in mythology, but in traditional beliefs.

For the Wind River Shoshoni life is a gift of the Supreme Being, Tam Apö. It originates with him and will finally return to him. Informants told me that at death "the soul returns to the Creator, who has given life," or they said that the soul returns to "Our Father who has given birth to man." Life is here and in other statements identical with the force in man that keeps him alive, the life-soul or *mugwa*. The cognition that this soul originates with the Supreme Being is common among many peoples in North America and is well articulated by the Shoshoni. It expresses the idea that one's whole life is in God's hands.

We may of course speculate about the possibility of Christian influences here, but they seem on the whole rather unlikely. Only the information that the soul returns to the high god after death may be disputed. Otherwise the Sun Dance has installed in the people a firm belief in Tam Apö as the source of the world and of human life.

The birth of a child was in the old days surrounded by ritual acts: the woman had to stay for thirty days in a particular small tipi at a distance from the camp, for she was in a dangerous, tabooed state. Many precautions were taken to help the expected baby; for example, the mother must not eat too much, for that would make the child fat and lazy. The father likewise influenced the child by his behavior. He bathed in a cold stream just as the baby is bathed in cold water, in this way making it easier for his newborn child. He rose early and moved around, thus making it easy for the child to do the same in times to come.

The naming was most important for the health and success of the child. A boy's name could be inherited from a deceased kinsman who was well reputed, or it was given by a brave warrior or hunter whose blessing was transferred with the name. If the name "was no good" but made the child sickly a medicine man could recommend that the parents throw it away and give the child a new name that had healthy consequences. A girl's name was taken from birds, flowers, and stars, or meaningless words. The name is even today suffused with power, and if asked to tell his or her personal name an individual prefers to let another person reveal it.

In order to succeed in life the man, and to a certain extent the woman, had to seek the protection of supernatural powers. There was not as in many other Indian tribes any rule that such powers should be sought at puberty. They could be gained at any time, and many Shoshoni, particularly the medicine men, tried repeatedly to augment the number of their guardian spirits. Women could approach the powers after their menopause. During their fertile years women could be a danger to the supernaturals; a menstruating woman who came close to the Sun Dance lodge would cause all the spirits there to flee the place.

At the time of my first visit to the Shoshoni the vision quest had already become almost obsolete. The old Basin idea of receiving spontaneous visions in dreams had become fashionable again after a medicine man had declared that the sought vision brought on only evil powers.[4] There were, however, still people around who had sought the powers up among the foothills. Those who had tried had, if they persisted and did not flee from the dangerous beings—real animals or monsters that they perceived—finally been visited by some spirit that granted them its protection and powers. The spirit was usually identical with one of the rock-drawings found in the vicinity. Indeed, it was not uncommon for the petitioner to direct a prayer for a blessing to the spirit depicted on a particular rock.

Not all the visionaries had the same luck. Some could not stand all the trials while waiting in the cold night beneath the pictographs, attacked or scared by animals, tortured by hunger and terrible visions. They rushed away in panic and, as I was told, became lame. Others happened to be visited by one of the evil-minded monsters that are said to haunt these high regions.

The powers of this ogre were all for the bad. A shy, mentally confused person was pointed out to me: this was a man who had received the destroying power of the rock monster. He was not able to control this power, but was himself overtaken by it.

The vision quest is thus a gamble, requiring mental and physical strength. In the old days when hunting and warring were part of habitual activities the quest for visions was a sine qua non. Today it can be dispensed with, and medicine men are the only ones who engage in vision seeking.

Old age was something that was both wished for and detested, and still is. Many vision stories tell us that among the good gifts with which a spirit could endow his client were white hair and many winters. The famous Chief Washakie was respected as "the white-haired boy." Old people have wisdom and experience; their counsels are sought and they are highly esteemed— as long as their wisdom and sanity can be upheld. Many of them, of both sexes, have been known as excellent storytellers. Old women are occasionally just tolerated, not more, particularly if they are widows and lack close relations. This is no rule, however; I saw many elderly ladies well cared for by distant kin. It is well known that the famous Sacajawea who accompanied the Lewis and Clark expedition to the Pacific was well cared for until her death at a very high age.

Death has never been feared, although of course precautions were always taken to avoid it or keep it afar as long as possible. The efforts of the medicine men were directed to delay, and if possible impede, the transition from this life to the next one.

In mythological tales it is recounted how death originated.[5] Here is one of the versions that I noted down:

> In ancient times, long, long ago, animals were human beings. The two most important were Wolf and Coyote. Wolf—the Creator—was easy to deal with, while Coyote always tried to go against Wolf's wishes. Wolf said that when a person died he could be brought back to life by shooting an arrow under him. But Coyote did not agree: he thought it was a bad idea to bring people back to life, for then there would be too many people here and there would not be room for them all. "No," he said, "let man die; let his flesh rot and his spirit glide away with the wind so that only a heap of dry bones will be left." Wolf agreed, but he decided within himself to let Coyote's son be the first to die. Therefore Wolf wished that the boy should die and by his very wish brought about the boy's death. Soon Coyote came and told Wolf that his son had died. He reminded Wolf of his statement that people could get a new life after death if an arrow was shot under them. But Wolf reminded Coyote in his turn that he himself had said that man should die. Therefore it would be so.

In this story Wolf appears as the Supreme Being, a reflection of the fact that in the Great Basin the primeval divinities are thought of as both animals and human beings. Coyote is as always the trickster and, more or less, adversary of the Supreme Being. In the version rendered above death is the result of an agreement between the two high beings. In another version Coyote is punished by the Supreme Being when he answers the latter disrespectfully by practicing ventriloquism. The punishment is mortality for all his descendants, apparently including mankind. Somehow this echoes the biblical story of the fall of man. A Christian origin seems most probable in this case.

The story in its first version was taken seriously by most traditionalists still in the 1940s. The idea of two wills competing over the destiny of mankind seems to contain vestiges of a philosophical discussion. Death is mysterious, but it was ordained in mysterious, primordial times when all human conditions and cultural ways were instituted. Man has to bow to this fact.

Death is surrounded by rituals that express a will to sever the dead person from the living more than real grief. For instance, coins are placed on the corpse's eyes and mouth if these have not been shut, a clear indication that the look of the eye and the open mouth represent danger. The personal belongings of the deceased follow him or her to the grave; a medicine man, for instance, has his medicine bag placed beside him. This custom may be interpreted as a consideration to the deceased person, but it may also be taken as proof of the old rule that what is contaminated by the dead has to go with them.

For some time the kinfolk are dressed in ragged clothes so that the ghost will be satisfied by their grief or—which is just as probable—so that the ghost will not touch them and haunt them. The excessive weeping after a death is no doubt to some extent a measure of true feelings of emotional attachment, but it has other aims. The weeping women pray that the dead person may follow a straight path to the land of the dead and not go astray. If this happened it would constitute a threat to the living, for wandering and lingering ghosts afflict their living congeners.

The feelings of care and love thus seem to stop before the final boundary line set by death. A further expression of this fact is the name taboo: as soon as a person is dead his or her name must not be mentioned for some time. I made mistakes in this matter and, to my regret, a sorrowful old woman, one of my best informants, avoided me for some weeks.

What happens at death? There are many opinions among the Shoshoni in this matter as there are among other Indians. Ideas of reincarnation (rare today), of life on earth as ghosts, or of life in another world such as heaven or a land beyond the shining mountains in the west, compete with each other. Christianity has, of course, turned minds to the idea of a happy existence in heaven. Some living persons are said to have gone over to the other side in a state of coma, and they have reported a life of "happy hunting grounds," with buffalo hunting on swift ponies. But such visions are not much credited these days.

It is interesting to find that the way to the other side leads over the Milky Way, an indication of a heavenly place for the dead. Some traditionalists even pointed out to me that the road along the Milky Way was identical with the center pole of the Sun Dance; its two forks stretching toward the sky stand for the forks of the Milky Way. This is a good illustration of how the cosmic scenery may be reduced in the cult to a ritual replica.

SHOSHONI IDEAS OF HEALTH AND WELL-BEING

Many of the passages of life show us how familial and personal care guards a Shoshoni Indian's health. The family always stands up for the individual from the time he or she is born. When sickness, wounds, and other physical tragedies occur the kinsmen do their best to comfort the patient. A relative is always ready to fetch a medicine man, an undertaking which was formerly done under the most intricate behavior. Stepchildren and adopted children are treated in the same careful way.

With the exception of lighter illnesses and misadventures it is a general conviction that all failures in health have their origins in a break with the supernatural world. The way to overcome this break, and a reliable way to reach the powers, is suffering. The vision quest deals with just that: a humble man prostrates himself on the cliffs on the foothills and, lying naked under a blanket for perhaps several days, he endures the hardships of the cold night, attacks from animals and other dangers, and abstains from food. The final vision is a confirmation that the powers have pitied him. So it is also in the Sun Dance: dancing through three nights with naked feet on the sandy ground and reaching for the Sun, the visible symbol of Tam Apö, the participants ask for commiseration and help. The suffering brings about a restoration of the balance between the individual and the mighty protectors of life, be they spirits in nature or the Great Spirit himself. One Shoshoni asserted that the one who receives blessings in the Sun Dance does not suffer because he has spiritual help, but this pronouncement is scarcely representative.

Seen from this perspective, man should be safe as long as he walks the way provided by society under the sanction of the Supreme Being. The Sun

Dance seems to reassure the Shoshoni Indian of this security. Each year the Supreme Being is praised and thanked for his good deeds to man during the year that has passed. He is asked to send continued blessings for the new year. The Sun Dance is also the occasion when diseases and weaknesses are swept away by those medicine men who take part in the ritual. First those dancers who ask for the blessings of health for themselves or their close ones stand up in a line before the center post, the sacred cottonwood tree. The medicine man touches his medicine feathers, usually an eagle wing, to the post. He draws the wing along the wood as if he were catching its fresh essence, the sacred power. Then he turns to his patients and brushes them, one after the other, with the feathers. It is not quite certain what this means, but some Shoshoni made me understand that a double interpretation is possible: power is transferred from the sacred post to the clients, whatever disease there is in the body is alienated. In other words, positive and negative actions are joined together in the progress, giving and taking are aspects of the same symbolic gestures. One Shoshoni told me, however, that the medicine man brushed the illness off with his feathers at the center pole; next he touched the pole again, as if loading the feathers with power, and transferred the power through the feathers to his clients. It seems that many interpretations are possible here.

After those dancers who so wish have been treated in this way by the medicine man it is time for the spectators to be blessed in the same manner. I saw an old woman with her little grandson in her arms receive the blessings. She had taken off her moccasins, for the place around the center pole is a sacred place. The medicine man swept her with his feather wing, raised his right hand over her head, and prayed over her. Health and well-being were granted her and her grandson.

It is possible that these blessing ceremonies, which take place on the day the Sun Dance culminates, at the time when it is most sacred, when many spirits are present, represent a late phase in the development of the Sun Dance institution. One thing is at least certain: the accent on health and well-being has become comparatively more important after the end of the great Indian wars and the coming of Indian reservations. People live longer, and their life-threads are no longer suddenly disrupted by warfare or epidemics. The concern of health has become the main concern.

The dangers that threaten the welfare of the Indian community today are related to economy and health, or, as expressed here, well-being and health. Beside poverty and lack of material resources—for reasons which cannot be discussed here—individuals and families are threatened by a high rate of homicides, suicides, and accidents from factors such as alcohol (drunken driving, carelessness with guns, and so on). While some of these disorders may be traced back to the relativization of values in a society that for several decades has been under the pressure of violent culture contact, it is obvious that there was a fragmentation, indeed, atomization of society already in the old days of independence. Today's factionalism is in many ways a heritage of the past, a leftover from the Great Basin–type society that existed before the Plains culture laid its veneer over it. Other disorders like tuberculosis and, in earlier days, trachoma, have of course a physiological background.

For the traditionally believing Shoshoni all these disasters are referred to supernatural factors. Such factors are particularly at work in the cases of failing health. Disturbed relations with the supernatural world, spiritual actions, and witchcraft through the action of human beings are the three main causes of disease. The individual is, in other words, never quite sure that he is safe from supernatural dangers. Despite continuous participation in the Sun Dance and other efforts to enhance one's situation in the eyes of the powers, every person may without knowing it fall victim to the operations of the supernatural world or human beings handling supernatural powers. It is obvious that in principle a good, moral life could lead to health and well-being; we are told that the spirits like certain people, that these people are good, kind, and responsible. At the same time, however, there are many risks everywhere and any time from supernatural dangers. The Shoshoni are faced with this dilemma, and they cannot resolve it.

CAUSES OF DISEASE

If we use the scheme of pathogenic causes outlined above we can state that one of the most important causes among the Shoshoni has been the disturbed relations between human beings and the supernatural world. Such disturbances are often identified with transgressions of specific taboos.

Taboo is a Polynesian word that denotes a code of prohibitions to prevent infringements against the religious and social order. The underlying beliefs are of religious and magic nature: whoever transgresses is supposed to be punished, mostly automatically, by supernatural powers. Shoshoni say that such a person is *omaihen*, "forbidden," "destroyed." A typical example of a taboo transgression obtains when a menstruating woman tries to enter the Sun Dance hall. Before the beginning of the Dance an announcer calls, "Whoever (woman) is sick, she must leave the lodge immediately." It is said that a woman who in this way is "unclean" obstructs the supernatural powers from entering the hall, so they linger outside it. A menstruating woman really should stay in a little hut, "the outside house," which has been erected for her in the periphery of the ordinary habitations. She is supposed to stay there some five to ten days. Men are afraid to go there, since they fear menstruating women; we hear that they do not receive clear dreams (of the supernatural) if they visit such women. At least it was believed in the old days that if a man entered the menstruation hut his blood would break out through his mouth or nose, and he would die.

On the whole, wrong ritual behavior makes the ritual omaihen and may bring on unfortunate consequences. It is, for example, fatal to tell somebody the contents of a personal vision if the vision is supposed to continue (in a new dream foreboded by the spirit). It is furthermore considered necessary that anybody who tries to drink while partaking in the Sun Dance has to leave the Dance immediately. Fasting belongs to the Sun Dance, just as it belongs to the vision quest. And so on.

Taboos are also contained in spiritual commandments. A general taboo imposed by the spirits is that a vision seeker must not flee from the place where he is expecting to be visited by spirits. If he does, frightened by animals or ghosts or monsters, he not only loses the power he hoped for, he becomes lame or will be obsessed by some other calamity (see the discussion below concerning Taivotsi).

Many places up in the mountains have been taboo, for instance, the geyser basins; to approach them has been dangerous. To point fingers at certain mountaintops has also been dangerous. If such taboos are infringed the human being stands the risk of being hit by the revenge of the supernatural beings. One does not question why this is so; one has to be content to know that there is another, supernatural world, and men and women have to adapt to its laws.

While human actions may upset the relations with the powers the latter may, on their own initiative, and for no obvious reason, make people sick. It is possible to see such measures as the inversion of the fact that some spirits take a liking to you—they take pity on a visionary who is humble and trustworthy, for instance. On the other side, a person who is not devotional or honest is often not just left aside at the vision quest by the spirits but is harmed by them. The result is a disease of some kind, such as lameness or blindness. In many cases, however, people are brought to suffering by the spirits although they have lived a straight and honest life. There are also supernatural beings that are invariably evil, such as the mountain ogres and the pygmy spirits. It has been recounted how the former make persons to whom they grant visions crazy. The mountain ogres are often dressed in clothes of stones and rocks and are supposed to be man-eaters.

The dwarf spirits, *nynymbi,* are dangerous because they hit you without cause when you are out in nature. They live among the willows close to big stones and creeks and are dressed in buckskin like old-fashioned Indians. They are as a rule invisible but can occasionally be seen and are then very small. They are equipped with bows and shoot their invisible arrows into people who come close to them. Many stories are told how they shoot riders so that they fall off their horses. The diseases caused by the nynymbi are usually heart strokes or tuberculosis. Only the latter cases can be cured.

Witchcraft by human beings is another cause of disease. The witches or wizards are mostly former medicine men who use their powers for selfish aims and do not hesitate to hurt others. A famous Sheepeater guide, Togwotee, was known to practice witchcraft a hundred years ago. He used to carry a doll wrapped in buckskin attached to his necklace. It represented his guardian spirit, a mountain ogre. It seems as if Togwotee had acquired this spirit intentionally, for he wanted power to injure people. He was feared during the Sun Dances when, it was said, he stole other people's souls. He was finally killed by magic by a Ute Indian medicine man who had a still stronger medicine.[6]

White people may also have the power to make people ill by witchcraft—this was at least the belief of many old people about 1950. These old people dreaded the camera and refused to be photographed. Younger Indians explained that the old-timers thought they were shot at when photographed. They also stated that after being photographed the old people did not live long. We know from other tribes that pictorial representations of a person mean that that person's essence, life, or soul is caught; whoever possesses the picture may destroy the person it represents.

The ultimate causes of the diseases that have been annotated here should not be confused with the operations through which diseases take hold of a person. It is true that some diseases, lameness for instance, may result automatically from taboo transgressions or angry spirits. Usually, however, diseases are mediated, that is, the revenging spirits work through two major means, intrusion of objects or smaller spirits, or soul loss—the latter also an effect of human witchcraft, as we have noted.

It is difficult to ascertain in the different cases whether an intrusion has been performed by an object (in some mysterious way) or a spirit into the body—in the reports there is a change from object to spirit and vice versa. The nynymbi shoots an arrow into a person's body, but that arrow may manifest itself as a living being, a spirit, as the following story by one of my informants, the medicine woman Nadzaip, tells us:

> On one occasion my brother [the medicine man Morgan Moon] cured my daughter who has now been dead for twenty years. A nynymbi had shot

her into the breast with an arrow from its bow, and she was close to death. That time my brother succeeded in healing her. He put his hand on her breast and sucked out a little humanlike being with arms and legs. He showed it; it had the length of a finger. The girl recovered, and played immediately afterward. She lived several years thereafter, but then died from "dry-up disease" [tuberculosis].

We may dispute to no avail what it really was that Nadzaip and the other spectators had seen. In any case, although my informant tried to separate the arrow motif from the little being her story made it plain that the object and the "spirit" were identical.

Intrusion is the common way of acquiring a disease, or at least it has been so in later times. Earlier there was also soul loss. There are tales about great medicine men, or shamans, known to fetch souls while in trance, but they seem to have died out during the first decades of this century. Other medicine men have used other practices, as we shall see. The dead could take the living person's soul away, but also evil human beings could do so. One informant said, "The soul exists in the top of the hair, about two inches high. When you sleep a man with witchcraft may take it away. You get crazy. If the soul never returns, you die. A doctor has to seek for the soul." It also happened that during a dream the soul alienated itself from the body or that during the last stages of a disease the soul loosened its ties with the body and wandered toward the realm of the dead.

In all these cases the services of a medicine man have been necessary.

THE SHOSHONI MEDICINE MAN

Traditionally it is the male specialist on medicine, the medicine man or *puhagan*, who cures people who are seriously sick. There are also medicine women who have passed the menopause, but they are few, and their powers are not as great as the powers of their male colleagues. The following account refers to the medicine men.

The Shoshoni medicine man is a visionary who has received more and stronger guardian spirits than other visionaries and whose power is specialized for doctoring. Sometimes he has deliberately tried to become a medicine man; sometimes it has happened without his will or wish that he has been blessed by the spirits that grant him curing capacities. Indeed, there are many ways that lead to the possession of power.

In many cases the power of doctoring is innate and even hereditary. The medicine man was born with this power. He needed, however, a vision of a spirit to have the power confirmed before he could start working with clients. Morgan Moon, mentioned above, was such a medicine man. His father was a medicine man, and his sister Nadzaip, whom I met during my first visit to the Shoshoni, was a medicine woman. Most informants make a clear distinction between medicine men with innate power and medicine men who have received visions; however, the fact that the former were also blessed by spirits, for instance in the Sun Dance, makes the distinction less clear.

Some people received their medical powers spontaneously, without having prepared themselves or even contemplated becoming medicine men. This is how Parukugare, or John Trehero, experienced his acquisition of medicine power:

> When I was a boy, about fourteen years old, I brought horses that we had west of the mountains to the east, for my mother. I took them over the mountains and arrived, in the evening, at a place at the uppermost run of the North Fork Popoagie. There are rock-drawings there, and I got a dream there. I didn't mean to go to sleep there; I slept there, I didn't know there were any drawings. In the dream I got scared; it was like having a nightmare. I wanted to wake up but could not do it—for you can't when spirits come in your dream. This dream was pretty near daylight. I saw a snake and a bear. Then I woke up and saw signs on the cliffs, among others, of bear and snake. I saddled the horses and went on.

After this dream John Trehero had the powers to cure snakebites and to kill people with bear medicine.

We notice that the rock-drawings were there when he woke up. This signifies that the place was sacred, for the spirits are supposed to engrave their own pictures on the rocks up in the foothills. Visions, sought or unsought, could be received at such places.

Lightning and thunder are responsible for many spontaneous visions. The respected medicine man Tudy Roberts had danced the Sun Dance, and he went up to the foothills behind Fort Washakie to sleep outside there. He had a dream and saw three spirits that were singing. They were dressed like Indians of today, "but had very clean clothes," and they had feathers in their hats. They were lightning spirits. They granted Tudy Roberts their power and said to him: "If anybody is hit by lightning, call upon us: 'black clouds and lightning,' and you will be able to doctor that person." Tudy told me that he blew the illness away with the aid of an eagle tail. The latter is marked with a sign of lightning grafted on it by the power—we may guess it is the scorching produced when the lightning struck.

Still another way of becoming a medicine man is to dance the Sun Dance. It is important, however, that the candidate does not seek power (although he may secretly contemplate the possibility of being selected by the spirits). The medicine man Morgan Moon was very sick in his youth. When the Sun Dance was celebrated he went in to become well. He danced back and forth to the pole, and he fainted. For a rather long while he lay there in coma before the pole. No one bothered him there. Finally four dancers came up and carried him back to his berth [the resting place in the periphery of the lodge]. He spent a couple of hours on his bed and then woke up. He related that he had received a vision in which an Indian had given him the power to become a medicine man and to cure the sick. He was assured by the spirit that he would retain this power until he died. From then on he doctored many people.

It is interesting to note that in his vision Morgan Moon saw an Indian slowly approach him and stop at his feet. The spirit handed over its power and its medicine song and then gradually faded away. Morgan Moon tried to find the spirit, but it was gone.

Nocturnal dreaming could also create medicine men. It is not the question of an ordinary dream but of an extraordinary one, characterized by clear visions and visions that cannot be interrupted. Medicine man Tudy Roberts confessed, "My visions have always come at night, in a dream." Once he dreamed that he had gone on horseback to the Milk Ridge Creek. There were many tents there, and he entered one of them. A woman was there, telling him that a child lay sick, suffering from a swollen throat. She declared that they had stuck a finger down the child's throat, but nothing good happened. Said Tudy, "I stuck a finger down the throat, and the child recovered. It received cold water and drank it without trouble. This is the way I got this power. These people were spirits. My finger is blessed. I stick it far down through the mouth."

Dreaming of medicine power was the general way to become a medicine man among hunting tribes of the western United States. The influence from other Plains tribes, however, convinced the Shoshoni that power could also be achieved through deliberate vision quests. Right up to the first World War it was considered normal for a man to ride on a horse to the cliff ledges up in the foothills where the rock-drawings are and stay there waiting for visions. As pointed out before, the rock-drawings—whose origins have fallen into oblivion by the historical Shoshoni—are supposed to represent self-portraits by the spirits. Fasting and praying to the spirit of his choice, the medicine man candidate could spend several nights there. Animals that in his imagination looked like monsters approached him and frightened him.

Typical in these respects is what happened to Taivotsi. He had many years ago a dream in which a spirit told him that, if he wanted medicine power, he should go the rock-drawings at the headwaters of Willowcreek. Once there he should bathe in the creek, thus cleaning himself from all dirt, and spend the night there, waiting for a vision. He did as he was told. He lay down there, early in the evening. He did not know if he slept but felt as if he was awake when an owl flew down and picked at him. The owl tried to scare him away, but he remained, and it flew from the place. Next there appeared a bear that tried to throw him around. But he was firm, so the bear gave up and went its way. Thereafter a deer made a leap at him several times, but Taivotsi stayed. A coyote came and bit him, but he was not afraid. Then a big rattlesnake approached him and rattled. Taivotsi, who had always feared snakes, jumped up and ran away.

That decided his fate. His grandson, who told me this story, assured me that if Taivotsi had persevered and stayed on the spot he would have received medicine power. His legs were crippled shortly afterward, and he had to walk with crutches. Many years later he participated in a Sun Dance, leaning on his crutches. He was blessed, and on the second day of dancing he could stand without his crutches. After that day he never used them again.

The grandson hinted at the possibility, as he thought it, that the spirit would have arrived and granted its blessing at the rock-drawings of Willowcreek as soon as Taivotsi had endured all dangers successfully. Usually the arrival of the spirit was preceded by such unpleasant experiences.

Psychologically the spirit appears when the trancelike state of dreaming occurs. One Shoshoni Indian explained, "The spirit works through your dream. It is like a dream, but not a dream—it is dreamlike. Your mind joins with that spirit that is going to take you away." Many vision narratives describe how the spirit is perceived first as a far-away something standing at the horizon, then as an approaching being of uncertain shape, and finally as a mostly animal-like person talking to the candidate, giving him its power (and the conditions for its use) and the medicine song, the singing of which will always provoke spiritual help. Often the spirit changes its form during its presence. Finally it disappears, dissolves as it were. One could say that it shares the characteristics of the dream. In this connection it is interesting to note that the soul when loosened from the body (the "free-soul") is identified with the dream—*navužieip* is the name of both free-soul and dream.

In former days this vision quest was a common way of achieving power as a medicine man. In particular, revelations of a bear spirit or a lightning spirit granted such power, but other spirits also could—if they so claimed— communicate it. The sincerity and good qualities of the supplicant were requested by the spirits. Since World War I this way of begging for power has been largely abandoned, perhaps as a consequence of the dissociation of the Plains Indian cultural overlay. In any case, the spirits of the vision quest have become regarded as less trustworthy, even dangerous to the petitioner.[7] The spontaneous visions of dreaming have become more important, indeed, as important as they were in the pre-Plains, Great Basin Indian days.

There was no initiation ceremony of new medicine men, nor was there a training period during which the candidate got versed in his profession. There are only hints that a new doctor studied casually what other, more experienced colleagues did. No one required, however, that he should have "learned" his profession. We are far away here from the institutional education typical of other societies.

The reasons are very plain. Socially there has never existed a professional corps that could handle such matters in a regular fashion. The individualism and factionalism of Shoshoni society, and, with the exception of military accomplishments, the traditions from the pre-Plains day precluded tendencies in this direction. Even more important have been the religious implications. A medicine man is a medical authority because he derives his efficiency from the spiritual powers. Spirits have told him what to do, how to cure the sick. No human being can teach him his trade. It is another matter that we, the observers, can find that there are fixed traditional rules governing his ways of curing.

INDIVIDUAL AND COLLECTIVE ASPECTS OF CURING

The individualism of Shoshoni medicine men accounts for the great discrepancies in their methods of curing, and their factionalism for the distrust that some of them meet in segments of their society. In relation to the latter point I was impressed by the very changing judgments of one and the same medicine man in different groups. The verdicts were running from "very good, reliable, with excellent results" to "an impostor, an unreliable person, worthless." Only one medicine man was above slander, a peaceful, reticent, conservative, and traditionalistic person, a representative of the old ways. Another medicine man who was charming but a bit unstable, although an old-timer and spiritually experienced, was discarded by many because of his joking character and womanizing. I found, however, that as a professional medicine man he was a very serious person and deeply respected by those whom he had treated. It is a strange fact that the two medicine men mentioned here usually worked together as rather good friends at Sun Dances, where both of them healed sick persons.

More pertinent to our theme is that curing methods deviated so much from each other simply because the spiritual commands varied so considerably. Some visions contained instructions that we should regard as preposterous, such as taboos against touching objects of metal or rules about the medicine man's body painting or dressing, which to us might seem eccentric. Some visions tell the medicine man to cure his patients in a very summary way, others give detailed instructions, still others restrict the circle of diseases that their client would be able to cure. Only the acquisition of a lot of specialized guardian spirits could vouchsafe a medicine man's abilities to treat all common serious diseases. One medicine man, John Trehero, said he was "loused" down with guardian spirits.

Sometimes the guardian spirit did not tell his client how to deal with a disease until just before he should remedy it. Tudy Roberts said that when he was about to cure measles he dreamed about a spirit that told him to refer to the bull elk (spirit), a medicine that he had acquired in the Sun Dance. He continued:

> When the sun rises in the morning I see in a [waking] vision the bull elk. It shakes me so that I see fires, I fall down and shake. Then I get up, shaking over the whole body. Then I am told what to do. I catch the measles by the palms of my hands, put it in the fire and burn it. If I don't burn it somebody else who is present will get the measles.

Tudy knew the nature of diseases through his spirit. "The guardian spirit tells me who is sick and what he suffers from."

In spite of the many individual variations there is a general pattern of curing methods inherited from times past but adjusted, in some parts, to modern conditions.

Particular rituals may be used when a medicine man is called upon. It is said that formerly the medicine man had to be asked to help with a certain phrase that his guardian spirit had given him in a vision and that he had made public. If a person wanted to be helped by the medicine man Charlie Myers he or his representative first had to get hold of a willow sapling, measuring between two feet and one yard, pare off the bark, and paint it red. Then he would attach the white plumes of the eagle to the staff and bring the latter to the medicine man. Handing it over to the doctor he would say, "I have come to get you so you can doctor —————— who is sick." Thereafter Myers accepted the stick and went to the home of the sick person. He could not refuse even if it were the middle of an abominably cold night with a blizzard raging outside.

In some cases the medicine man "knows" mysteriously from what disease the patient suffers, and in others the guardian spirit has revealed it to him, as we have seen. Very often the medicine man has to examine the patient and then give a diagnosis. We hear of medicine men who can see right through the body and thereby discover the disease agent. One medicine man could see the disease not through the body but through a black muff. He put the muff on four sticks between himself and the sick person and stretched it tightly. The disease shone in the dark. "It is like television," said this medicine man, to whom I was very close. Tudy Roberts moved his beaver skin over the patient's body; when the fur became hot he knew where the disease was located. It is a common notion that a disease makes the body hot—another way of expressing the fact that the patient has a fever.

Occasionally several medicine men, one after the other, tried to cure a sick person. More common has been the presence of many men and women, in latter times as engaged spectators, earlier as a choir. I was told that they were singing "prayer songs" directed to the medicine man's helping spirit. Morgan Moon had the tent full of singing people when he cured his patients. They sang very softly the medicine song that belonged to him and that he had received in a calling vision. He owned two or three songs acquired from different guardian spirits. When I visited the Shoshoni in 1948 one medicine man, Tudy Roberts, started his curing with a prayer and a prayer song, but he used no choir. The song calls on the spirit to be present and lend its power to the medicine man. Medicine men claim that they see the guardian spirit as they are curing.

METHODS OF PROFESSIONAL CURING

It should be evident from the foregoing description that most diseases handled by medicine men are oriented from an etiological explanation of intrusion and soul loss. The methods applied to remedy the diseases are more or less adapted to their respective etiologies. This is very obvious in the case of intrusion diseases.

Intrusion, whether by disease spirits or disease objects, generally calls for the removal of the pathogenic agent. The real connections between this agent and the spirit or person who is responsible for its actions are not always clear. We know, however, that dwarf spirits and wizards-witches shoot an arrow into the patient's body. From all appearances other disease-giving beings use the same device. The medicine man removes the intruding spirit or object by different operations, and often he destroys it.

One of these operations is the medicine man's stroking the patient with his feather wing. It has been shown here how this is done in the Sun Dance. The disease is swept away, at the same time that fresh power is infused into the patient. According to what I was told, this way of curing is not original. Perhaps it was introduced with the arrival of Plains culture, in which feathers and feather symbolism have a high value. Singing while swinging feathers and applying these feathers on the patient's body are common among medicine men today, even outside the Sun Dance. The symbolism of feathers, particularly eagle feathers, is quite clear: the feathers belong to the beings that come close to the celestial world. The eagle is in Shoshoni belief a "pure" bird, messenger of God, and carrier of supernatural qualities.

Another, equally common operation is sucking and biting. The medicine man sucks at the afflicted place or at any place where he feels the disease may exit from the body. We saw how one medicine man, Morgan Moon, placed his hand on his own elbow and the latter on the patient. By sucking through his hand he thought he could extract the patient's disease. John Trehero used to suck the evil out and then spit it into a vessel. From here it was thrown on the fire. Most people have never seen the disease. Nadzaip, Morgan Moon's sister, confessed that she had never seen the disease. She meant that only a medicine man has the power to see it. (She was herself a medicine woman!) Nevertheless, she was aware of the fact that when her brother cured her daughter everybody present had seen the disease spirit (see the account above). She reported that everyone standing around the sick girl—that is, all the people that had sung the medicine song—could see the little being that he had sucked out when he held it up. Then he threw it away.

A third curative method is to draw the disease out. It may be exemplified by a case in which medicine man Charlie Myers was active. He arrived at a lodge where there was a very sick man, delirious from fever. Myers brought the willow stick that had been given him. He wore a necklace with a large looking glass in buckskin and red feather pendant. He prayed over the patient, looked at him through his looking glass, and said, "A little man [the dwarf spirit] has shot you through the lungs with an arrow, close to the heart." Then he took his stick and put it toward the sick man's chest. He laid one hand on the stick, and with the other hand he lifted the stick from the chest. The bystanders heard a gargling sound from the patient's chest, of a thing falling down. Shortly afterward the sick man raised himself on his elbow and said, "Oh, are you here, people?"

A more subtle way of curing by drawing was represented by Tudy Roberts. He touched the sick spot with his eagle wing and then drew the disease out, "with my willpower." "Only I can see the disease," he declared. "It is a round thing, and red. If I can't get it out in a right way it returns to the patient."

The fourth way of doctoring intrusion is the laying on of hands. This method was to my knowledge primarily used by John Trehero, who among his many guardian spirits had the beaver. This is what he told me:

> I dreamed about the beaver; I kept dreaming about him every now and then. Finally he told me how to use his power. The beaver said, "Here is my power," and he showed me his front paws. This spirit, it is very strong and powerful. If a person has pain I feel with my hand on him, and that pain comes in my hand. I use my own hands for beaver paws.

This quotation shows clearly that John Trehero identified himself with the spirit when curing; how this identity was experienced we cannot know. We also notice that the disease went over to the medicine man, an exceptional matter. It is not impossible that Christian healing had originally given the impetus to the laying on of hands.

Twice I was myself exposed to this kind of curing. In both cases John Trehero was my medicine man. On one occasion I complained about pains in my cheek—I had an infection in the left oral cavity. John lifted his hand, pointed it at my cheek, and regarded it with a resolute determination. Then he quickly lowered his hand and touched my cheek. He held it there some second, and then, swift as lightning, he drew it back again. It was my impression that he had mobilized a great amount of psychic energy.

On the other occasion Trehero cured rheumatism in my left shoulder. First he used some peacock feathers that I had given him, laying them against my shoulder. Then he removed them, put his right hand on my shoulder, and ordered me to put mine on top of his. Thereafter he removed his hand and put it on top of mine. Suddenly he quickly withdrew it and asked me if I had felt the power enter me. He wanted me to feel his power, so he extended the palm of his hand and asked me to put my finger in its center. I did so and felt the quick pulse. That, declared John Trehero, was the power. Later he told me that while curing me he had seen the beaver. It was with the beaver's power that he had healed me.

The effects of the cure? Well, for some four years I was without rheumatic pains. It may be that, together with a certain "scientific" skepticism, I half believed in my medicine man's capacity. And faith can do wonders.

A fifth means of extracting intrusion phenomena is to blow them away. Tudy Roberts blew the disease away with his eagle tail. Sometimes he first drew it out and then blew it away. A medicine man before my time, Bogori, was known to blow away a lot of diseases. He prayed to his guardian spirit, the elk, and then in some mysterious way put the diseases on the prongs of the elk's (a living elk's?) horns. They never left that place. There was also the saying that a medicine man could blow away dangerous spirits from the bodies of patients to the whites on the other side of the big waters (the Atlantic).

The diagnosis of soul loss corresponds to medical devices designed to retrieve the forlorn soul. These methods are no longer used; the last medicine man who used them regularly, Morgan Moon, died in 1944. During this century there have been differing opinions about the application of the diagnosis. Morgan Moon could refer a patient's state to soul loss at the same time as his younger colleague, John Trehero, denied the actuality of this diagnosis: if the patient's heart was still beating, how then could his soul have gone away? This account shows that Trehero had lost the implications of the old soul dualism, the dichotomy between a soul that keeps the body physically going (or the life soul) and the soul that represents the individual and may leave him in states of dream, trance, and coma, the free-soul. This dichotomy goes with shamanism and is the prerequisite for the soul-loss diagnosis.

The regular way of curing soul loss in the old days was for the medicine man to put himself into a trance. It was said that his guardian spirit had given him this capacity. The medicine man—or shaman, as we may call him in this case—lay half an hour or an hour like a dead person, without any sign of life. His own soul had left him and was on the path to the other world, trying to intercept the fugitive soul of his patient that had taken this direction. After some time he moved again: his own soul had returned, and he had brought back the patient's soul. Then the patient recovered.

There is a current story of the son of an Indian policeman who was cured in this way. He was sick and lost consciousness. The medicine man was sent for. He declared that the soul (free-soul) had gone, and only breath (symbol of the life soul) remained. This was a serious situation. All that was left for the medicine man to do was to "die" (go in a trance) and catch the lost soul in the realm of the dead. Said he, "When I have died my soul will go to the world of the departed to hunt the boy's soul. But in order to bring me back to life you bystanders must give me three kicks in the back."

So he died, and lay dead on the ground. After half an hour he received three kicks in the back. The people standing around could hear him give a deep breath; his soul had returned. After the medicine man regained consciousness, he told of his experiences in the land of the dead. He said that he had found the boy's soul on the other side of the (western) mountains, playing with dead boys over there. The medicine man had great difficulty in persuading the boy to come back with him to his home again. At last the boy consented and went with the medicine man. The medicine man assured the policeman that the boy had come back and that he would be quite well again. The boy recovered and grew up to be a man. This event took place at Trout Creek about the year 1900.

It should be noted that the young boy went away in spirit when he had lost his consciousness. This is typical for most cases of soul loss: it is primarily a diagnosis valid in cases of trance, swooning, and coma. The mind is gone; only the body or life soul keeps the person alive.

Such trance cures were still remembered by many people in the 1950s. People have told me that as children they were sometimes advised by the folk coming out of a sick person's tent not to play close to the tent. Their argument was that the patient's soul was outside the tent, and the youngsters might come between the soul and the medicine man working in the tent.

Today's medicine men fear such trance journeys. "We medicine men nowadays don't come that high," commented John Trehero. "If I should try to cure that way, the spirit will destroy my medicine." This is probably another way of saying that he lacked the spiritual sanction to pursue this medical method. He used another technique to catch a soul that had just left its owner: "I catch it with the fast-traveling lightning medicine and blow it back into the back of the person's neck." In other words, he prayed to the lightning spirit to fetch the lost soul, and then he reinstalled the soul by blowing it into its place.

Such techniques remind us more of the curing of diseases due to intrusion spirits, although in the latter case it is the disease spirit that is blown, and blown away. An entranced shaman like Morgan Moon could resort to similar methods when curing soul loss. A Crow Indian mother had lost her little girl, who was three or four years of age. Morgan Moon's sister said, "The child is dead; there is nothing to do." But her brother retorted, "No, the soul has just temporarily left the body. I shall bring it back." He touched the top of the child's head, stroking it round the crown. The child opened her eyes and looked at him. Her soul was close to the body and entered it through the top of the head. Next day the girl was playing again. She was quite well.

In this case, as in Trehero's, the girl was close by. Otherwise it is probable that Morgan Moon would have been forced to make a dangerous soul expedition. The application of intrusion therapy in a case of soul loss gives evidence of the dominance of this therapy in late Shoshoni medical thinking. The use of the guardian spirit as a restorer of a fugitive soul reminds us of similar methods at Puget Sound.

Despite these exceptions Shoshoni professional therapy is instructive, because it presents us clearly with the reasons for different medical techniques.

It also demonstrates the close connections between diseases and religion, and therapeutic methods and religious beliefs.

SHOSHONI NONPROFESSIONAL FOLK MEDICINE

Shoshoni patients do not always turn to professional medicine men. Minor ailments may be taken care of by experienced tribesmen or people who know traditional cures, and sometimes by the patient himself.

Wounds and smaller physical afflictions can be remedied by wise old men and women who adjust bones and put herbs and decoctions of herbs on one's bad spots. Well-known "herbs" like juniper needles, sagebrush twigs, and sweet grass also give a health-bringing fragrance. They are, according to the Shoshoni, sacred medicines.

A particularly potent herb is a primrose of great beauty that grows up in the mountains: shooting star, the American cowslip. This flower, with its shifting colors, is to the Shoshoni "tough medicine." Those who want to get hold of this medicine—which both may give help to its possessor and become dangerous to others—have to perform certain rites, including bathing and sleeping at night close to the flower. Just before sunrise they ask the flower for its blessing, such as help against disease. They dig up the root, put it in a small buckskin bag, and bury the flower where the root has grown. Whoever makes a mistake in the ritual procedures is mysteriously strangled to death. Whoever succeeds in the ritual program has a tremendous powerful medicine at his or her disposal.

During the last hundred years new religious movements have often furthered the idea that the human being may be healed through supernatural power without the intervention of doctors. The peyote herb, for instance, which is supposed to have a healthy influence, is taken internally both privately and in a ritual collective connection. It is worth observing, however, that the peyote cactus is not a medicine in our sense of the term, but a powerful, supernatural being or thing.

Another health cure is supplied by participation in the Sun Dance since the 1890s. Many dancers take part vigorously to improve their own health or the health of family members and friends. Faith in the success of the Sun Dance and strenuous dancing may guarantee future health. Medicine men may, as we have seen, strengthen a dancer's health by symbolic curing; but the dancer may improve his own health if his faith is good.

CURING AMONG THE ARAPAHO

We now change the scene from the Shoshoni to their close neighbors in Wyoming, and former enemies, the Arapaho Indians. These once full-fledged Plains Indians belonged during the Indian wars of the 1860s and 1870s to the mighty Sioux-Cheyennee-Arapaho military alliance. In spite of their warlike appearance the Arapaho have been known as a most religiously inclined tribe. Their Sun Dance is possibly the finest of all Plains ceremonies, their devotion to religious powers impressive. More than their allies the Arapaho have been ruled in their decisions by religious considerations.

The Arapaho are counted among the large Algonkian linguistic family that we made acquaintance with when dealing with Ojibway and Cree health and medicine. The closer relations between the latter tribes and the Arapaho are not well known, but there is certainty that the Arapaho have come from the north. Some of their customs, including the original Spirit Lodge ceremony, attest to their affinity with Canadian Algonkian culture. The general features of their medical complex, however, have an outspoken Plains character.

Thus, the concepts around the medicine man remind us of those we found among the Shoshoni. The medicine man usually receives his powers on a vision-quest expedition. It happens, nonetheless, that the blessing spirit reveals itself in spontaneous dreams. In some cases the medicine is bought or received from a relative. This is at variance with Shoshoni customs but is in accordance with customs among other Plains tribes. Power may also be offered to a person by spirits but rejected by this person because it is too dangerous to possess. A strange idea is the tenet that a medicine man cures with the aid of disease objects kept within his body. A. L. Kroeber, a well-known expert on the Arapaho, has commented on this belief:

> A medicine man who sucks ghost arrows [that have intruded into the patient's body] increases his power, if he swallows and retains these objects after extracting them from the patient's body. It is probable that such beliefs are connected with the feeling that the ability to produce various objects at will, by vomiting, is an evidence of supernatural power. It has been stated in one case, and seems to be generally believed, that medicine-men with this power keep such objects permanently in their bodies.[8]

This account confirms my observations of similar ideas among some Shoshoni medicine men.

Sucking, bloodletting (cupping), and brushing are, according to Kroeber, common means by which a medicine man removes a disease. The patient may himself improve his health by wearing protective amulets or using sweat-lodge facilities: sweating out the impure, the disease.[9]

Kroeber also tells us of Arapaho attitudes toward insanity.[10] Some of his information reminds us of the ancient Scandinavian berserks, a sort of warriors ("bear-coats") who fought in battles with the frenzy of bears. There is, for instance, the story of a man who made a charge in battle and thought himself a wolf. Afterward he ran about like one, but later recovered. One Oklahoma Arapaho imagined he was a deer, and he was called Deer. He cried like a deer, leaped like one, and his eyes looked different. It seems that originally he mistook a deer for a pretty woman. When he saw it was an animal he touched he felt ashamed. Soon afterward he had the delusion that he was himself a deer. At last he recovered from his mental illness. In cases like these we are not told how the recovery came about.

The old practices of healing are even today resorted to in frustrating situations, although it is more common to seek the help of specialists in Western medicine. One ceremony, however, has survived as a powerful remedy, the Spirit Lodge.

THE ARAPAHO SPIRIT LODGE

The Spirit Lodge is a Plains application of the Algonkian ceremony of the Shaking Tent, which we have observed in an earlier connection. In contradistinction to the Shaking Tent, it has no particular tent for the acting shaman and is mostly (nowadays) enclosed in a wooden house.

The Spirit Lodge is also known by its Lakota name, *yuwipi*, since it has been retained particularly well among these Sioux Indians.[11] And, in fact, it was a Lakota shaman who reintroduced the ceremony among the Arapaho from whom it had been absent since 1881, according to the report of the then Indian agent. This reintroduction took place in 1954, and it is a remarkable example of how many forgotten Indian rituals have come back in our days. The events that I experienced took place in August 1955. The Arapaho who figured as host of the ceremony, Buster Crispin, was extremely satisfied after it. "This is the old Indian way," he confirmed.

This ceremony was held in order to save the health of Buster Crispin's cousin ("younger brother") Steve Duran, who suffered from a nondescript disease that caused him indigestion after eating. The ceremony could be characterized as a form of curing, as it is so regularly among the Lakota. We remember that the Shaking Tent primarily was arranged for divinatory purposes, although occasionally it could serve medical ends. As usual among North American aborigines, this trend to reinterpret rituals as basically curing rituals belongs to the period after the end of the great Indian wars.

An Oglala Lakota shaman performed the ceremony. His name was Mark Big Road, and he was a descendant of great war leaders but also of medicine men. After the séance that will shortly be described I sought him out to receive information about his medicine. He fixed his friendly, calm eyes on me and told me how he had become a medicine man. He had inherited his medical capacities, but he was empowered by the spirits out in the field. He had gone to lonely hills, fasted and kept awake on his bed until the spirits had revealed themselves. His particular helping spirit was Skadi, who was the ghost of a white man. Skadi had become so indianized that he now spoke the Siouan language. Skadi had helped Mark to achieve other helping spirits, some of them small spirits used for discovering and bringing back lost possessions, others mighty spirits like Thunder, and one spirit said to be seven thousand years old. Several people came forth to tell me or show me how they had been cured by Mark and his spirits. Buster Crispin, for instance, pointed at a young boy who, according to an X-ray taken in the hospital, had had a tubercle in one ear. Mark treated him, and a new X-ray taken shortly afterward proved that he was now well. Indeed, Mark's power was legendary, and he was popularly credited with having innumerable spirits—the figures 227, 300, and 427 were mentioned to me by different informants. The most dependable was, however, the "control spirit," Skadi. Practically all spoken prayers in the séances were directed to him.

The medicine ceremony I attended was, fortunately, performed through the medium of the English language. Arapaho and Lakota are not mutually understandable, so the "colonial" language had to be used.[12]

The room that made up the wooden house was filled up by people, seated on blankets and mattresses along the four walls. The western part of the room was taken up by the men, the eastern by the women. Four drummers, who were also singers, took their place on two mattresses in front of the men. Buster Crispin informed me that the coming ceremony was no play, nor was it religion: it was a curative act administered by a doctor. Furthermore, the patient, Steve, suffered from a severe disease; this ceremony was therefore more important and serious than any earlier ceremony. "The spirits," he said, "won't come and stay unless you participate in the praying. You must believe and pray, pray to God and the spirits that he has sent." It was important, he emphasized, to pray not only to God, as we do in church, but also to the spirits.

The ceremony opened in the late evening by Helen Crispin, the host's wife, handing a ceremonial pipe to Mark Big Road with the following prayer:

I am Steve's sister-in-law. I ask you, Mark, help me, help my sister, and all of us, to have him cured. He walks toward death, and his many children may become orphans. Our hope stands now to you. I fuse my tears in my prayer. Help us to keep Steve, we love him, his children need him. Mark, help us, I am so desperate, you can help us, please have misery with us!

As a token of acceptance Mark seized the pipe, lit it, and smoked.

Buster Crispin then stood up, exhorting everyone to pray together for Steve: "It is not enough with Mark curing. We must all sing or pray, and we must have faith. We are just weak beings, we don't know how to do everything right, but we must try to believe, not doubt, not wonder, just pray to the ninety-six spirits that tonight will be present here." "And," he added in a Christian fashion, "I ask for blessings from God and the Holy Ghost." These words attest to the infiltration of missionary ideas in an old traditional tribal ceremony.

Water was poured over hot stones, and the room was filled up with steam like in a sweat lodge. Indeed, it functioned as one, purifying all present—a necessary introduction to all large Indian ceremonies. Everybody passed around the sacred place where the heated stones were, walking clockwise, in the sun's direction.

A floor altar was now constructed. The medicine man unfolded a mat in the center of the room, about 50 × 50 centimeters, on which he sat down. Around this mat were arranged two ceremonial pipes, tobacco pouches, gourds, and an enclosure of a string fixed to seven flags of bright colours and 147 red tobacco pouches. A gourd with flags and eagle feathers marked the most sacred place on the southern side of the altar. Incense of sweet grass was spread out over the ritual objects by the medicine man. As the drums were sounding and the songs taken up, he stood up with naked feet on the sacred altar ground, holding each pipe in turn toward the cardinal points. Two barefooted women now raised themselves to make self-sacrifices of their own flesh. One of them, Buster Crispin's young daughter Helena, placed herself on the altar. Mark Big Road touched her left arm with sweet grass, held up his hand blessingly, and prayed. With a razor blade he then chopped out one slice of flesh after the other, while the drumming went on and the people prayed with lowered heads. Blood poured from the young girl's arm, her face was twisted in pain, but not a sound come from her lips. She was succeeded by the medicine man's own wife. The flesh of the two women was put in a gourd on the altar ground. The voluntary offering of one's own flesh is the finest gift to the spirits and makes them show pity for the people.

The true medicine drama could now begin. Mark Big Road removed his shirt, and the host and another man wrapped him up tightly in a blanket, so hard that his hands became red. In a suffocated, strained voice from the interior of the blanket the shaman shouted, "I call Skadi, I call Skadi." Now and then his calls were broken off by the sound of the owl, "Hu, hu." (The owl is here as everywhere in aboriginal North America a representative of a dead person, and Skadi is as we know a ghost.) The shaman was bound with ropes all over his body by the two men and then placed upside down on his mat. All the time he continued calling and singing. Then the light in the ceiling went out.

The drums started thundering, men and women were singing, the room was filled with sounds. After a while a rattle was heard in the middle of the clamor. It sounded now here, now there high over our heads. The drumming and singing silenced, some moaning sounds came forth from the medicine man on the floor. Then Helen Crispin's voice was heard:

> Oh, Skadi and you other spirits, please, pity us. We are here to ask you to take care of and to cure Steve, my brother-in-law, who is very ill. Help him to get well. We believe in you, Skadi. Please cure him, allow him to be with us, let him take care of his family. Skadi and you other spirits, we ask you from all our heart to make him well.

Agreements were heard from everywhere, and one and another confirmed with an "amen." Then followed prayers from others who cared for their sick relatives in the white man's hospitals. It should be remarked, however, that not only diseases were the subjects of these prayers. Some mothers asked the spirits for advice concerning their small children: should they really send them to school?

Some further prayers convey the impression of honesty, submission, and trust. Here is another prayer by Helen Crispin:

> Skadi, take away the evil from Steve, place it somewhere out in space where there are no people and where nobody may be hurt by this evil. And think, Skadi, of my niece who is sick and weak, and cure her.

A young woman prayed,

> Skadi, I am not a full-blood Arapaho, but I believe in this, and I have given [in the past] seven patches [of flesh]. Please take care of my small

ones, one of them has TB, please save the child, Skadi and you other spirits.

Finally Buster Crispin:

> I feel that we must pray for pity on us, our incompleteness and our ignorance. We should do so, for that is the old Indian way. Skadi, and you other spirits, have mercy on us.

The events that followed next were anticlimactic. Under his cloak the medicine man was muttering that Thunder was present, but not Skadi who had been delayed in his journey from Rapid City. There were some minutes of expectation, and then drumming and singing set in, deafening and violent. Again Skadi's "hu, hu" was heard (how it could have resounded before was never explained), and heavy steps boomed from the floor. The seated crowd was asked to move away from the walls so that the spirits could pass. The host exhorted Steve to stand up against the wall. After some time he announced that Steve had been cured by Skadi, who had now left for his home grounds.

How Steve was cured was never disclosed. It is possible that the spirit—however we want to interpret this figure, machinations by the inspired shaman seem probable—performed some sort of drawing out the disease. Afterward nobody could tell me, or dared tell me.

There were now some jokes about Skadi among the people sitting there in the dark. They illustrated how very close humor and serenity are in Indian religion. Then the light was put on again.

The scene that met our eyes was surprising: Mark Big Road was seated on his sagebrush mat, which was neatly rolled together, and drops of sweat floated down his naked upper body. The rope was well coiled up, but the blanket had been thrown over a skeptical white woman who was present. It was now just after midnight. The light went out again, and soon singing, drumming and rattling penetrated the room. The medicine man announced that Skadi had seen to the sick, that Skadi had promised to make Steve recover, but that he had made it plain that Steve must always think of Skadi. Outcries of joy were heard. Helen's voice was raised, saying, "Thank you, thank you, Skadi." After a while the light was lit again. Everybody was now at ease; they laughed and looked happy.

The pipes were passed for smoking, and the participants prayed, "Bless my relations." As usual in Indian ceremonialism the session was concluded with a good meal. It was almost three o'clock in the morning when the sacred meeting was called off.

What strikes us in this ceremony is the rallying of people around the sick person—although of course the dramatic spectacle as such serves as an attractive magnet—and the intenseness of the tender feelings for the patient and other sick people. Close family emotions and sentiments of intimate friendship gush forth during the act, and prayers are accompanied by tears. There is no discordance in these feelings; they are universal and pervasive. All present seem to constitute one wish, one hope, one trust.

The Arapaho session invites us to certain comparisons with the North Algonkian Shaking Tent ceremony. It is obvious that it is the same phenomenon, slightly changed. The particular tent or booth of the medicine man is gone, and with that the characteristic shaking movements at the entrance of the spirits. We do not listen to conversations betwen the spirits and the conjurer, or to the voices of spirits on the whole: the medicine man tells the public what the spirits, inaudible to the people, tell him. Most importantly, spiritual messages concern human health, and only occasionally common divination. Among the Arapaho the old divinatory ceremony has become a curative ceremony.

The simplication of the ceremony, and its major use for medical purposes, signifies the change of many Indian ceremonies in post-Reservation days. Health (not wars or economic pursuits such as hunting or horticulture) has become the main concern of Indian families.

THE PAWNEE: THE BLESSING OF THE ANIMAL LODGES

The Pawnee and their linguistic relatives, the Arikara, Caddo, Wichita, and others, occupy the southern and middle Plains. All evidence seems to testify that that they have been settlers in this area from pre-Columbian days. They have been planters, although buffalo hunting has also occurred. Until 1874–75, when they were moved to the Indian Territory (Oklahoma), the Pawnee lived in the Platte and Loup valleys of Nebraska. Their villages were spread over the region.

In many respects the Pawnee deviated from other Plains peoples. They were, in fact, more adjusted to the tall-grass prairies on the eastern fringe of the Plains area and to an agricultural life-style than were the roving nomads on the high plains. Their lodges were large round mud houses, their ceremonies intricate and similar to those of the Eastern Woodlands. Maize and fertility were important issues in their ceremonial life. The Pawnee are well known for their calumet dance, a peace ceremony in which the participants danced with long-stemmed pipes decorated with animal symbols and feathers. On the other hand, they lacked the Sun Dance, and their ceremonial organization was different from that of the other Plains Indians.

It is therefore not surprising that their medical ideas and usages differed from the patterns of other tribes. If we want a general idea of medical notions in the Plains and Prairie area, we cannot ignore the deviating Pawnee data, so interesting in themselves.

The main ceremonies relating to fertility and war were administered by priests, or ritual servants who had learned the myths, songs, and ritual movements. In agricultural societies priesthoods are more important than medicine men, if the latter exist at all. The Pawnee knew both categories, but in general used medicine men—that is, supernaturally inspired religious officers—only for medical functions. It is true that those who had been blessed by visions of spirits could achieve capacities as diviners and conjurers, but usually they only appeared as healers. In this they deviated from all other Plains visionaries. As a logical consequence, people never sought power unless they wanted to become doctors. At the same time, it should be emphasized that Pawnee medicine men were widely respected and known for their extraordinary feats. Indeed, their capacities were derived from the highest god, the celestial *Tirawa* himself.

In Pawnee cosmology all power stems from this exalted deity, and it is said that he infuses all beings. Sun, moon, and stars are gods who act on his behalf. One of the stars, the so-called Black Star, has delegated his particular powers, which are powers of medicine, to the collectives of animal spirits. These are the spirits that inspire men through visions and dreams, and make them medicine men. Now, we must not imagine that it was a single representative of an animal species that blessed the visionary with medical powers. As a matter of fact, the animals appear as a plural crowd and sit together in "animal lodges."[13] The candidate is in his vision conducted into a mysterious lodge where animals of all sorts sit together. They are arranged in the same order as the medicine men have in the Pawnee medicine societies. The Pawnee know many such animal lodges, and they can locate some of them on their former hunting grounds. Obviously these lodges are thought to be situated where ancient visionary places exist. Mounds and riverbanks are supposed to contain holes through which the shaman candidate in his vision can slip into the mostly subterranean animal lodges.

Tradition tells us that the animals initiate the candidate into their medical knowledge. The information, songs, and dances parallel the esoteric performances displayed by Pawnee doctors in their medicine societies. Different animals in turn tell their powers to the young man and thus mediate them to him. Although there are believed to exist several animal lodges, usually each lodge is composed of a series of animal species. Only in a couple of cases do we hear of lodges taken up by one single species, the elk or the bear. Initiated medicine men, however, belonged to medicine lodges each one consisting of visionaries blessed by a certain animal species.

In spite of the importance of trance visions, most medicine men had not had any vision but had been taught by older medicine men. The training was long and circumstantial. Probably there is an influence from priestly education in this training system. The candidate succeeded to the office of medicine man on the death of his teacher.

All medicine men, whatever their background, belonged to medicine societies. Doctor candidates and ritual functionaries could also belong to these societies. Finest of them all was the Doctors' Lodge, composed of the leading doctors of the other societies. Every lodge was an imitation of the animal lodge, and the ceremonies copied the initiation performances in the animal lodge. The doctors had a common fifteen-day period during which they visited the sick and exhibited their magic tricks.

These doctors, however, could also cause diseases. In other words, they practiced witchcraft. By sleight-of-hand tricks they might project disease objects into a person's body. Such objects could be parts of the skin of a dead body that had been greased with buffalo fat to make them slide right into the victim. Painted all over with red paint and tied very tight with horse hair, they were kept in the medicine man's eagle-wing fan. By shaking the fan after midnight the doctor could dispatch the disease object and make it fly through the air into the mouth of the victim. Another doctor would be called upon to heal the sick person. The doctor put some emetic medicine into a cup of water and had the patient drink it. This caused the patient to throw up fragments of the witch-pellet. The latter was then burned in fire.

Diseases and injuries were not always the effects of witchcraft. An American linguist and anthropologist, Gene Weltfish, tells us how some time in the 1860s a Pawnee of the Skidi band, called by her Boy Otter, as a young boy broke his left leg when he fell from a horse.[14] A medicine man who was one of the four leading officers of the Doctors' Lodge was called upon. He placed four splints around the bone and tied them together with four straps of tanned bison hide, but to no avail. A kinsman of Boy Otter then substituted deer-hide straps for the buffalo hide, for he had received supernatural power from the deer. This did not help either. A good bone and leg doctor, Old-Man-Good-Land, and his assistant and son-in-law, White Fox, then took over. They blew medicine on the leg and tied it up with cloth. They also said that the boy was not allowed to use knives—taboos against using steel or metal are common in instructions given by supernaturals. Unfortunately,

Boy Otter transgressed the prohibition, so the bone stuck out. Old-Man-Good-Land did not give up. He gave Boy Otter medicinal plants to chew. Then he pulled out the bone, cooked certain leaves in water, and blew the concoction down into the hole left by the bone, again and again. Two weeks later the boy was much better. The medicine man received two horses, blankets, and cloth for his important service.

It remained to set the boy psychologically free from his suffering. Four doctors, among them Old-Man-Good-Land and White Fox, sat down at the patient's bed with their medicine bundles, gourd rattles, and eagle-wing fans. Old-Man-Good-Land announced that the animals of the animal lodges would all listen to the songs they had given for healing bone fractures. "Now Boy Otter is going to get well." Next evening when the doctors were assembled Old-Man-Good-Land addressed them again, mentioning all the sacred objects that are symbolic of the animals and their curative power. He said, "Now today we are here as doctors. The objects you see here are the animals, that is, their medicine. They have consented to have him live." Thereupon White Fox made a smoke offering with his pipe to all sacred objects, the doctors, the presents received, and the cosmic directions. At the meal given afterward Old-Man-Good-Land declared, "I had this medicine, and these animals have blessed me and they have given us this their goods. . . . Now the animals have blessed us. Now we have smoked. Now we have eaten."

This is a medical ritual that was used long ago and apparently is not reproduced today. It is nevertheless mentioned here because it refers to a different Prairie culture of high age. In its ritualism it points to the Indians of the Southwest, yet in its concern with animals and animal spirits it shows affiliation with the Indians of the Southeast.

·5·

Traditional Medicine in the Southeast

Although most Indians of the Southeast were removed to the Indian Territory (Oklahoma) at the beginning of the nineteenth century, remnants of the original tribes like the Seminole, Choctaw, Catawba, and Cherokee are still around. Our attention here goes particularly to the Cherokee, who are renowned for their medical system. We may rightly characterize this system as aboriginal, but it is in fact a final result of many historical strands, white culture among them.

Let us quickly look into the historical background.

The Southeast is an area where horticulture and tendencies toward high civlization developed early. In unknown ways a culture of distinctively Mesoamerican stamp spread over the Southeast some twelve hundred years ago. This culture was characterized by a highly developed agriculture, each household having a garden where they planted corn, beans, squash, pumpkins, sunflowers, and tobacco. More particularly, society was both diversified and hierarchical. It was fractured into phratries and clans, and structured into classes, at least among some leading groups. The Natchez on the lower Mississippi, for instance, had both a sacred king and an aristocracy, temple mound foundations, and an elaborate sun worship. These "Mexican" features disappeared with their defeat by the French in the 1720s. Since then, the remaining Natchez people have been living with the Creek and the Cherokee. The Southeastern tribes retained their basic social organization, but without the exalted position of supreme chiefs and the temple service. Indeed, during the last centuries their political structure was less centralized and less autocratic, the tribes being more confederations of "towns" than solid units.

This more leveled organization was particularly at home with the Cherokee, a southern branch of the Iroquoian linguistic stock. Their kinsmen, the Iroquois proper, had their main dispersion in the western part of the state of New York. The Cherokee territory was the Great Smoky Mountains in Tennessee, North Carolina, and northern Georgia. Their country was famous for its rocks and caves. A remnant of the tribe lives in this region even today.

It seems certain that the Cherokee, who were peripheral to the Southeast area and originally probably shared a more democratic political system with the other Iroquoians, in historical times constituted a federation of independent villages under chiefs. During the eighteenth century they built up a kind of a state where their priests became dominant. The tribe was divided into seven (earlier fourteen) totemic clans; seven was their sacred number. Like their southern neighbors, the Creek, the Cherokee had sacred towns of refuge where no human being could be molested, such as Echota on the Little Tennessee. This was the ancient "capital" of the nation. A central council hall was situated here. It is known that a female dignitary, "Beloved Woman," was allowed to enter this hall and speak in councils there.

These Indians, like their Iroquois congeners and most Eastern Woodland tribes, kept their heads shaved except for a roach or scalp lock in which they fastened their feathers. Notable was their use of blowguns for the killing of birds and rabbits. They lived in square houses of poles or logs, plastered with grass-tempered clay; these were furnished primarily with beds spread with bear skins. Opposite the front door was a sweat house where the inhabitants purified themselves from disease by sweating it out. They also had open arbor-style buildings. Like all Southeastern Indians the Cherokee had a large open place for games and an immense festival and council hall in the form of a rotunda. They had a strange reputation of eating cold food, but this was probably based on a misunderstanding: the fact is that salt and hot food were prohibited for sick people—a general taboo the origin of which is not known.

It is possible to say that the Cherokee had no cultural profile of their own. They have been regarded by anthropologists as weaker copies of the Creek Indians.

The Cherokee lost their independence during the eighteenth century. At the same time they gradually turned into one of the "five civilized tribes" of the Southeast, incorporating large parts of white man's cultural heritage like orchards, beekeeping, cattle, horses, and the use of slaves. Repeated clashes with the white government ended with the exterritorization of most Cherokee to Oklahoma and the surrounding area at the beginning of the nineteenth century. A conservative group stayed back in the old country, however, and it is mainly from them that the interesting medicinal recipes have been obtained. Since about the time of the western removal the Cherokee have had an alphabet of their own, created by Sequoyah, and a lively press. This cultural achievement, extraordinary in Native American history, made it possible for aboriginal doctors to write down their cures in notebooks. It is through the study of these books that we get interesting information on the Cherokee medical ways.

THE MYTHICAL INTRODUCTION OF DISEASES

In principle the Cherokee think that, unless the individual has been bewitched, each person is to blame for the diseases he or she contracts. The direct causes may be natural or supernatural, but the individual is, through his or her conduct, responsible; however, the very fact that there are diseases is a consequence of decisions made by mythic beings in the far past. These decisions were provoked by the unexpected spread of mankind in those days and are to be seen as acts of vengeance from the mythic beings. According to myth the latter were all animals—not the animals of today, but their gigantic, wise, and divine prototypes.

In the myth "Origin of Disease and Medicine," it is recounted that the people increased so rapidly that the poor animals found themselves cramped for room. Moreover, the people slaughtered the larger animals and trod upon the smaller ones. The bear elders held a council in their townhouse under a certain mountain, and the old White Bear chief presided. When all present had complained over the human behavior it was decided to begin war against the people. White Bear suggested that his kind should not fight since they could not manage bow and arrows. The deer held a council of their own under their chief, Little Deer, and they decided to send rheumatism to every hunter, unless he asked pardon for the offense. (The myth is here referring to the animal ceremonialism in which the hunter asks the killed animal for forgiveness.) A hunter who did not behave this way would be struck with rheumatism by Little Deer. The fish and reptiles held a council together and determined to send awful dreams so that the victims sickened and died. Birds, insects, and smaller animals finally met under the leadership of Grubworm. They voted that man was guilty and named a number of diseases that should befall him. The outcome, however, would have been that the human beings would be entirely eradicated, so all these diseases

were called off. In the end the animals decided to make menstruation sometimes fatal to women.

The plants, however, were friendly to man, and they agreed to furnish a
cure for some diseases. This is the way plant medicines came about. "When
the doctor does not know what medicine to use for a sick man the spirit of
the plant tells him."[1]

We receive the impression from this myth that animals only concurred in
plaguing mankind with diseases. Yet this is not correct. The animals could
also be helpful in curing diseases. To obtain this help the practitioner had
to watch that he called on an animal that had not caused the disease. For
instance, a clogged throat passage has been caused by water insects (which
are supposed to be ghosts), and the doctor calls on the large fish that prey
upon these animals to come in from the great water to disperse them.

The question is, of course, what "animal" stands for. Is it the common
animal in the wild, its mythic prototype, the master of the animals (a concept
distributed among many peoples both in and outside of America), the spirit
of the animal or a spirit in animal disguise, or possibly a ghost? It is difficult
to know. The literature on the Cherokee contains all these forms, but it is
doubtful if the Indians make clear distinctions between them. In this matter
they do not seem to deviate from other North American Natives, who usu-
sally put us in the same perplexity.

THE IMMEDIATE CAUSES OF DISEASE

The Cherokee consider that diseases may be caused not only by animals
(or animal spirits) but also by powers like the Sun, the Fire, the Moon,
the River, Thunder, and the little people, and by ghosts, witches, dreams,
neglected taboos, and, in the case of epidemics, contacts with human disease
agents.

The powers may send a disease as punishment, but may also, on another
occasion, help the same individual to overcome another disease-sending
spirit. There are as far as we can see only two exceptions to this rule: the
Moon is never asked to dispel disease, and the little people are rarely
friendly. The River—that is, any river—becomes insulted if people throw
rubbish or urinate into it, and it then sends diseases. In a way the animated
River functions here as an ecological guard, a supervisor of man's behavior
when he or she confronts nature. Thunder only rarely causes disease; he
primarily expels disease. The little people appear in groups. They are only
occasionally visible but are often heard singing and dancing. Although kindly
disposed to lone travelers they like to make children sick.

As in all other Indian cultures human ghosts provoke sickness. They feel lonesome in their western realm, the Night Land, and long for their living kin. Neither vengeance nor jealousy drives them, but love and affection. Their devotion results in the living kinsman becoming sick and languishing, and finally dying. As noted before, ghosts of slain animals that have not been treated correctly in the hunting ritual or have been tred on are also originators of disease. Indeed, our foremost authority on the Cherokee, James Mooney, asserts that most diseases are ascribed to the influence of animal ghosts, in particular those of insects.[2] (Calvin Martin's sensational assertions that according to the North American Indians epidemics were caused by the vengeance of the animals are based on such records.)[3]

Witches attack people who have insulted them, quarreled with them, or provoked their jealousy by making them sick. They like to be close to the dying person to catch his or her vital power and add it to their own. Also menstruating women exercise a disease-causing influence.

Some dreams cause disease, or they are omens of disease. Thus, dreams of the little people, the Sun, and various animals mean oncoming disease, in some cases a specified disease. Dreams of certain scenes, such as ball games, train journeys with companions, and burning cabins signal that friends will sicken and die. This preoccupation with dreams is typically Iroquoian: the Iroquois at the Great Lakes have always made the dreams rule their lives.

We need not here discuss neglected taboos, which have been illuminated in the last chapter, or causes of contagious disease that are obvious and close to our modern Western medicine. Perhaps it should be remarked, however, that in Cherokee medicine the mere looking at some fish is supposed to bring smallpox.

THE CHEROKEE DOCTOR

Whatever the diseases, almost any Native doctor is supposed to be able to handle them. If some doctor is incompetent to cure a certain disease it is probably due to the fact that, in his training, he or she has broken off medical studies too early, the Cherokee think. The emphasis here is on what you learn, not on spiritual experiences. This does not mean that such experiences have not existed among the Cherokee doctors—we shall soon see some vestiges of them—but they have little place in the acculturated modern milieu. It is another matter that no one will be accepted as a doctor unless he manifests great spiritual capacity. The Cherokee doctor is a practitioner who in many respects imitates the white doctor without, for that matter, unreservedly agreeing with him. Indeed, for a long time the two colleagues seem to have been bitter rivals—at least from the Cherokee perspective.

The Cherokee doctor, who is generally a man (women are midwives and sometimes expand their medical activities), enjoys a high reputation. The disintegration of Cherokee society after the wars at the beginning of the last century, not least the decrease of the chief's authority, has made the doctor socially and politically important. He is respected both because of his medical knowledge and his learning in botany and oral traditions (myths and other stories); however, he does not seem to be surrounded by the same air of mystery as supernaturally endowed medicine men. He is more like a ritual servant, a priest. Like all other Southeastern tribes the Cherokee had priests during the ancient days when their traditional religion was fully operating. A priest may or may not be blessed by supernatural experiences. His main distinctive feature is that he or she has learned, through tradition, how to deal with supernormal powers. In the same way the Cherokee doctor has learned his trade from other doctors and from notebooks. The doctor does not exclusively practice medicine. He plants corn and harvests it like anyone else in the tribe. He is just distinguished from all others by his medical wisdom and his resource of practical knowledge.

A young Cherokee who wants to become a doctor seeks a reputed older doctor and asks to become his disciple. Sometimes the older man refuses him, because he will not contribute to the diffusion and therewith weakening of the sacred lore. If the candidate is accepted he stays with his teacher as long as necessary or as long as his teacher agrees. The young man has to learn all the lore about diseases and their curing methods. Before he starts his learning he has to drink a decoction so that he will remember everything he is taught. The decoction is made from some insect or from the leaf of the pitcher plant. The candidate is also required to boil and drink the decoction for four or seven days while he rests in a secluded place in the forest or in the mountains. We know that a hundred years ago this isolation was combined with fasting and contemplation, and most probably visions. Here then we have a clear indication that at least in part the doctor is an heir of an inspired medicine man.

Since the days of Sequoyah the apprentice has also been able to learn medical lore through notebooks (formerly the instruction was exclusively oral). Against a certain payment the candidate is usually allowed to copy his master's notebook, containing a mythically founded formula and an explanation. The practical devices, and the reference to paraphernalia to be used, are also given in the teacher's instruction. Some people are able to convince a doctor that he should sell them a whole notebook, or parts of it, so that in the future they need not turn to the doctor in cases of disease.

THE TREATMENT OF DISEASES

When a person is struck by disease the family, and the whole neighborhood, are anxious to take care of him. Thus, if the head of the family is sick the neighbors provide for his family by chopping firewood, plowing his fields, and planting his corn. If the disease goes on for a longer time the other community members see to it that a little informal committee is created to make their contributions to support the afflicted family. Mutual aid is a self-evident concept among these people.

Meanwhile, doctors are called for. They decide among themselves if they can help the patient. Sometimes a doctor considers himself incompetent in the particular case, and another doctor takes on the job. The first doctor may stay to keep out dangerous witches. For instance, he smokes his pipe as he walks around the sick person's bed. The smoke of the sacred tobacco prevents witches from approaching.

Some doctors are diviners and can decide the nature of the disease. They resort to "examination with the beads." In such a case the doctor holds a black bead between the thumb and index finger of his left hand, and a white or red bead between the forefinger and thumb of his right hand. If the bead in his right hand moves briskly, this is an affirmative answer. If it is motionless the answer is negative. It is also possible for the doctor to make inquiries of the patient, asking him whether he has infringed upon a taboo or whether he has had dangerous dreams or omens.

The curing itself is ruled by the formulas. For instance, if a person has sharp pains in the breast the doctor recites a formula in which it is stated that a ghost from the land of the dead has caused the pains. It is also said in this formula that good spirits from the land of the Sun have arrived to get rid of the disease. "Relief has been caused." After having read the formula the doctor blows four times upon the breast of the patient. By means of a blow-pipe made from the trumpet weed he sprays medicine, usually taken from a plant, over the patient. Then he gives the patient a medicine to drink, composed of a concoction of bruised snakeroot and ginseng root. The rite is repeated four times, for four consecutive days.

The cures suggested by the formulas vary greatly. Beside using plants for decoction and infusion—plants which are often selected for their particular qualities, such as their pungent smell or their strange growth—the doctors rely on vapor baths, massage, extraction of the disease by sucking, scarification with an arrowhead or a tooth from the rattlesnake, the patient's vomiting, or his change of name. The background to these procedures is supernatural, but the moment of the supernatural is less manifest than among other Indian tribes.

The medical prescriptions of the Cherokee may in many cases appear "rational," but we must not lose sight of the fact that they are based on formulas that are in themselves sacred and grounded on mythological facts. Now and then soul flights to the land of the dead figure in our texts, but there is no illumination of how, why, and when. We discern in the distant past an inspired medicine man who could cure both intrusion and soul loss; however, the impact of Southeastern priest administration and modern acculturation seem to have quenched the original medical spiritualism.

·6·

Traditional Medicine in the Southwest

There are many fascinating natural and cultural Indian areas in North America, but one may question whether any one of them is as attractive and enchanting as the large variegated Southwestern area of the United States. This region is a country of dramatic topography and beautiful colors, and the fantastic landscape has its counterpart in the mosaic of very diverse Indian cultures. Anybody who visits cities like Albuquerque or Santa Fe, who regards the scenes of the Rio Grande Indian pueblos, or who strolls through traditional Navajo settlements can testify to the truth of this judgment.

As a matter of fact, it is surprising that such a span of Native American culture forms, and some of them of a most exalted nature, could be represented in this area, which is, from the ecological point of view, rather dry and apparently unproductive. In the north there is a highland populated by the well-known Pueblo Indians. It is cold in wintertime but reasonably warm in the summer. It may be characterized as a steppe covered by juniper and sagebrush, surrounded by mountains clothed with pines. In the southern regions there are desert conditions, and here live the Yuman and Piman tribes. Their country is a lowland with sometimes excessive heat, and only water-saving plants like the creosote bush grow there. Over much of the area a third population, the Southern Athapascans, is strewn: the Navajo have their living grounds in between the pueblos (towns, villages), and the Apache may be found on the outer periphery of the Pueblo Indian settlement area. One Apache group, known historically as the fiercest one, the Chiricahua, lives in the desert zone.

Culturally the Indian Southwest reaches its esthetic climax among the highly advanced but secretive and enigmatic Pueblo Indians. Their well-developed ceremonies and attractive costumes are widely known for a magnificent display of colors. Other Southwestern groups, in particular the Yuman and Piman Indians, often give evidence of a traditional poverty. We are reminded here that the Southwest is ethnographically one of the most complicated culture areas in North America, with ties to both Mexican Indian and Canadian Indian cultures. The whole span of Native American cultural forms, from hunting and gathering to incipient high culture, was found here not so many years ago.

In fact, the ethnographic contours of the Southwest exceed the present boundaries of New Mexico and Arizona, and of the United States as well. Within the United States the Southwest comprises, beside New Mexico and Arizona, the southern parts of Colorado, Utah, Nevada, and California. South of the international border large parts of Northwestern Mexico—Baja California and the Sierra Madre region—are also included in what has been called the Greater Southwest. This chapter will focus primarily on the groups living north of the Mexican border. We shall be dealing with the multifaceted Pueblo Indians, outlyers of the Middle American high civilizations; with the numerous Navajo Indians, Athapascan late arrivals from Canada; and with the Pima-Papago Indians, village farmers possibly related to earlier high-culture developments (the Hohokam culture, with earth wall constructions and irrigation canals) but during later centuries very much impoverished. Today nothing remains of their old associations. The Pima and Papago are the Indians who in our survey span the international boundary.

One considerable population in the western part of the area, the Yuman tribes, will not be discussed here, because the available information on their curing methods does not give us much more than what we have learned from other North American peoples. The medicine man, who in fact is the only person among them experiencing visions, sends out his soul to retrieve the lost soul of a sick person or removes the disease-object that has intruded into the patient. Among some Yuman tribes soul loss is also treated with the medicine man's blowing and singing—most probably a secondary development, an influence from practices used when handling diseases from intrusion. A curious detail, characteristic for a Yuman tribe like the Mohave, is that the whole procedure of curing may be supposed to be experienced beforehand in the medicine man's dream.[1]

The other three groups to be dealt with here have more profiled ways of disposing of disease, ways which have only been touched on in the preceding chapters. First we have the sedentary Pueblo Indians with whom medical corporations are active in healing patients. There are of course exceptions to the rule: individualistic curing occurs among the Taos Indians in the extreme northeast of the Pueblo area, among the Hopi Indians in the far west, and, as we shall see, partly also among the Zuni Indians east of the Hopi. The Indians of the Zuni pueblo are otherwise excellent examples of the collectivistic medicine way.

Second, the Navajo constitute a remarkable mixture of individualism and collectivism in their curing practices. Since in their curing acts they identify the patient with the cosmos and its powers we may here speak of "cosmological healing."

Third, the Pima and Papago have some very peculiar concepts of disease—they talk about diseases that stay, and diseases that disseminate. It is worth looking into their somewhat unique etiological system and associated therapy.

THE ZUNI RELIGIOUS SYSTEM

The Pueblo Indians are known for large clustered houses or "towns" of masonry and adobe, intense horticulture, pottery, ceremonial chambers, masked dancing societies, priests, and elaborate rituals. Much of this has been taken over from their famous neighbors in the south, the developed cultures in the Valley of Mexico. It is probable that influences from these quarters reached them over the highlands of Sierra Madre. This happened long ago, before the rise of the Aztec empire. It is very possible that the Zuni have lived in the area they now occupy for the last thousand years.

The pueblo of Zuni to which we shall now turn our attention is situated on the north bank of the Upper Zuni River, close to the western border of New Mexico. The valley surrounding it is covered by greasewood, yucca, and cactus. Today the pueblo consists of a conglomeration of small houses, often with adjoining gardens. Since early times the Zuni people have cultivated corn, squash, and beans, traditionally cared for by the men. Men also weave cotton on looms—there have been cotton fields since the arrival of the Spaniards. The close sedentary living together has stimulated the growth of unilinear family relations and matrilineal clans with totemic names (although no religious totemism can be discovered). Hunting plays a great role as a subsidiary economic pursuit, but it has not had any great effect on the general style of life.

Indeed, the collectivism of the Zuni is a logical consequence of their horticultural way of life. As I have pointed out, man in a hunting society is an inveterate individualist, relying on his own capacity and on the guardian spirit that gives him protection. The man in a horticultural society, however, needs the collaboration of his tribesmen in the settlement where he lives together with them. Not unnaturally, therefore, his religious help comes through collective ritual action. It has often been pointed out that the emphasis in hunting religions is on belief, and the emphasis in horticultural religions on ritual. Whether we accept this statement or not, ritual in itself usually calls for human cooperation. The Zuni are excessively ritualistic. This is apparent in their maize ceremonies and in their medical procedures. There are no lone doctors, but whole societies of experts in medicine to whom the individual has to turn. The single professional recedes behind the collective forces of the social institutions.

This interpretation must not be simplified to the extent that it appears that all individuality has been lost. There are strong personalities, and some individuals have a prominent ritual position. The frequent accusations of witchcraft against deviant or powerful personalities reveal the factual importance single individuals can have; however, the very prominent institution of witchcraft persecutions gives us evidence of the strict social adherence that is expected from everybody in a rather rigid social and ritual system.

The predominance of collective societies and rituals has in fact eclipsed somewhat the development of religious conceptions of Zuni gods and spirits. Elsie Clews Parsons, one of the leading experts on the Pueblo Indian religions, commented on this tendency: "In a religion as highly ritualized as is Pueblo religion, the Spirits tend to become negligible, for the observer, if not for the believer."[2] There are certainly gods and spirits in Zuni faith, but they are very much hidden behind the ritual display. For instance, the spirits of the dead, the *koko* (a more familiar name is *kachina*, the general technical term for these spirits in the Pueblo area), are known through their appearance in the masked dances of the kachina society. It is believed that the dead live in a sacred lake southwest of Zuni but come to visit their living kin and then are present in the masks carried by members of the said society. The spirits of vegetation and fertility also somehow disappear behind all the rituals that accompany the growth of the vegetation according to the rules of the calendar. The koko may indirectly be counted among the spirits of fertility, for they are supposed to bring rain from the clouds that enclose them.

The ceremonies still take place in ceremonial chambers *(kiva)* and on the open plaza, in spite of the presence of the Catholic church; the Zuni have, like the rest of the Pueblo Indians, managed to hold on to their old religion.

One reason for this successful conservatism is the secrecy that surrounds so many ritual occasions, exactly as in other pueblos. This has impeded white researchers from taking part in important ceremonies. Like other rites, the medicine rituals have been hidden from outside eyes. Indeed, Elsie Clews Parsons doubts that any outsider has been able to witness a curing act.[3] She is probably correct, for curing ceremonies are very secret, and we know that only officers of medicine societies are allowed to be present at these ceremonies. It is true that we have received some glimpses of such a ceremony from an older ethnographer, Matilda Coxe Stevenson, but her claim to have been present at a ceremony seems doubtful. On the whole, the Zuni are cautious in giving full information on sacred things, particularly curing; if one tells about these performances their efficacy will be lost. It is therefore only with difficulty and through indirect means that we are able to discern Zuni medical lore.

COLLECTIVISTIC HEALING AMONG THE ZUNI: THE MEDICINE SOCIETIES

All medical activities are thus based in the medicinal societies, and we can begin with an account of their protective deities, which represent an interesting development from the guardian spirits of hunting societies.

In the atmosphere of secrecy and restraint that the scholar encounters it is of course rather difficult to gain a clear picture of the powerful beings that endow doctors with curing powers, the "beast gods." They are the patrons of the curing societies who, according to mythology, were transformed into stone fetishes at the beginning of the world by the so-called twin gods—the gods who once ordered the world. We are told that these fetishes live and that their powers come from their living hearts. The fetishes are preserved in the ritual chambers of some societies and families. Ideally, however, the beast gods live in the place where once in the beginning of time the people emerged from the underground, Shipapolima, in the east. (In this agricultural society human beings are supposed to have originated from the netherworld, just like the plants.)

There are six species of animals represented as beast gods, all of them conceived to rule about the six cardinal directions—six, because zenith and nadir are added to our common four directions. They are the mountain lion, the most powerful of beast gods, residing in the north; the bear, in the west; the badger, in the south; the white wolf, in the east; the eagle, in zenith; and the prey mole, in nadir. Each of these beings is represented at the remaining five points by a younger brother, so that, for instance, all the six brothers of mountain lion are represented at different points and have different colors: yellow, blue, red, white, spotted, and black according to the order given above.

All this symbolism, so typical for the Pueblo Indians, is clearly the product of their systematizing and symbol-forming mind. It is obvious that the whole world of symbolic medical patterns, with symbolically tinged society patrons and rigidly organized doctors' societies, makes a very different impression from the loosely structured curing models of the hunting Indians. Still, there are interesting indications of closer connections between them.

The prey or beast gods are not only medical patrons but are masters or guardian spirits of the hunting animals as well (that is why they are called beast gods). Hunters have to turn to them if they want luck in hunting their clients, the animals of the species they represent. Now, among predatory tribes living on hunting such animal spirits are more or less identical with man's personal guardian spirits. We have seen how the latter serve the medicine man when as a visionary he is blessed by the spirits. The guardian spirit imparts its power into the medicine man in a vision. Vision quests do not occur among the Zuni, and spontaneous visions, although they do exist, cannot create doctors; however, the Zuni beast gods impart their powers into the medicine societies they protect. The recipients are no longer the individuals, but the collective organization.

At the same time there is a reminder of the old hunting vision complex in one remarkable detail: each member of a society has his or her personal fetish, that is, a feathered ear of corn that is placed on the altar of the respective society. This is the remainder of the original hunting medicine pouch.

More important, however, is the stone fetish belonging to the whole society. The beast gods and their societies are collective transformations of the original guardian spirits and their human clients. The societies are constellations of individuals with the rights to handle curative medicine powers.

It is now time to take these societies into closer observation.

There are twelve curing societies, most of them comprehended under the designation "societies of the completed path," and all of them sometimes called "the cult of the beast gods." These societies have in common that their members had once been close to death due to illness, accidents, or effects of taboo violation. They therefore had to ask for the protection of the beast gods and in this way entered the societies. As society members they thenceforth have to assist in curing sick tribesmen.

Although the medicine societies primarily cure the sick and infirm they also have other responsibilities. To some extent they are supposed to control the weather. The oldest medicine society, the Priestly people, also takes care of rain ceremonies, and the Clown society chief plays a role in dramatic rites describing the recovery of the Corn maidens and thereby the revival of the growth of maize. All this is natural in a setting of agriculture and fertility values. It is surprising, however, to find that there are no less than twelve curing societies, most of which also perform some rain ceremonies. That actions for rain could be associated with a curing society is not so startling in a dry country, where the ground itself could be judged as sick, but why so many societies for curing? The fact that one curing society, the Red Ant people, also engaged itself in war rituals not so long ago underscores the multifaceted role that the curing societies have had in Zuni life.

The curing or medicine societies are rather specialized. The Coyote society consists of people who are excellent hunters and who cure illnesses that have been caused by deer. The Red Ant people, also called the Knife society, helps people out in removing ants from their bodies and in curing skin diseases. The Sword-swallowers (also called Wood) cure a sore throat. The Cactus society cures wounds from bullets and pointed objects (formerly arrows, presumably); its members have killed but not scalped an enemy. The Eagle-down society cures smallpox and pulmonary maladies. The Helis people treat convulsions. And so on. All of these societies excel in various sleight-of-hand tricks of a shamanic type, such as swallowing fire, dancing on a bed of hot coals without getting hurt, swallowing wooden swords, and so forth. Even in such details the societies reveal their one-time origin in the medicine man and shaman of hunting cultures.

There are also specialized orders that intersect many societies, such as the order of the magicians in five of the fraternities. The men of such organizations impersonate the foremost god of curing, the bear. The curer draws bear paws over his hands and then treats the patient. It is not quite clear whether in this ritual the doctor is in ecstatic frenzy or not; at least one professional observer (Parsons) emphasizes the "orgiastic" potential of Zuni character.[4]

It remains to point out that the societies have a very strict organization under a chief and several officers. The order particularly occupied with curing is always the foremost section of a society. Every society has a richly decorated altar in its meetinghouse. The altar exposes the stone fetishes of the beast gods and various other sacred objects, such as the feathered ears of corn that are the personal fetishes of the members, given to members at the time of their initiation.

The formation of the medicine societies has affected other societies. The witches are said to have imitated the curing societies in their program of actions, but they do everything in reverse. Instead of curing people they are thought to send disease objects into them (see below). The kachina society, a society into which practically every male Zuni is introduced, is organized like a curing society. It is reputed to have patrons who both cause and cure disease. In the kachina dances (or ceremonies) one of the supernatural masters or koko—that is, spirits of the rains, clouds, and the dead—helps people to get rid of venereal diseases: a person who is masked and dressed like this spirit purifies the men so that if anyone has venereal disease he may be cured and not give disease to the women.

Much has been written here about men. What about the women? We know that there are female members of the medicine societies, although they are rather few. They cure sometimes but not often. In the Clown society, for instance, women may certainly be members, but they never attend public rituals, nor do they doctor. Their roles are thus very uncertain.

It could be said that medicine societies are remarkably prominent in the Zuni organization of societies, but the Zuni do not stand alone here. Pueblo Indians farther east who speak Keresan languages display a similar orientation. In scholarly circles it has been presumed that the original function of Pueblo societies was curing and that with the growing importance of agriculture the societies also turned to rain ceremonies. I shall not further enter into this problem here. It is true that such a theory could explain the Navajo emphasis on medicine (see below), but against this bold interpretation could be argued that collective societies for the furthering of agriculture are a natural phenomenon in many agrarian civilizations.

It seems to me more appropriate to see the development of medicine societies as the expression in a highly organized community of people's deep affection for the sick and their heartfelt care of them. That this is an important concern among Zuni Indians is well testified to in anthropological experience. For instance, one white visitor to a Zuni man's sick bed observed the tender care provided him: "His head was pillowed in the lap of his little old white-haired mother, who was gently stroking his forehead and talking to him in the endearing phrases of mothers to little children."[5] The sick person is generally in the care of the whole family, the neighbors, and the medicine society that is treating him.

This eagerness of the Zuni to save a sick kinsman or friend from the jaws of death could possibly seem surprising when we learn that after death the person will be well received as a koko under a mysterious lake. There he or she will spend a very happy life and occasionally return to earth in order to help surviving relatives. So what is there to worry about? The answer is indeed obvious: feelings of love and care, and longing for deep fellowship, are all human emotions that demand that a dying person stays in the circle of family and friends.

ZUNI WAYS OF CURING

For the Zuni diseases usually depend upon the actions of human witches, but they may, as we found in the discussion of the koko, also be the results of the operations of supernatural spirits. We have also noted that members of one society, the Clown society, are able to cause disease as well as to cure it. Most disease symptoms can be traced to the presence of malignant objects in the body, but there are cases where the "heart"—the soul—has been stolen and must be retrieved. Here as elsewhere in North American aboriginal medicine the method of healing is connected more with the origin of disease than with the symptoms themselves. Sometimes the doctor can tell who the disease-giver is. If witchcraft is suspected the supposed witch is exposed to torture (at least it was often so in bygone days) and urged to confess. If the doctor mentions the culprit's name, or the witch through torture is forced to admit the crime, from then on the witch has lost all access to supernatural power.

Some diseases due to intrusion obviously call for some surgical operations. The scholar Frank Hamilton Cushing, who, a hundred years ago, was accepted as a member of the Zuni nation, recounts how he was asked to assist when two Zuni doctors treated a man suffering from a swollen foot. The doctors found that the patient had a "decaying condition." With great skill they removed the inflamed flesh, washed away the pus, and bandaged the man. Cushing's role was to administer a medicine containing an opiate.

All this sounds rational, but the premise of the operation was not—the decaying flesh was thought to be infested with worms, or turning into worms, and the infusion of the roots and bark of the willow, of a bright, red color, was considered the source of life and of flesh-forming blood.

It happens that an invalid turns to a single doctor to get well (this doctor being a member of the medicine society). The disease is then not considered fateful. A kinsman of the patient, often the father, goes to the doctor with "prayer meal," made from maize, and part of the doctor's fee, a thread from a blanket or shawl, all placed in a cornhusk. These things are also supposed to be offerings to the beast gods. With this prayer the kinsman asks the doctor to help out. If he accepts the doctor goes to action. He smokes (cigarettes), sings a sacred song, and mixes his medicines in a bowl. Thereafter he massages the patient with ashes. With the help of a power object—

his crystal, or a vision-producing drug—the doctor is able to see where the pain is. He breathes out his animal helper (the beast god), which he sends into the patient's body. Then he sucks out the disease-causing object obviously sent by a witch.

We do not know for certain if the retrieval of a lost soul still occurs or, if so, how it is carried out. It is possible that, like the Keres doctor, the Zuni doctor goes after the heart soul that is hidden somewhere in the surroundings. As we shall see, soul loss plays a role in collective society healing, but then only as a theme to be prevented.

After curing a former patient waits till the winter solstice, when he goes to the house where the doctor, and the society to which the doctor belongs, is quartered. The patient's head is now washed, and he is adopted as a "child" of the society, a ward to care for.

When the patient is plagued by a very serious disease his family calls on the whole society to come by. The society arrives in a group and declares its intention to spend four nights with the sick person, from midnight to dawn. During the four days the society members prepare the sacred ritual of initiation into the society, which takes place on the last night. This initiation is necessary, for without it the patient remains vulnerable and has no guarantee that he will survive. It is a very expensive business to join the society, or some of its orders.

The preparations for the initiation include setting up the society's sacred paraphernalia, singing the particular songs of the society, invoking the beast gods, and alienating the disease from the patient's body. The common methods for this are extraction, massage, sweating, bloodletting, and the use of drugs. The initiation ceremonies follow the treatment. The patient receives a face and body painting that is supposed to transform him or her into a powerful being, an "animal," a "bear." All society members are actually called bears, since bears are supposed to own the strongest medical powers. The ritual of initiation is in fact a death-and-revival ritual: the novice "dies" (he eats and sleeps little, and is untouchable) and comes back with bear power (marked by the body painting).

Such transformations are well known from other rituals in North America and are connected with the reception of visions (as on the Plains), the acquisition of medicines (as among the Ojibway), or the manifestation of socially controlled powers (as among the Kwakiutl of the Northwest Coast). Their import is the change of individual status from a person of ordinary capacity to a person invested with supernatural power. The new doctor of the Zuni becomes so exalted that by his title—bear—he is more or less equal with the most powerful of the beast gods, the bear. It is said that in the ritual of initiation he impersonates the bear that gave him power, "becomes a bear." When he then in his turn treats patients he paws and claws them like a wild bear. We are informed that in this condition the doctor is particularly enabled to see the nature of the hidden disease by gazing into a crystal.

The healed patient becomes a new member of the society (or order) and learns the prayers, songs, and medicines that belong to his fraternity. Usually, however, only the chief of the society is charged with active curing, while the other members are more passive assistants. Women appear less frequently in curing, as was pointed out above; some societies do not allow women to doctor at all.

The new member of a society has to take part in its rituals whenever the society is called to a curing performance and an initiation of another patient. In most societies all members, sometimes including women, have to assist in sucking the sick person. At the time of the winter solstice the society arranges communal cures free of charge to which anybody may come and be treated: they are sucked, brushed, or given a drink of medicinal water.

Although the Zuni tend their societies and rituals with an almost mechanical precision there is no doubt about the religious feelings of the society functionaries. Here is an example of a prayer directed to the powers by a chief of the Little Firebrand society:

> Lion of the North, give me power to see disease.
> Bear of the West, give me power to see disease.
> Badger of the South, give me power to see disease.
> White Wolf of the East, give me power to see disease.
> Eagle of the Zenith, give me power to see disease.
> Shrew of the Earth, give me power to see disease.
> Thou, my Sun Father, give me power to see disease.
> Thou, my Moon Mother, give me power to see disease.
> All ye ancient ones, give me power.[6]

To be acquainted with the nature of the disease is the necessary condition for curing the disease, in American Indian as well as in Western medicine. The difference between them is, inter alia, that the Zuni Indian refers to magic or revelation, the Western doctor to scientific fact (or presumed scientific fact).

ZUNI SYMBOLISM OF RITUAL CURING

The main feature of Zuni ritual curing is its detailed symbolism. Matilda Coxe Stevenson, who, according to her own statement, witnessed a medicine

ceremony in the Big Firebrand society, closely describes parts of the ceremony that (if authentic) disclose its remarkable formal character.[7]

In this case the patient suffered from a swollen throat. He was placed on
a pallet in the middle of the floor. Masked men impersonating the powerful
koko spirits danced for a while on the roof. About dusk they were led down
into the chamber by a woman who had made a road of sacred meal for them
to follow. Four times the koko circled round the patient while the choir was
singing. With four fingers one koko ran a line of meal from the patient's left
shoulder to the waist, and another ran yucca leaves over these meal lines.
Then the first koko drew meal lines from the right shoulder to the waist,
whilst his colleague stroked the patient with the yucca. This marking and
stroking was repeated for knees, back, arms, and palms. A koko mask was
placed on the patient's head. He then spat through the small mouth hole.
(Spitting is a rite of exorcism.) The members of the society danced and
encircled the patient, and they continued their symbolic actions, such as
laying bread over the patient's heart. Finally they dipped yucca suds on the
head of the former patient, now a new member of their society, whereupon
a woman washed his head. Gifts for the ears of corn and the prayer feathers
were then exchanged, and a feast followed.

It is easy to recognize the sanctification of the patient and his purifcation
from evil influences in these actions. Another example of this ritual symbolism is provided in a Zuni story about a "sick" girl who was cured from an
intruding disease. (Since we have a drought of information from observers
we are forced to adduce such indirect sources.) This story tells us of a young
boy who brings home a young girl to be his wife. She is, however, "raw,"
that is, supernatural, and has to be treated by a medicine society to become
"cooked," that is, human. The medicine society members arrive with a medicine bowl, an ear of corn, and eagle feathers.

> They sat down facing the east. The grandmother rose. She took a package
> of prayer meal to the headman [of the society]. He moved her hands to
> the six directions. She said, "I have needed your help to cure my daughter
> [her grandson's woman]. She is a raw person and cannot eat as cooked
> persons do. You are powerful and can cure her." She gave him the prayer
> meal. The headman made a cross of meal upon the altar and set down the
> bowl. He spread a blanket and laid the girl upon it facing the east. He
> went four times to the altar and prayed. He growled like a bear and ap-
> proached the girl. He sucked out insects and bugs and spat them into the
> circle of meal. At last there was nothing more to suck. She was cured. He
> said, "Now you can eat like cooked persons. Get up." She sat up. Four
> times he gave her water to drink. He took water in his own mouth and
> spat it out on his hands. He rubbed the girl's body. He took water from

the altar to the boy and his grandmother and they drank. He took the
cornhusk full of insects and prayer meal and went out to the east and left
it there. The girl was cured.[8]

We notice how full of ritual symbolism this Zuni account is: there is the
use of corn and corn meal as sacrificial gifts, the cross as a design of the
universe, an eastern orientation for connections with beginning daylight
and life, four as a sacred number in prayer and other sacred action, bear
impersonation as a sign of medicine power, and water as a life-giving source.
All these elements present a typically Pueblo form of religious expression,
indicating that healing is part of a cosmological performance.

So far we have been dealing with diseases caused by the intrusion of an
object. But what about soul loss? The evidence is meager, unfortunately,
but it is there. A woman told an anthropologist how she caught the measles
and fainted—"died," she said, for the same word is used for faint and die.
While "dead" she dreamed that she was going to the country of the dead in
the west. It was a very nice country, and she was happy there with her
deceased relatives. The dead asked her for feathers, which obviously symbolize the breath of life. When she woke up from her coma her folks were very
worried that she should go back with the feathers and thus forfeit her life.
They therefore called on a medicine society and had her initiated there.

In this account the society was apparently unable to cure the patient, but
they could prevent her from becoming sick again by giving her a "new
heart."

THE NAVAJO WORLD

The Navajo are the largest Indian population in North America, and their
tribal lands, which stretch over four southwestern states (Utah, Colorado,
New Mexico, and Arizona), constitute the largest of the Native reservations
in the United States. Scientific attention has therefore focused on these
Indians during the twentieth century. Anthropologists have tried to pene-
trate the difficult symbolic systems in Navajo culture and religion; psychia-
trists have been fascinated by their personality structures, and students of
religion have been puzzled by their ritual systems and the difficulty in analyzing their religious concepts.

Together with the Apache tribes, the Navajo belong to the Southern Athapascans. These tribes broke off from the Northern Athapascans in Canada
and arrived in the Southwest some time during the fourteenth or fifteenth

century. They were then primitive hunters and gatherers, prone to assault the Pueblo Indians and to rob them of their attractive horticultural products. The Navajo soon adjusted themselves to the agricultural pattern in the Southwest and became called *Apaches de nabaju,* "Apaches of the cultivated fields." This name distinguished them from the other Athapascan groups that remained "wild Apaches." Through their long acquaintance with the Pueblo Indians and, from the seventeenth century, with the Spanish people the culture of the Navajo gradually changed. They acquired horses, sheep, and goats, and they became excellent weavers and silver workers.

At the same time they retained in part their old life style, now and then harassing Spanish, Mexican, and later American homesteads. Once the harvest had been brought in the raiding was on. In 1863–64 the U.S. army under Kit Carson defeated the Navajo in Canyon de Chelly and brought the whole tribe—at that time some eight thousand people—to Fort Sumner, Pecos River, where they were to be "civilized." Neither schooling nor missionary activities worked, however, on the stubbornly traditionalist Navajo, and after four years they were removed back to their own isolated plateau and mountain country. Raiding ceased then, however, and the Navajo resumed their herding and farming life. They multiplied rapidly and are now about 160,000 individuals.

They should have prospered if water shortage and sheep grazing had not threatened their existence, so that in the 1930s they had to drastically cut down their herds. Today we see the numerous Navajo communities or bands spread out over the wide country, with picturesque, mostly octagonal wooden houses, hogans, coexisting with more modern buildings. It is in these houses that the famous ceremonies that fill up so much of Navajo time take place. These ceremonies are the main expressions of Navajo religion.

As noted above, Navajo culture changed form when the people became acquainted with the flowering culture of the Pueblo Indians. Most important were the changes in their spiritual and ceremonial life. During the great Pueblo revolt against the Spaniards at the end of the seventeenth century many Pueblo Indians became refugees among the Navajo. They taught the Navajo many things, so that their hosts' ceremonial life was enriched.

From then on the Navajo became known for their long and remarkable ceremonies; for their masks, altars, praying sticks, and use of cornmeal as sacred matter and for their sand paintings as visual charters of the universe. A series of "chantways" developed, song rituals which could last between two and nine nights (with the daily ceremonies in between included). The same chantway could correspond to several myths of origin. The original religion with its shamanism, puberty rites for girls, and fear of the dead thus changed, but to some extent only formally: the shaman remained as an ecstatic ("hand-trembling") diagnostician, the puberty rites were incorporated and expanded in the new ceremonial system, and the traditional fear of the dead is still a surprising and prominent feature in Navajo life.

All this rich ceremonialism contrasts oddly with the simple social structure.

The foremost Navajo origin myth describes the arrival of the ancestors from the underworld, and it is clearly taken over from the Pueblo Indian mythology. It takes its beginning in a primeval underground world that is dark and black. Taboo infringements, mainly of a sexual kind, infuriate the gods of this somber world so they cause a great inundation. The people (who at this time are ants, bats, and other insect beings) flee through a hole in the ceiling to a second world that is blue. Similar taboo transgressions occur and compel the people to move to a third, yellow world. For the same causes that drove them away from the preceding worlds they have to enter a fourth, red world, and finally a fifth world, the present one. Here the Sun combines all the colors of the different underworlds into the daylight we have today.[9]

This origin myth plays a vital role in Navajo religious life. The dark underworlds represent chaos and death. In the night, and at death, the individual returns to the same conditions that the first people experienced at the beginning of time. It is characteristic that the ceremonies, the chantways, begin in the night, reenacting mankind's gradual emergence from the underworld and attainment of the light and the beautiful morning world. In the healing chants, it is the patient who is being restored to health who, as one writer puts it, is "going to greet the rising sun."

The dominating beings in Navajo mythology and religion are Sun, his wife, Changing Woman, and their progeny the Twin gods, primordial beings who once ordered the world. Changing Woman is the most beloved of Navajo divinities. She is associated with earth and vegetation, and as her name suggests she changes her appearance with the seasons. She is the goddess of regeneration, and she was the first woman to undergo a puberty rite. Other divine persons are Spider Woman, goddess of weaving; Salt Woman, who rules over a salt basin; Deer Owner, who is a powerful master of the animals; and Talking God, a protector of corn who appears at dusk.

The absence of clear ideas of existence after death is a typical Athapascan phenomenon. Indeed, most Navajo declare that they do not know what will happen to them after death. Their concerns are about this life, which they try to make as harmonious as possible. There are, however, different traditions about conditions in the next life, like the tradition of a return to the darkest underworld, and there are reports of people who have come to the other world in trance experiences. Such tales do not have the same truth value for everybody. It is said, however, that the human being's "inner form," a wind soul, returns to Dawn Woman (who could be the same as Changing Woman) after death.

NAVAJO THEMES OF MORALITY, PHILOSOPHY, AND HEALTH

Like all other Indian nations the Navajo value hard work in a positive way.[10] They lend help to other people who are in need, but loyalty to one's own family takes precedence over other loyalties. Moderation is recommended in all matters. Thus, it is good to assemble a fortune so that ceremonies can be held to ward off or cure illness, but it is bad to have too much wealth, for that may raise suspicions of witchcraft. It is a pity, but a very poor person is thought to be lazy and incompetent. (The parallel with current American mores is obvious.) In the same spirit, sex is valued highly as a matter of enjoyment, but sexual promiscuity is disapproved. Indeed, there are ceremonies to remove inordinate sexual passions.

It is evident that there is an order of things that has to be followed to avoid unhappiness. This order may by its very universal determinism be called supernatural;[11] however, it is not dependent on supernatural beings. On the contrary, gods and spirits are subordinated to the same general law. It is true that in mythological accounts the supernatural beings—generally comprehended as "the Holy People"—often do things that are not allowed according to mundane ethics. For instance, they enter into all kinds of sexual alliances, and they take part in theft and fraud. Here as in many other North American mythologies there is a gap between mythology and religious and social norms.

This supernatural cosmic law has its counterparts in many other religions; consider, for example, concepts such as *rita* for the Vedic Indians and *tao* for the Chinese. Our concept of fate seems to come rather close to these ideas.

Navajo Indians wish for themselves and their dear ones health and long life. In order to achieve this goal they have to keep to the inherent law of the universe. If they infringe upon this law they certainly do not expect punishments in the next life, but they expect bad consequences in this life: health deterioration, and a shorter life span. Their outlook is rational; there is no feeling of sin as in Christianity, no personal guilt. A person who commits what is considered a serious crime—say, rape, theft, adultery, or murder—has done so because he or she is "out of order," not in harmony with the cosmic balance that rules our lives. The person does not regret what has been done but tries to correct the error. Otherwise health and long life are in jeopardy.

Before more is said about the principle of balance some remarks should be made about the kind of transgression implied. It is not limited to the action itself but encompasses both mind and action. Thus, there is the silent injunction that it is not only the pronouncement that a person shall die that constitutes a transgression—the very wish that this person shall die has the same import. In a most enlightening book the American Navajo specialist Gary Witherspoon asserts that according to Navajo philosophy a person's mental and physical phenomena are inseparable.[12] Not only the speech but also the thought can have a powerful impact on the world of matter and energy, Witherspoon argues. Words and thoughts both have a creative power. In ritual creativity the thought is the inner form, whilst the speech that realizes the thought is the outer form. Navajo Indians labor with these concepts, which come close to the animistic separation between soul and object, soul and body. All objects—for instance, a mountain—have an inner form.[13]

We see here how different the Navajo conceptual world is from Euroamerican thinking. This difference is possibly even more pronounced where the principle of order or harmony is concerned. It is necessary to pay further attention to this principle, for the adherence to the principle of cosmic balance determines a person's health and length of life.[14]

Hozho, the beautiful, pleasant, and healthy environment including the universe, and existence—has been called the central idea in Navajo religious thinking by specialists on the Navajo world view. When hozho rules, everything is in harmony. Deviation from this principle, which for the sake of simplicity we may call beauty (as others have done), brings about disease and death. The harmony through beauty is put out of order by the human being's contact with dangerous things, by his or her evil thoughts and deeds. The individual may be little responsible for these accidents: witchcraft, for instance, may destroy the harmony in a person when it influences him or her. There is only one means to overcome such a critical situation, and that is to find the right ritual for a correction of what has gone wrong. These rituals usually end with the phrase, "beauty has been restored."

The health of the human being is thus not an isolated case; it is a matter of the whole universe. By contributing to the upkeep of beauty, and by having it restored when it has become lost in individual cases, each man and woman work for the universe at large and its basic order.

COSMOLOGICAL HEALING AMONG THE NAVAJO

It is possible that concerns about health and long life among the Navajo are so pronounced because of their uncertainty as to the reality and qualities of life after death. By placing the cases of disease in the middle of a cosmological perspective they derive from religion as much as they can to keep the individual physically and mentally sound. If religion cannot effect an insurance for a happy next life, at least it can safeguard the present existence to a certain extent. At the same time it is possible for us to discern that in the hope of a unity with the supernatural powers of the universe there is a longing for longevity and, indeed, equality with the unlimited happiness of these powers.

This religious conviction and the thought that the promotion of health and long life is part of a cosmological ceremonial system are of course of Pueblo origin. The whole ceremonial organization of curing has probably been taken over from the Keresan and Zuni pueblos. It was linked with original Navajo shamanism and received here a prominence and a status that almost ousted other features in Navajo religion.

This does not mean that all ceremonies are directed toward healing. Navajo ceremonies have many purposes. Some mark transitions in human existence, such as puberty rites, or war and peace rites (now more or less obsolete). Others are connected with vital economic pursuits: they call on corn and rain, or invocate the powers of the game. The medicine rites for curing the sick are, however, the most frequent and most important. It should be mentioned that many ceremonies that are not primarily designed for the rehabilitation of sick persons also safeguard people against the danger of disease and death. Before we enter the different ceremonial ways, let us look into the structure and meaning of them.

Navajo ceremonies seem at first glance to engage a collectivity of functionaries, but this is not so. They involve a diviner, a ritual specialist, sometimes helped by an assistant, and the recipient of the ceremonial blessings. Whereas other peoples' rituals often are expressed as dances, Navajo ceremonies mostly take the form of song recitals and dramatic performances. The ceremony takes place in the hogan, which is supposed to symbolize the universe. The fire in the middle of the lodge represents the sun.

In a medicine ceremony the roles of the acting medical people are related to the way in which the disease came about. As mentioned, the general motivation is that the harmony of the universe has been upset by events that have happened to individuals. In every particular case the cause of the disharmony is diagnosed by a so-called hand-trembler. This individual is a shaman who through ecstasy or trance ("hand-trembling") and various devices perceives which one of the available ceremonies should be used. Then follows the healing ceremony, performed by a singer. Every ritual drama has a myth that illustrates the supernatural origins of the ritual and also gives rules for its performance. The myths are grandiose creations, encompassing series of well-organized tales referring to mysterious events in the primordial world. In this way the great myths are bound up with the ritual procedures. They are presented as songs of great poetic beauty performed by particularly educated singers who not only sing but also recite them. Every part of the ritual has to be rendered correctly; otherwise the person who is sung over will get hurt (unless the ritual is immediately repeated again by another singer). Considering the fact that one and the same ceremony may contain several hundred songs, the danger of mistakes is obvious. No wonder a ceremony that normally only engages one singer but may take as many as nine nights (and days) to perform often requires more energy and memory than a human being can stand. Nowadays singers forget single episodes more and more, so that ceremonies have been abbreviated. Often singers are assisted by masked men who represent the Holy People (the gods) and act out mythical events.

There are over sixty ceremonies (chantways) for blessing, curing, and purification. They can be enacted any time during the year. The blessing ceremonies safeguard the Navajo land, the sheep and crops, the homes, and human beings. They are important for the avoidance of events leading to weak health. The curing ceremonies take care of mental and physical disorders; they are the central medicine ceremonies. The purification ceremonies purge all objects, places, and human beings that have been soiled by contact with dangerous things and beings. These dangerous elements—potential sources of disease and misfortune—are animals, wind and lightning, ghosts and dreams of ghosts, wrong behavior during a ceremony, bewitchment, breaking some taboo, and so on.

THE BLESSINGWAY CEREMONY

Among the blessing ceremonies Blessingway stands out as the core of Navajo ceremonial activities. It is said that it sets the pattern for all other rituals. It is a kind of a charter of Navajo national identity, for it concentrates on the Navajo land between the four sacred mountains, and it deals with the convention of the gods in pristine days. Its aim is to restore a person to the proper way of living and bless his life. The Holy People who in mythic times did things in a proper and exemplary way are described in the songs, and this makes the person sung over restored and happy. The very words of the songs have this creative result. All blessing ceremonies strengthen hozho by attracting and incorporating the goodness and power that belong to the gods.

The Blessingway ceremony is a preventive ritual, and it is arranged when a person is so inclined. It lasts only a couple of nights and is of surprising simplicity. It may include prayers, the use of cornmeal and corn pollen, and—at the end of the ceremony—a ritual washing with yucca suds.

At least this was the case at the following ceremony, noted down by anthropologist Charles C. Case.[15] On this occasion no special costumes were required, and there were no sand paintings (but actually a cornmeal painting), and no masked figures. The doctor or singer asked the client to place all objects he wanted to be blessed on a particular cloth. The family hogan in which the ceremony took place was also blessed by the doctor. Both the client and his family blessed themselves with corn pollen that the doctor sent around in a clockwise direction (because the sun goes this way). The participants touched a pinch of pollen to their foreheads and another to the top of their heads. The doctor delivered a prayer that the client had to repeat, word for word. Then he purified the patient with yucca suds as he sang about how in primeval days Talking God washed the first client with yucca. During all these actions spirit visitors may silently be present to watch the ceremony. Sheep skins and blankets were reserved for them on the floor of the hogan.

Late the second night the doctor started singing about the First House, about the Blessingway ceremony held there, and about the gods who took part in it. Throughout the rest of the night he sang about the making of the earth and the universe, about the physical features given to the earth, about the creation of the animals and, finally, humankind. Nobody was supposed to sleep during these performances, for that would have spoiled the ceremony.

In many Blessingway performances the singer or doctor passes clockwise inside the hogan, thereby marking its four posts with cornmeal. This ritual demonstrates that the hogan is identified with the four cardinal points, that is, with the universe, and that the ceremony itself is a recreation of the world, or rather, identical with the original creation. The cosmological symbolism of the whole ritual procedure is thus underlined. Another ritual performance, the purification of the client, may take the form of a "bath" in which cornmeal is applied on his body. Cornmeal or corn pollen is in Navajo as in Pueblo ceremonies sacred matter.

Particular attention should be paid to the prayers. In Navajo religion prayer is an act not of supplication or worship but of identification with the gods and their power. The prayer signalizes that the individual is in control of divine power. Scholars who have studied Navajo prayers interpret them as magic and compulsive or as "performative utterances," meaning that the utterance of the words effectuates their intended actions. Indeed, the Navajo prayer is supposed to be a powerful thing, and it is said to appear as a Holy Person with a strong personality. We are reminded here of what was said before: words and thoughts have creative power.

Blessingway rituals are particularly used for at weddings, for pregnant women, and for girls passing through their puberty. In the puberty ceremony a girl becomes the Changing Woman, this most beloved divinity, the symbol of regeneration, rejuvenation, and beauty.

THE HOLYWAY CEREMONIES

The curing or Holyway ceremonies are resorted to when the person has already fallen sick. Their aims are to transform the evil influences sent by some powers into good influences, thus creating immunity against the evil in the patient. Holy People are potentially dangerous, but their powers can be used in such a way that they promote blessings. Like other rites the Holyway ceremonies reenact the creation of the world as it is told in the myths. This is done through song, prayer, and drama in which the patient is placed in the middle of the recreated universe and identified with the hozho as expressed by the deities.

There are several curing rites that are called Holyway. Their common denominator is that they are all attributed to the Holy People. The Holy People are said to be offended if a person trespasses taboos and rules of life given at the beginning of time. As a punishment the holy ones cast a spell on the offender, and the latter cannot recover until the spell has been removed. This certainly sounds as if it were a case of mere disease intrusion, and there is reason to think that it was originally so; however, no recovery can be made without the restoration of the disturbed balance and the patient's identification with the harmonious cosmic powers. Only through such a procedure will the offended Holy People be inclined to withdraw their curse.

A person who is sick and does not know the origin of his disease sends for the hand-trembler whose task it is to try to reveal what afflicts his client.[16] Through different techniques he solves the problem. He sits outside the sick man's or woman's hogan, listening to the winds, the animals, and the spirits. He also guides his hand feelingly over the body of the patient, and when he knows the nature of the disease his hand starts trembling. This capacity is a gift from a poisonous lizard, the so-called Gila Monster known to shake its forelegs.

The diagnostician then informs the patient and his or her family what ritual is needed for a restoration to health. If the patient suffers from bodily damage the seer will recommend the Lifeway chant. If the disease has been provoked by an encounter with a bear, and it is wintertime when Thunder is asleep, the Mountainway chant is the right treatment. For most diseases, however, a Holyway chant is the adequate ritual.

The patient or the patient's family calls on a singer or doctor who has mastered the appropriate ceremony, which may last up to nine nights. The singer's protracted training, up to a decade or two, should guarantee that he will accomplish his task well. The chosen doctor decides when and where the ceremony is to take place. There are then many arrangements for the family of the sick person to make: the hogan where the ceremony will be held has to be cleaned, and the food for the occasion has to be prepared.

The ceremony begins with the performer's blessing of the hogan and proceeds according to a pattern already described for the Blessingway chant. The Holyway ritual refers to the Emergence myth (like all other rituals). The central personage is one of those heroes who are supposed to have ended the mythical time and who figure as human ancestors. The myth tells how this hero visited forbidden places and committed acts that were wrong—in sum, he transgressed all the taboos set forth by the Holy People. Consequently, disease and even death struck the unhappy hero. The Holy People were now brought to his rescue. By identifying himself with these cosmological beings, and even by executing compulsive control of them in prayers, the disorder of disease could be overcome.

This mythical drama is repeated in the curing ritual of today's patient. The latter is identified with the mythic hero who is said to have contracted his disease in the same way. In all particular ritual acts the patient imitates the hero, sings his songs, and performs (with the help of the singer) his prayers. In other words, the patient *is* the hero. In the prayers the Holy People are beseeched to remove their spell and remake his or her whole person. Indeed, the patient even anticipates this blessed state by hinting that it has already been realized. This is the result of the deep identification with the deities.

The ritual drama receives a particularly strong effect in the symbolism of the sand paintings that are made during the fifth to eighth nights of the ceremony.[17] The Navajo probably learned the use of sand paintings as a model of the cosmos from the Pueblo Indians. Among the Zuni the young candidate to the koko society is initiated by, among other things, treading on a sand painting representing the supernatural powers. His identity with these powers is further demonstrated by the painted sand being rubbed onto his arms. The same ideas and practices have been adopted by the Navajo.

The sand paintings of the Navajo curative ritual are performed by knowledgeable men under the direction of the singer. The paintings are of varying size and consist of pigments made from sandstone (red, yellow, and white), cornmeal, plant pollens, flower petals, and charcoal. The artist makes these pigments drip down between his fingers on a base of clean sand that covers part of the floor. The paintings he accomplishes depict the sacred world, the supernatural beings, and the mythical episodes discussed above. The sacred world is described in its normal state as an ordered world with which the patient can identify him- or herself.

The apex of the sand painting ritual occurs near the end when the patient is himself included in the painting. That is, he or she is drawn into the sacred, ordered sphere by sitting down in the midst of the painting, naked as much as is considered decent and with his or her body parts placed as far as possible on the divine counterparts. The chanter applies sand from the depicted body parts of the deity to the corresponding parts of the patient. This completes the identification process. Members of the patient's family may also take some of the sand and apply it on their own bodies, as a form of blessing. When the ritual act is over the sand is collected and deposited at some distant place in the north, far from human paths.

It may happen that these ambitious rites fail to cure the diseased person. In such cases the failure is considered due to some mistake in the ritual performance. Perhaps the diagnosis has been wrong, and therefore the wrong ritual has been used. Or the ritual has been performed in a deficient manner. For instance, the prayer formulas have not been delivered in a correct way, or parts of them and the songs have been forgotten. One thing is certain to the Navajo: a ritual that has been presented without errors never fails to have a positive effect.

THE EVILWAY CEREMONIES

In the third type of ceremony involving human health, the Evilway ceremonies, a sick person is restored to hozho after he or she has become afflicted by evil powers, usually sent by malevolent supernatural beings. The remedy is exorcism of these powers. The malevolent spirits are the ghosts, the rapacious specters of dead people. The original "ghostway," as it is called, the true Evilway, or Upward-Reaching Way, deals with Navajo ghosts. There is also another ghostway, Enemyway, which is directed against ghosts of non-Navajo peoples. Formerly there were ghosts of fallen enemies; nowadays the ceremonial is also aimed at Navajo who have been too much in touch with white people.

The idea behind Evilway ceremonies is that it is necessary to avoid the dead. It is not a question of fear of death as such; rather, it is avoidance of the dead because contact with them may mean disease and premature death. The curing ritual here is therefore not so much concerned with a restitution of disturbed order but with removal of the pathogenic power from the patient's body. As in other ceremonies there is a recital of the Emergence myth, with particular reference to the ghostland and the first ghost. The ritual is characterized by its exorcism of the bad power and imitative shooting of arrows against ghosts. Sometimes the singer and the patient travel together in prayer to the realms below. The ghost is talked down into ghostland, while the patient is talked upward out of that place.

As has been suggested, it is possible that Holyway chants have been derived from the Evilway ceremony. The latter, with its intrusion theory of disease, is certainly much closer to the intrusion techniques among the Northern Athapascans of Canada, the original congeners of the Navajo.

It is remarkable what a place the Navajo disease concept has in tribal life. Navajo religion is dominated by extensive ceremonies and the mythology attached to them. Most of these ceremonies concern diseases and their healing. It is indeed a great riddle how this ritual and mythological complex could play such a conspicuous role in Navajo life. There is certainly a patterned fear of ghosts and diseases in this society, and there is the uncertainty of life after death, but why this disease complex was developed to such an extraordinary extent we do not know.

THE PIMA AND PAPAGO OF THE SOUTHWESTERN DESERTS

Until recently the etiology and therapy of diseases among the Pima and Papago, on both sides of the international boundary in the southwestern corner of North America, attracted little attention. New discoveries by Donald Bahr and his associates have revealed that their medical doctrines are quite unusual and therefore ought to be observed here.

The Pima and Papago are two neighboring groups with close linguistic bonds. They have many cultural and religious traits in common, and it therefore seems appropriate to deal with them here as a unit. Their country is the rough Sonora Desert, dry and forbidding in the west, more useful to human life in its central parts, and quite acceptable along the Gila River. This natural division corresponds to three groups of Piman population, the Sand Papago who were collectors in the western periphery, the "Two Village" Papago in the center—their name taken from the fact that they have both winter and summer habitations—and the "Riverine Pimans" at the Gila River, or the Pima proper.

The former Sand Papago were simple food collectors in a land of creosote bush and white bursage. They relied on mesquite, paloverde, and other "food plants" on the mostly arid arroyo banks, and they had some access to bighorn sheep, mule deer, pronghorn, and rodents. They lived a poor life, moving around and sleeping in temporary windbreaks. They are now largely gone.

The Two Village Papago had their winter dwellings in the foothills of the mountains, next to springs, and their summer houses at washes (arroyos) on the plains and in the valleys. Their winter houses were round and their summer houses rectangular brush houses. These Papago lived on beans (such as mesquite beans), acorns from oaks, and nuts from piñons, and they could hunt the many deer that grazed in their vicinity. After the summer rains they farmed at washes where they built dams.

At the Gila River the Pima proper had a more affluent existence. They lived off a rich variety of plants, hunted animals, and tended to agriculture, partly with the help of canal irrigation.

It is the Papago, once the Two Village Papago, to whom we shall pay attention here. They do, of course, live today in modern houses, sometimes frame houses, sometimes adobe buildings, and they are often wage laborers. The old society, dominated by headmen and medicine men or shamans, is mostly gone; however, some vestiges of the old order remain. Thus, there are patrilineal moieties subdivided into clans. We scarcely find headmen any more, but the medicine men who indeed were expected to disappear long ago are still well represented. A recent calculation attains a ratio of approximately one medicine man per hundred people.

The medicine man is well paid and is often wealthy. If he is well known he attends to two or three patients a day. Whereas in former days a medicine man could arrange ceremonies and use all kinds of magic, not least divination, today his area of professional action is mostly restricted to healing. He is trusted with respect, but he runs the risk of being killed when he is held responsible for epidemics.

The medicine man's position is reflected in the figure of the culture hero, Elder Brother Shaman, who is portrayed as an ancient medicine man or shaman. In his last speech to the people, before withdrawing from human affairs at the end of mythical times, he warned humans not to destroy the earth. They should be deferent and thus enjoy health and avoid sickness. The Anglo-Americans on the other hand, he prophesied, would kill the earth, and that would be witnessed by the Indians. When he had said that the culture hero withdrew. But some medicine men can probably still meet him, for they are reputed to be able to journey to the sky and the under-world.

DIFFERENT DISEASES FOR NATIVE AMERICANS AND WHITES

Like the Navajo the Pima and Papago are thus very much linked to the therapeutic side of human existence. Indeed, there is much that all these tribes have in common, like the use of sand paintings at curing rites and the differentiation between diagnosticians and singers. It is interesting to note, however, that in contradistinction to the Navajo pattern the diagnosti-cians are considered to be the true medicine men among the Pima and Papago, a kind of inspired healers, whereas the singers are laymen who have learned the songs given in revelations to the diagnosticians. In some cases the medicine men manage to restore a person's health during the diagnostic rites, but mostly they refer the curing process to the singers.

Typical for the Pima and Papago is the distinction they make between "wandering" and "staying" diseases.[18] The wandering diseases are those that are infectious, spreading with germs, and that originate from foreigners. Such diseases (in former days, smallpox, and today, measles, chicken pox, and different types of flu) disappear as the germs spread to new regions. They often appear as epidemics and are considered very bad: the people personify them as evil spirits. Aboriginal doctors do not treat these diseases; they have to be cured by Western doctors.

The staying diseases are of a different kind. They only afflict the Pima and Papago, no others, and they always stay around. They are not contagious. They are caused by "dangerous objects," which react when human beings transgress against the dignity and propriety of these objects. There are about forty such objects mentioned and known by scholars, and there are certainly many more in indigenous beliefs, a heritage from the Elder Brother. Among them are all kinds of animals, such as badger, bear, butterfly, buzzard, cat, coyote, deer, dog, eagle, frog, Gila monster (the lizard), gopher, hawk, horned toad, owl, rabbit, snake, and turtle. Each animal mentioned repre-sents its entire species, not a single individual. (We could perhaps say that it is the essence or spirit of the animal that is at work.) We also find plants like jimsonweed and peyote; lightning, water, and whirlwind; and an invisible, two-headed snake that lives underground and can fly for long distances. All these beings or objects may turn upon man with what is called their "ways" or "strengths." This could be easily understood when it comes to a snake, for instance. But snakebites are not involved here, nor are such afflictions as indigestion, constipation, broken bones, or for that matter sorcery: these are "nonsickness" afflictions and injuries.

The expression "their ways" conceals the fact that the actions of the dangerous beings or objects are dependent on a commandment of superior order, probably instituted by Elder Brother. There is an intrinsic norm, or harmony, in existence that cannot be transgressed, something these objects have to control.

It is not always known how trespassing takes place. Only a medicine man can find it out through his diagnosis. It is supposed that a more or less substantial thing, or "strength," enters the patient's body and creates the symptoms of a sickness. The strength permeates the body and moves toward the heart. If it reaches the heart the patient will die. Often the strength that causes pain in a patient is very old, lying deep in him, and overlapped by other, later strengths that have not yet attained the same permeation.

As mentioned, the treatment is divided up in two parts, the diagnostics, which may be a very drawn-out and complicated process, and the curing itself, partly performed by the diagnostician–medicine man, but mainly administered by the singers.

The diagnostics are difficult because the diseases are covering each other inside the patient's body and because they may try to elude the medicine man by hiding away from him. It happens that several medicine men try to discover the ailment, but fail one after another. The task of the diagnostician is primarily to discover the earliest strength in the patient, for a strength does not start creating symptoms of disease until it has been covered by later strengths. He also tries to move it back from the heart so that the patient will not die. The medicine man blows on the sick person, massages him (to separate the strengths), sings spirit songs, and tries to suck out the hidden disease. He also brings forth a crystal through which he can illuminate the strength. He fans the patient with an eagle feather, he shakes his rattle, and he blows smoke. Obviously the song calls on the helping spirit of the medicine man; it was given him by the spirit when the latter once came to him and instructed him. Since a medicine man has been initiated by many spirits (probably in visions), the songs invoke many spirits. The spirits are, it is said, very happy to listen to the songs they once gave away. It seems that the spirits communicate the nature of the disease to their client.

All through the night these diagnostics go on. In the morning, the doctor names the sickness. Having learned its identity the patient is admonished to recall the occasion when he or she became sick. The patient then remembers some transgression in the past, perhaps several years ago.

It is now that the curing sets in. The medicine man may have removed the strength by his sucking, but the final elimination of the disease falls on the ritual singers. The latter use singing, blowing of smoke, and the putting of objects (fetishes) on the patient. Such objects may be horse tails, horned toads, and other things that represent the causal disease agent. With their songs the doctors try to persuade the wronged spirit to stop the disease; with the blowing they introduce breath into the patient's body; and with the placing of the fetish on the patient they make him receive the curative strength of the fetish.

The ritual singers may use the songs of the medicine men about the "way," blow smoke, and fan with feathers like the medicine men, but they lack their powers. Once the diagnostician has settled the cause of a disease its removal from the body seems to be certain. The ritual singers accomplish this operation by their actions. In addition to the actions mentioned they may also perform dances, eat the flesh of such dangerous objects as the rabbit and the deer, or make sand paintings. Sand paintings are common in those cases where wind, owl, or horned toad are vindictive disease agents.

In many ways the Navajo and Pima-Papago means of healing are similar, but the importance of the singer is much higher in Navajo therapy.

·7·

Medicine in New Religions

Hitherto we have observed what expression medical ideas and concerns have taken in traditional Native American religions. It is natural that today attention to aboriginal medicine and concepts of health primarily centers on such medical systems that were part of old-time Indian ideology. We must not forget, however, that many tribal religions at the present time are obsolete or nearly so, or, at least, that new ideological directions have taken their place. Medical ideas and practices have consequently changed. The change has not resulted in a secularization of the traditional medical complex. On the contrary, Indians have steadfastly held that health and curing are basically in the hands of the supernatural powers. The ways may shift over time and place, but the connection with the other world is always there.

New religious ideologies have, as we know, sprung from the cultural and psychological changes brought about by pressure from Euroamerican sources, by war, conquest, epidemics, and the like that caused social, cultural, and political disintegration as well as great personal suffering. In a situation of deprivations of all sorts the Natives tried to build up a new spiritual defense. They retained their religious vision of the stucture and meaning of the universe, but they combined this outlook with new cultural and ideological contents taken from the knowledge and experiences of the modern Western world. Out of the culture contact, or acculturation, new religions were born, strange compositions of original Native ideas and new, foreign traits. It may surprise us that the Indians accepted thoughts and beliefs originating among their enemies and oppressors, but it was in fact rather natural: the old ideologies had broken down in essential aspects, while the new experiences and insights demanded changed ideological worlds.

The formation of new religions began in the eighteenth century. Prophets appeared whose messages were eschatological, revealing a new heaven and a new earth. Often old rules of medical cure fell into disrepute, because the prophets demanded it, or because the span of time before the collapse of the world was considered too short for attention to bodily disorders. Thus, the old medicine societies of the Seneca Iroquois disappeared or went underground when the prophet reformer Handsome Lake (active 1799–1815) changed the face of Iroquois religion in the first years of the nineteenth century.[1] Only with time, as the "new religion" became a rally point of the conservative tendencies in Iroquois religion, did these organizations rise to importance again. Handsome Lake's religion was strongly inspired by Quakerism. It recommends confession of sins as a means of alienating diseases, impurity, and other bad influences.[2]

The last major prophetic movement, the Ghost Dance, had another character. It did not present an alternative religion, like many of the other prophetic movements, but offered an addition to the old traditional religion. It has left its imprint on Native religions in many areas right up to the present day. The Ghost Dance, named after the round dance through which the believers thought they could hasten the return of the dead, had two great outbreaks, in 1869–70 when it erupted among Indians of Nevada, California, and Oregon, and in 1889–90 when it spread from the Nevada Indians (Northern Paiute) eastward to the Plains. In the Plains area the Ghost Dance released emotions that resulted in the Sioux "uprising," the killing of the Lakota chief Sitting Bull, and the battle of Wounded Knee.

The central message of the second Ghost Dance, as promulgated by its originator, Wovoka, implied the end of the present world, the return of the dead and the game animals, and a lasting peace with the whites (or their destruction by natural catastrophes). Since the perspective was short-term the care of the sick was kept in the background. Wovoka himself, a Paiute medicine man, refused to lend help to the sick Paiute around him. Only in later times, when the Ghost Dance had been transformed into a ritual within the frame of traditional religion, could the tribal leaders of the Dance also operate as medicine men.[3] This was, for instance, the case with the Shoshoni medicine man Tudy Roberts, whom I met in the 1950s on the Wind River Reservation.

PEYOTE CURING

A spiritual revitalization movement of another type is the peyote religion mentioned in chapter 4. It is centered on a kind of sacramental meal, which due to its qualities as a drug gives extraordinary mental experiences and fosters friendship and sympathy among those who partake in the meal. The sacred substance is peyote, a cactus *(Lophophora williamsii)* which grows along the Rio Grande del Norte and further south in Mexico. The background of this sacramental eating was a Mexican Indian ritual in which peyote was taken for specific supernatural goals; this ritual was transformed into a religion of its own, mixed with Catholic elements. The peyote ceremony was brought to the southern parts of the present United States by Apache, Tonkawa, Kiowa, and Comanche Indians during the eighteenth century. No prophets appeared; the end of the world was not in sight. Here was simply a sacramental religion that could satisfy the immediate religious needs of peoples whose cultural and spiritual world was on the verge of dissolution. During the twentieth century this new, pan-Indian religion spread over the United States and southern Canada and partly replaced tribal religions. On many reservations today a third of the Native population are peyote worshippers.[4]

Peyote is a universal potency. There is indeed a cult, for the cactus is regarded as a god, or a "medicine." Medicine is, as we know, a vague term for what among American Indians primarily refers to supernatural power. As such it also includes the power inherent in its curative functions. Peyote is a power that has such medical values. Through the use of peyote a person is supposed to be healed from any physical or mental ailments. Some people even carry peyote along with them and take it for internal application as soon as they are in precarious health. This comes close to the common use of medication in Western civilization; however, the supernatural energy involved is as a rule not forgotten. The sacred character of peyote is pronounced in the more common ritual sessions. A whole ceremonial system has been built up around the psychotropic cactus, with officers (road man, fire man, and so forth) and a carefully ordered sequence of ritual actions. People who join the cultic groups do so primarily because of the therapeutic values of peyote. Indeed, it can be shown that the first "missionaries" of peyotism were influential people who had been cured from some difficult disease by peyote.

It is therefore not surprising to find that many peyote rites have been and are being arranged to heal sick persons. In principle the same ritual pattern is followed as in the more ordinary peyote ceremonies, but there are some small deviations motivated by the specific goal of the ceremony. According to a well-known student of psychotropic botany, Richard E. Schultes, the following scenes occurred when a patient suffering from tuberculosis was treated in a Kiowa peyote meeting in Oklahoma. The acting personages are the leader (road man) of the ceremony and his assistant (fire man) who among other things attends to the fire.

> Leaving his place shortly after the ritual of the Midnight Water, the leader walked to the patient, lying at the side of the tipi. The fire-man handed the leader a cup of water, and the leader offered several prayers in which the words Jesus Christ were frequently used. He handed the patient four-teen mescal buttons [that is, pieces of peyote] which he himself had partly masticated before the treatment. While the patient was swallowing them, the leader waved the cup of water in cedar incense produced by throwing dried juniper needles (*Juniperus virginiana* L.) into the altar fire. He also wafted this incense to the patient's bare chest with an eagle feather fan. Following this, he chewed several more buttons, expectorated them into his cupped hands, and anointed the patient's head with the saliva while praying. Then he picked up a glowing ember from the altar fire and, placing it almost in his mouth, blew its heat over the patient's chest. The ritual ended with a long prayer.[5]

It is interesting to watch how the peyote leader here appears as a medicine man. He may have been a professional medicine man, but it is more likely that in his office as peyote leader he was entrusted with the capacity to heal people through peyote. Deep down it is not his own supernatural adherence, but the patient's indulgence in peyote eating that brings about the wonder of healing. The peyote leader is perhaps more adequately called a priest or doctor. Some techniques in his curing otherwise remind us of the Plains medicine man, such as the sweeping of the patient with an eagle wing, the use of incense, and the anointment of the patient's head.

In the past, among the Mescalero Apache in the Southwest, medicine men were organized under the peyote leader when they participated in the peyote ceremony. The Navajo Indians feared that peyotism as a disease ideology would threaten their own traditional religion, which, as we have seen, was built up around the curing complex. Students of Navajo culture have observed that peyote ceremonies have been preferred to traditional curing ceremonies because they are shorter in duration and less expensive than the latter. In recent times the Navajo have tried to integrate peyotism with the old rituals, in this way disarming its aggressive divergence.

It is particularly interesting to study peyote's role as a healing power among the Washo, a tribe in the region of Lake Tahoe, on the border of Nevada and California. Here one can say that peyotism, because of its inher-ent medical potentialities, ousted shamanism.[6] Washo shamans were very powerful. They received their powers from spontaneous dreams in which they saw animals of different kinds and, in particular, water babies. Shamans could have many guardian spirits. The first one a shaman received was the chief helper (or controlling spirit). All power emanated from this spirit. People who suffered from diseases—often originating in dreams—turned to the shamans to be healed. A curing ritual took four nights. The shaman danced with rattle in hand, sang songs, talked to his or her spirit power, and sucked out the evil agent. There was always the risk that the latter took possession of the shaman, who then became unconscious for a time.

These shamans were, because of their powers and medical capacities, the mightiest people in Washo society. They were feared for causing sorcery; accusations of sorcery were common. They also broke Washo rules in other ways; they called attention to their importance in an unabashed manner, and they showed contempt for sharing virtues. If many of a shaman's patients died he or she was easily under suspicion. In ancient days such a shaman was killed.

The unpopularity of the shamans paved the way for peyotism. From about 1932, when peyote was introduced by a Ute Indian married to a Washo woman, the peyote religion was the foremost foe of shamanism. It has been stated that 90 percent of those who went over to the new religion did so because they believed in peyote as a help against all diseases. It seems that peyote was regarded, and still is regarded, as particularly important in medical matters because it enabled its leader, the road man, to diagnose the disease. The road man who has consumed peyote can look into the patient and see his disease. He fans the sore spot and prays that the disease will leave. The patient is then expected to vomit up the disease.[7] We notice the difference from traditional religion where the disease object is sucked out or removed in other ways by the medicine man.

It is an amazing thing that among the Washo so many shamans became peyotists. Not least the shaman candidates moved over to become peyote functionaries, probably because of the collected hatred toward shamans. Indeed, the first convert to peyotism was a shaman who in a dream had been told to abolish his shamanhood and go the sacred road of peyotism. Most shamans were, however, violently opposed to peyotism.

The fight between the two camps was bitter. The peyotists denounced the leading role of the shamans and emphasized that anyone could cure diseases [that is, if he were a road man] on his or her own initiative. While the peyotists accused the shamans of witchcraft, the shamans made the same accusation against the peyotists. At the same time, somewhat illogically, they claimed that the peyotists lacked power. The end result was that the shamans who initially had had some successes in their efforts to root out the peyote religion in the course of time diminished in numbers and finally almost ceased to exist.

It is possible to say that peyotism acts as a frame of medical treatment among its clients, substituting its own therapeutic wisdom for more traditional medicine. Today, however, the peyote religion is decreasing in many places, often yielding to a reawakening of selected parts of traditional religion.

THE SWEAT LODGE MOVEMENT

The latest pan-Indian religious movement, the sweat lodge movement, is, like the peyote religion, a revival that in principle embraces the total blessing and welfare of the tribe, but particularly brings blessings to the participants. From about 1970 or, according to some informants I have consulted, as late as 1980 this new movement has diffused over much of the west, including California, the Great Basin, and the Plains. The basis of the movement is the Indian sweat lodge, a structure that has existed in different forms among many North American tribes for hundreds of years.[8] It has its counterpart in the well-known Finnish sauna and in other similar buildings in the North Eurasian world. There is, however, one important difference between the North American and the Old World sweat houses: the former emphasize spiritual cleanliness, the latter bodily hygiene and pleasance. Of course, in distant times the Eurasian sweating ritual may also have been directed toward spiritual goals.

In North America, provisory sweating lodges from animal hides and canvas have existed on the Plains, and similar structures covered by mats of bark have existed in the north. In Alaska and California the Indians constructed larger houses of wood and earth that were used more permanently and also served as men's club houses (and sleeping places for unmarried men). Apparently the latter houses were used more for personal well-being and less for religious purposes. Another difference was that the small lodges in the interior of the continent were connected with water vapor sweating, whereas the Alaska-California houses were associated with a direct fire sweating technique.

All Indians did not use sweat houses. They were conspicuously absent among Numic peoples (such as the Shoshoni and Paiute), although their neighbors the Washo possessed them. The Numic absence is remarkable considering the fact that the new sweat lodge movement has one of its strongholds among Numic communities.

The traditional sweat lodge of the interior is in most places a small, low, round, and dome-shaped hut with a pit in the middle and a door or opening toward the east, the sacred direction. Stones are heated over a fire outside the lodge and then carried to the pit. When water is poured over them an immense vapor fills the lodge. The heat can be exceedingly strong, almost unbearable. There are ritual prescriptions how to behave in the lodge, for instance, how to smoke in a sacred rite, and how to pray and sing.

Now, in the old days people used sweat lodges as a preparatory rite before a major ritual, such as the Sun Dance on the Plains. The sacred sweating was supposed to clean people spiritually for the great ceremony. Among some tribes, like the Plains Cree, this sweating could be undertaken several times a day, thus keeping the individual in a mentally clean mood. In the new sweat house movement the sweating ritual is itself the main ceremony, making the sweating persons sound and healthy, happy and content. Sick persons are healed in small congregations, as a part-blessing of all the welfare that can be granted by the powers. In other words, as in the peyote religion the restoring to health is a consequence of the general infusion of power and well-being brought on the participants in the ritual group.

In retrospect, this understanding of medicine is typical for the religiously based medical thinking of the North American Indians. Medicines taken from particular plants or animals may have a specific healing effect, but medicines originating in religious visions or supernatural power are part of the general blessings granted by these powers. It is true that a certain animal spirit, like the bear, may have a particular capacity to cure certain diseases, but he may also confer other blessings. Healing that springs from a religious source is always an application of the mysterious, multifaceted blessing sphere of the divine.

·8·

Transcultural Medical Relations: The Interaction between Native and Euroamerican Curing Methods

Both the traditional medicine and the medicine in the new religions have their roots in ancient American Indian ideas and practices, and both systems are now used by Native Americans. It is true that they have occasionally been transferred to white persons, in particular when the latter have been regarded as guests or as people in danger. I suppose there are quite a few of us who have been helped out by Indian medicine men.

Today, however, Native Americans have become progressively incorporated into white Euroamerican civilization. In many cases this acculturation is perhaps not so pronounced, but there is an increased presence of white people and their institutions, not least medical care. On reservations today most Indians have the option of being treated by a traditional medicine man or a Western doctor. Many accept both, or accept that some diseases are handled by a medicine man and others by a modern doctor. Indeed, they may also think that their own medicine, and the practitioners of this medicine, the Native medicine men, should operate among people outside their own tribal circle, whether these patients are members of other tribes or whites or blacks.

It is all a matter of the evaluation of the indigenous medicine, in the eyes of the Indians as well as in the eyes of the Euroamericans. Two cultural worlds stand against each other, two value systems, two medical systems: one, a religio-holistic system as represented in Native American societies, and the other, a Western scientific system represented by academically trained doctors in white societies. When these systems cross each other's boundaries we may talk about transcultural systems. Insofar as such situations occur on most reservations today, Native North Americans may be said to use transcultural medical procedures.

We are little concerned here with the attitudes of white doctors to Native medicine; however, the same evaluations which, as we shall see, Indians hold toward white medicine are expressed by these doctors vis-à-vis Native medicine: there are cases of devaluation, tolerance, and positive evaluation. With some exaggeration one could say that these attitudes represent a gradual change from a condescending to a more sympathetic view of Native doctors and their arts. (This is said with the reservation that many doctors schooled in Western medicine repudiate all nonacademic medicine.) Some modern doctors, like Andrew Stanway at the Institute of Complementary Medicine in London, distinguish between two sorts of medicine: first, conventional or allocative medicine, which regards the body as a machine, a motor with many parts, and second, alternative medicine, which may also be called complementary or holistic medicine (the latter term preferred in the United States) since its practitioners regard the human being as a wholeness of spiritual and physical traits. Apart from herbal medicine and such surgical work as occurs, Indian medicine may be said to be of the latter type. It is "faith healing," taking into account the patient's need to believe in the medical procedures, since spirit and body are interdependent. This healing is very close to the "folk healing" in Euroamerican societies. At modern medical congresses and in scholarly publications this folk healing is the object of much attention.

Anthropologists and others investigating "primitive medicine" have noticed that diseases caused supernaturally are referred to indigenous practitioners, while smaller mundane diseases are treated at home, and more important nonsupernatural diseases (for instance, tuberculosis, or appendicitis) are treated by modern physicians.[1] This grouping agrees fairly well with what we know about North American Indian medical practice in present times, although there are of course divergences from this schema according to the state of communications between Native and white medical practice. Another important distinction is the one suggested for the Lakota by their provocative observer, William K. Powers: the distinction between "whiteman sickness"—diseases brought by Euroamericans—and "Indian sickness."[2] We have seen how the Pima and Papago in fact apply such a division to their diseases.

Let us now look at how the North American Indians arrange their medical cures when they are confronted with white doctors and medicines. Only some few snapshots can be given from an abundantly rich material. The principles of division will be the ones mentioned before—Indian devaluation, tolerance, and positive evaluation of white practitioners and their medicines. At the same time we shall scrutinize how traditional medicine may survive in the modern world, and how it even is designed to replace white medicine.

INDIAN CRITICISM AND TOLERANCE OF EUROAMERICAN MEDICINE

The general Indian attitude to white physicians is that they are clever in curing mundane diseases, although not quite reliable. Many are found to fail in their efforts to help out the patients, but so do the traditional medicine men; so the dilemma is the same as in traditional society. An investigation of some Ojibway Indians from Manitoba shows that, when a white physician has been unsuccessful, a medicine man or woman is consulted. He is then often asked to ascertain whether the illness has natural causes, and therefore may be treated by the physician, or supernatural causes so that the patient has to be cured by an Indian doctor. We notice here that the etiological aspects of the disease are most important. If a medicine man among these Ojibway states that the disease is caused by witchcraft, or due to an earlier maltreatment of animals, or to a contact with menstrual blood, it can only be dealt with by an Indian doctor.

One example given by Dr. L. C. Garro at a medical department in Winnipeg is illustrative. An Ojibway man awoke one morning to find that he was lame in his legs and his hands. He was transported to a hospital, but the doctors there were unable to explain his disability. They gave him a pair of crutches and some arthritic pills, and then they sent him away. He was home for a week, without experiencing any improvement. A medicine man was called in. He could state that the man's illness was due to witchcraft, brought about by a jealous individual. This individual had injected foreign substances into the patient's members and thus incapacitated him. The medicine man sucked these objects out through a tube that he put on the afflicted places. The man soon recovered and has since then not suffered from similar pains.[3]

It is easy to understand that occurrences like this one do not strengthen the belief in Western medical potential. According to Native understanding diseases are not inexplicable; they have ultimate causes that may be of a spiritual nature. If an Ojibway woman has a miscarriage, or a child born deaf, the physician may not be able to tell why this is so, but the medicine man will know. A Navajo hospital nurse told an interviewer that the trouble with a white doctor's curing is that it only affects the symptoms of the disease—it does not reveal the causes of the disease.

The rule is, however, that the physician is well credited, that he is trusted to give valuable help. On the other hand, the psychotherapist who directly intervenes in the medicine man's business is not accepted by the Indians. William Powers states that the psychotherapist is not popular among the Oglala Lakota. He informs us that according to the Oglala the psychotherapist looks down upon the Indians, does not understand their language, stays only temporarily, is more or less crazy and ignorant of Indians, and is often young and inexperienced. The Oglala point out that the medicine man of the *yuwipi* rituals cures much more quickly, in one to four hours.[4]

There is thus a much higher confidence in the Native medicine man and shaman than in the alien psychotherapist. The medicine man anchors his psychic (and physical) therapy in the supernatural world, the psychiatrist in the profane world with a system of references that for the Indian is definitely less creditable. Dr. Wolfgang Jilek, whose discussion of Salish medicine ceremonies we have observed above, makes the following remarks on the Indian evaluation of the inadequacy of Western medicine. It can be defined as "(a) lack of holistic concepts and practice; (b) overvalued focus on physical biochemical aspects, paired with neglect of psychosocial and cultural aspects of ill health and treatment; and (c) superiority of indigenous therapies in the utilization of dissociative mechanisms and in effecting positive personality changes."[5]

Whereas the modern physician cures physical diseases and injuries with means that are superior to traditional remedies (although little understood by the Indians), for instance, efficacious medicines and surgery, his psycho-therapeutic colleague cannot offer a meaningful help to his Indian clients. This means that while cases of physical suffering may be referred to white hospitals the medicine men retain the services for those patients who in their estimate need a holistic-supernatural treatment.

The conditions among the Crow of the Northern Plains as described by their anthropological expert, Fred Voget, may illustrate this:

> The challenges of hospitals and modern medicine are countered by finding a place for hospital medicine along with curing in the Sun Dance. Indeed, Sun Dance leaders make use of the hospital for particular remedies such

as cough and heart medicines and salves. They also refer patients to the hospital if they get a message that their powers are not strong enough for that particular illness. At the same time, medicine men know that they have cured or prolonged the lives of people who turned to them when the hospital appeared to offer no help.[6]

Similarly, it is reported from the Washo that patients with psychoneurotic disorders do not first consult a white doctor but go to a shaman, while most other patients first consult a physician. By referring to the shaman as a "faith healer" the patients recognize that he or she is capable of handling psychoneurotic disorders or disorders with psychosomatic components. The Washo shaman cures his patients by removing the spirit or inanimate object that has intruded into his patient's body and that dries out the body of its water and blood content.[7]

In many quarters there is a more balanced view of the competence of Indian and white doctors. The modern Cherokee, for instance, think that the two medical systems are complementary.[8] The Navajo consider that both types of medicine are essential for their health needs.[9] This seems also to be the judgment of their Western doctors, for after their treatment of a Navajo patient they occasionally permit the Indians to have a singing ceremony in the hospital. This reminds us of conditions in British hospitals where sometimes healers work by the side of professional doctors.

The introduction of Native American healing into hospitals has meant a major growth of prestige of this therapy. Indeed, in one sense the shamanic cure sometimes has taken over the hospitals. One of my disciples who investigates shamanism on the Northwest Coast, C. J. Gurt, relates a remarkable recovery of a Nootka woman from Vancouver Island who was hospitalized after a car crash and was close to death. In her dizzy state she saw a spirit frog land on her breast. It sang a song and said that she would become a great shaman and after her recovery cure sick people. This woman is now a shaman and is said to be able to make soul journeys.[10]

Another example of the invasion of shamanism in American hospitals has been offered by a modern Oglala medicine man, Wallace Black Elk. His account, which mixes a traditional perspective with modern medical terms, shows his ambition to merge Native American and Euroamerican medical traditions. At the same time, he and his people thus attain a higher status for the Native medicine man and his medicine. The shamanistic setting of his account is the Spirit Lodge, or yuwipi ritual, which we have earlier observed in the description of Arapaho medicine ceremonies above.

The patient in Black Elk's report is a young boy who shortly after his birth was taken to a hospital in Denver where he had to stay for four years.

He was incapacitated all over: he could not drink, cry, sit up, or walk. He received food through a tube down his throat. The hospital doctors were unable to heal him although they tried everything. According to Black Elk, they did not know what was wrong with the boy.

Black Elk and his team then tried to intervene. On the recommendation of the doctors the board of directors allowed the Indians to arrange a healing ceremony. Many of the hospital patients asked to witness the ceremony, and that was granted them. All windows and other sources of light were blocked with plastic and tape. An altar was arranged and a drum brought in. Everything was ready.

The Indians started singing calling songs, and then thunder was heard and a flash of light went through the room. Something shaped like a man, surrounded by a glow of light, came in. "It was like a ghost." He asked why he had been called. Black Elk then answered that it was because of the sufferings of the little boy. The ghost went forth to where the boy was, lying in a crib between the doctor and the nurse. The ghost examined him and then said that an unknown power had taken a spider web and tied knots around the nerves. He said that the spider spirit had to be called in.

The Indians now sang a spider song, and red spider, the leader of all spiders, entered. His information was that medical science was unable to understand the cause of the disease because they cannot see the web with their microscopes or X-rays. After another song he went over to the boy and untangled the web. When that was done the boy could make sounds and move around. The spirit was thanked, and tobacco ties and robes were given to him.

When the lights were turned on the child was standing, and he enjoyed drinking milk out of a cup. He walked laughingly back and forth in the room. The other patients attending the ceremony had also been healed. The spirit had been among them and fanned them. He had given them water, which removed the poison and the bacteria they had.

Black Elk finishes his narrative by pointing out that the offering gifts designed for the spirit were gone when the lights came on, and by pitying the doctor who should make a report on what had happened—how could he do that? It remains to be said that the account reproduced here was presented by Black Elk in his autobiography. How the hospital doctors experienced the two hour session is not known. This is, however, of little importance in this connection. The account is reproduced here to prove how Indians legitimize their medicine ways in modern hospitals and try to demonstrate their superiority to Western medicine. [11]

With this statement we approach another modern tendency in Indian therapeutics, the conquest of shamanic medicine among the white population.

THE EXPANSION OF NATIVE AMERICAN MEDICINE INTO WHITE SOCIETY

The realization that aboriginal American medicine and medicine men are just as skillful as their academic colleagues in hospitals, if not more so (the truth value of this opinion disregarded), has convinced many Indians that they can expand their medical field of action into the white world.

It is today not uncommon to find Indian medicine men at work in white people's homes. For instance, Lakota medicine men from South Dakota are active in white districts in nearby Rapid City. Some medicine men take more extensive journeys. The Crow medicine man Tom Yellowtail, for instance, has visited patients as far away as California, Wisconsin, and New York. It is obvious that this expansion would have been impossible without an enhanced susceptibility to the efficacy of Indian medicine on the part of the white population. People who in other connections turn to white folk healers have included Indian curing in their health program. While formerly this happened now and then when white trappers and coureurs de bois were out alone in the wilderness with Indians as their closest neighbors, today the medical trade takes place on a more general and businesslike level. The inclusion of Indian medicine at hospitals has strengthened the transaction.

To the Indians this is not only a national victory. It is the sign of a more meaningful medicine where the connections between medical etiology, social care, and religious faith are closely tied together. The white man is caught in an Indian religious universe that is nonetheless wide enough to include his own religious values, or nearly so. It is not that he is facing an inperialistic religious attitude that expels Western Medicine from the scene. An example from the Woodland Cree in Canada will show that the Indian attitude can be more open and tolerant.

As described by a team of anthropologists from Edmonton, Russell Willier is a Cree healer from northern Alberta who wants to revitalize Cree society so that it can take its place in the multicultural Canadian world. As a medicine man—who has inherited his medicine bundle from his great-grand-father—he has tried to incorporate ideas and techniques from the white society. He thinks that his medicine craft is good for everybody and therefore offers it to the whites. This has provoked both protest and approval in the Indian communities, and in white circles as well. Willier is quite open about his methods. He has been filmed in action, and academic doctors are welcome to watch his medical procedures.

Willier's methods include diagnosis with the help of guardian spirits and treatment with herbal teas and ointments according to the directions of these spirits. It happens that the spirits in his dreams change old traditional herbal compositions. All treatment is accompanied by tobacco offerings. Willier does not think that otherwise his herbal medicine will be efficacious. The diseases he takes care of are of multifold kinds. Psychsomatic diseases take a prominent place, but organic diseases like cancer also fall under Willier's treatment.

This Cree medical activity has had such a successful result that Willier has instituted his own health center where other Indian healers are also at work. He is aiming at cooperation with Western doctors. He is convinced that he can do what they cannot achieve, and that they can do what for legal reasons he cannot achieve. Although some orthodox doctors refuse to have anything to do with him he persists in his conviction that cooperation between the two medical worlds is necessary. Cooperation, not integration. [12]

This is only one example of an attitude among modern Indian medicine men, but in my experience it is very characteristic of the interaction between traditional and modern medicine just now.

It seems obvious that traditional Indian medicine, in modified forms, will persist in the multicultural world that is embracing us. Authors who take another stand—and there are several who do—take for granted that an increasing acculturation will nullify Native American medicine. For instance, it has been argued that an increased Euroamerican schooling and the demands of wage work will bring about the demise of the traditional Navajo healing system. [13] Considering the resilience of traditional medicine as seen in accounts like the foregoing, this is scarcely probable. Only indigenous cultures whose traditions die out and which are swallowed by the overwhelming white majority culture will face such a fate. The Navajo do not belong to those minority cultures. In a larger perspective, Native American medicine will live on because it appeals to all those who cannot find a holistic religious interpretation of their ailments in present Western medicine.

Conclusions

As we look back at the material collected in this volume the impression is close at hand that there is a wealth of information available on North American Indian health and medicine. Only a fraction of the material has been collected on these pages, but it certainly conveys the understanding that there have been many different ideas of medicine and medical practice that have had a direct relationship to religious thoughts and attitudes. Indeed, the diverse medical practices may to a large extent also be characterized as religious rites.

A FIELD OF DIFFICULTIES

While this may seem to be the main outcome of the present book we should at the same time be aware of the many caveats that this survey includes. First of all, it has been difficult to know exactly to what extent traditional medicine lives on today. There are so many ethnic groups in North America, and our knowledge of them is so uneven. I have found that even modern field researchers are little informed about the medical culture in their own areas of interest. In some cases there is substantial modern research; in other cases we have only older information at our disposal, but a general knowledge that old customs survive. In some areas medical practices observed during the seventeenth century still persist, while in others it is uncertain if medical ideas and rituals noted down during the last century are still valid. I have used my best judgment, but I obviously run a considerable risk in these evaluations.

Second, due to their richness and complexity it is next to impossible to summarize the various ideas and practices surrounding the medical complex in indigenous North America. Nevertheless, what follows is an effort to catch some characteristic features that should bring out the particular profile of the data and stress the close connections between medicine and religion.

157

THE CONCEPTS AND PRACTICES OF NATIVE MEDICINE

In spite of the diversified nature of the medical material presented above it has an easily discernible shamanistic background. In other words, a religious etiology predominates.

This is of course what could be expected from a survey written to stress the religious aspects of Native American medicine, but it is in fact the picture that one receives from a general study of American indigenous medicine. It is true that there are medical practices where ulterior motives never surface. Thus, herbal medicine is applied without reference to supernatural factors. It is also true that herbal medicine occupies a large part of medical activity in aboriginal North America, as it does in all folk medicine. There have been bulky volumes published on the ethnopharmaca of different American Indian tribes. Their plants have served as internal or external medicines whether they have been handled by medicine men or wise old men and women. It is, however, not uncommon that the herbalists use magic strings of words that transfer their curing into a supernatural field of action. We have seen good examples of this among the Cherokee.

It is quite natural that smaller wounds and aches have not given rise to metaphysical comments. We are not well informed whether those surgical operations that sometimes occurred not so long ago were interpreted as provoked by supernatural agents, but this may very well have been the case, as Cushing found among the Zuni.

In any case, serious diseases that in the long run might threaten the patient's life have always been taken care of by medicine men or doctor societies. They are supposed to be caused by spirits, and the connection between doctors and helping spirits ensures the safe outcome of a disease and a curing that is in the hands of the supernatural powers. In reality disease and disease healing is a religious transaction.

As already noted, this is emphasized by the fact that shamanism everywhere appears as a basis for advanced medical cure. In some places the doctors are by definition true shamans, ready to fly to the other world or to call on spirits. In other and, in fact, most places it is the pseudoshamanic medicine man who is active, a person who initially through a vision or a nocturnal dream has been invited to become a healer, and who can use supernatural means to remove the disease spirit or object. The boundaries between the two classes of doctors are often very fine. It is possible to say that both have developed from a shamanistic view of reality. This means that their actions are intended to correct disorders that are caused by supernatural agents or that impede the supernatural channels to man.

The shamanic substructure is obvious everywhere, and particularly so among those Indians who until recent days have been hunters and fishermen. True shamanism, with the doctor performing soul-catching journeys, is reported from the Algonkians of Canada, the Northwest Indians, and the Great Basin Indians. On the southern Northwest Coast it is the individual's guardian spirit that is lost and restored by the shaman's guardian spirit. A strange development of Coast Salish shamanism is the psychodramatic spirit canoe ceremony, an imitative shamanic séance in which souls caught by the dead are brought back to the land of the living.

Another form of true shamanism, involving the calling of helping spirits to the vicinity of the shaman and the patient, is known from the Algonkians and occurs in a somewhat changed form (yuwipi) among northern Plains tribes. Medicine men who primarily suck out disease objects (or disease spirits—often spirits turn into objects and vice versa) are to be found almost everywhere, except in parts of the Southeast and the Southwest. As indicated earlier in the text, where soul-loss and intrusion therapies coexist soul loss curing mostly refers to diseases that affect the individual's consciousness and lead to his slow demise if no cure is set in (therefore the Native words for unconsciousness and death are the same in wide parts of North America). In other places intrusion diseases or soul-loss diseases are dominating disease etiologies, in other words, forming patterns that exclude other types of explanations.

The shamanic disease ideas become less palpable toward the south. Soul-loss theories exist, but soul-catching expeditions by the shaman are seldom heard of. Such expeditions are, as the Wind River Shoshoni point out, exhausting for the healer. Even in the north we find them substituted by mimic performances (among the Salish) and soul catching in the woods (among the Tlingit). The use of wooden soul catchers on the Northwest Coast should be seen in this context. The collective song to the guardian spirit at the curing séances among the Shoshoni is an interesting relic of the old Arctic shamanism. We have noticed that shamanism is practically absent in the Southeast and large parts of the Southwest. A remnant of shamanism may be found in the instituion of diviners so common in the Southwest (we have seen such professionals among the Navajo, Pima, and Papago, and some Zuni doctors also have specific divining functions when they make a diagnosis after consumption of visionary drugs). In the Southeast the Cherokee have diviners, but they are common magicians.

There is no doubt that the most common doctrine of disease in North America, and in the traditional world at large, is the idea of disease due to intrusion of an object or spirit. In several places this intruding agent is equated with power (consider, for example, the *migi* of the Ojibway, the "pain" on the southern Northwest Coast, and the arrows swallowed by Arapaho medicine men). The sucking medicine man or woman is therefore sometimes well remunerated for the risk he or she takes, since an intruding thing or spirit represents supernatural power of some sort. Beside the common ways of extracting the disease through sucking, biting, sweeping with feathers, drawing, or making the patient vomit, there is also verbal exorcism, as among the Tlingit.

Both shamans and common medicine people may don special articles of clothing received by them through instructions in visions and dreams from their guardian spirits. Mostly it is the skin and symbols of the spirit—that is, the animal in whose form it has appeared—that are worn by the visionary and medicine man or woman. In many cases the visionary is adorned with symbolic equipment, for instance, feathers of a bird (spirit), necklace of grizzly bear teeth, or face painting depicting a water animal. Both Plains medicine men and Pueblo doctors dress themselves in bear hides to impersonate the bear, for the bear has the strongest medicine—a conviction that is rather general in North America. It is also common that a bear doctor in curing behaves like a bear and growls like a bear. The connection between the bear spirit and the person who impersonates him is, in ritual curing, almost one of identity.

On the Northwest Coast the shaman wears the mask of his guardian spirit, and he is then possibly possessed by the spirit. Masks have also been used by other medicine men—for instance, among the Iroquois and the Pueblo Indians (in the medicine societies)—but it is difficult to analyze the relations between the person and his or her mask. Whatever their import in different tribes and to different individuals, the attire of medicine persons enhances their supernatural and therefore medical powers.

In the southern areas of North America indigenous ways of curing show different patterns deviating from the shamanic and pseudoshamanic patterns of the north. In the Southeast, the acculturation with white civilization has reduced the original religious basis of the medical cures to a minimum. Among the Cherokee, the idea of spiritual agents of disease is present, but the curing methods (formula recitation, blowing of medicaments, or their infusion) are, except for the ritual moments, devoid of religiously inspired treatment. Knowledge, not visionary experience, directs medical actions.

The situation is quite different in the Southwest where old traditions still subsist; however, the medical picture has here changed with the introduction of agriculture. There is aboriginal agriculture also in the Southeast and the Eastern Woodlands, but the early destruction of culture in the Southeast and the often weak structuralization of horticulture in the regions more to the north have restrained agrarian influences on extant folk medicine. Still, we perceive some common medical traits over the whole agricultural area. Individual medicine persons have here been incorporated into medicine societies or even replaced by curing societies, for instance, among the Iroquois, Pawnee, and Pueblo (Keresan, Zuni) Indians. (It is also probable that the curing societies of the Ojibway and Central Algonkian midewiwin, in the outskirts of agricultural North America, have the same background.) As noted in earlier chapters, such collectivizations of professional activities seem to be part and parcel of horticultural civilizations. Among the Pueblo Indians these trends have reached their apex.

The collectivization certainly expresses an outlook, but it does not reduce the religiosity behind individual views and actions. It means, however, a changeover from subjective experiences to conforming ritual approaches. A person does not become a doctor as the result of extraordinary visionary experiences, but because he or she has been initiated into a medicine society. Indeed, as we have seen among the Zuni, such an introduction may also restore a sick person to health. (Compare the same situation in the Ojibway midewiwin.) Here as in other connections there is the phenomenon of "the healed healer," the basic idea being that the healer undergoes a transition from a weak human state to a powerful, supernaturally endowed state—an ideological heritage from ancient shamanism (as we have seen among the Coast Salish). The ideas of guardian spirits and the curing processes in Pueblo society convince us that the religiocultural basis everywhere is shamanism, transformed into sacerdotal ritualism. The particular healing methods used in collective curing may change from sucking out an intruding object or spirit to forcing a witch to confess (which makes the disturbing element effete) to transformation of the patient into a revitalized being through a death-and-revival ritual. All these methods have their antecedents in various forms of shamanic healing.

The medical systems of the Southwest, and occasionally other horticultural or neighboring Native areas, have another characteristic trait, and that is what has been labeled here cosmological healing. The disease state is seen as an aberration from life and the world as it should be, that is, in balance with the cosmological powers. Every little detail of the universe is judged from this perspective. This idea has rooted firmly in horticultural societies, where the symbolic order plays a great role—witness the intricate ceremonialism in parts of the Eastern Woodlands, the Plains, and the Southwest. Cosmic symbolism, as we may call this system, also characterizes some Athapascan tribes, like the Navajo. Diseases are considered to be deviations from the sacred norm and may be destroyed by integrating the sick person with the universe through the use of symbolic actions, for instance, by identifying the patient with the sacred universe. As shown in the foregoing, this is often done with the use of sand paintings or the anointing of the patient with sacred lubrication.

The old ways of curing still persist, but they are more and more mixed with Western medicine or are supplemented by the latter. As a holistic medicine with a religious etiology the Native medicine is bound to survive wherever the Indian national ethos lasts, unless, of course, other holistic medicine—of Christian or other religious provenance—gets the upper hand.

It is the basic religious interpretation of disease and its curing that has been observed in this book. Other aspects of Indian medical practice, and some *in et per se* interesting details, have here attracted little attention, because they lie outside our main course; however, a few of these other aspects and details might be mentioned here.

Several authors have pointed out that the institute of confessions is known in many parts of Indian North America, and it is apparently pre-Christian. Such confessions may dissolve the disease that is harassing an individual. We have occasionally seen in the foregoing how they operate and what kind of curses they annihilate. There are two particular groups of offenses that are retracted through confessions. The first concerns the violation of some taboo or supernaturally valid prohibition. Sometimes the violator is the sick person, sometimes another person in the circle of kin and friends. Sometimes the violator is aware of the transgression, but often he or she is unaware. We have seen how among the Pima and Papago the patient has to try to remember taboo violations in the past that might have called forth the disease—a procedure that actualizes the process of Freudian psychoanalysis. Among the Wind River Shoshoni and others, mistaken ritual behavior brings about a disease.

The other kind of offenses consists of (another person's) witchcraft activities. The Tlingit ascribe all dangerous diseases to witchcraft. Among the Zuni prominent personalities have been accused of causing disease, and among the Pawnee doctors were known to make people sick through witchcraft. In all of these cases only confessions of guilt from the supposed culprit could cancel the disease. Confession here means saying the strong, right word at the right time, causative and creative. It changes conditions, unties the person who is tied, and neutralizes and immolates evil forces. It has a liberating effect—it is not a sign of submission as is the case in the Old World religions of salvation.

The medicine man has been presented rather fully in the preceding text, but some further features could be stressed in this comparative perspective. We notice that the medical training and learning among inspired doctors may proceed along several lines. It may happen that the candidates are shown in their visions how they should cure a patient; or they are told by their guardian spirits in visions how to do it; or they try as best as they can; or they learn from older practitioners. The last is less frequent when medicine men operate alone but is sometimes the rule when the doctors work together in medicine societies.

Payments for the services of the shaman or medicine man vary from tribe to tribe. In the old days Plains doctors usually expected to receive blankets and horses from their clients or the relatives of clients. In our days they receive money, often substantial amounts. Some medicine men demand more and larger fees than their Euroamerican colleagues would expect in a similar case; others have been instructed by their guardian spirits to heal their patients free of cost. It is important to remember here that a medicine man is always a part-time doctor: he is also a hunter, fisherman, or planter like the rest of his people.

Some of the shaman's "medical" instruments deserve our attention. The drum, usually used to excite doctor and participants and to accompany dramatic and exalted states, has been used in the north of North America and on the Plains, but elsewhere in the United States it recedes before the more common rattle. The tendency is that shamans have drums, and common medicine men rattles. Another instrument is the piece of crystal that in the western part of North America is treasured as a power object and inserted into the visionary by his spirit helper. In the Southwest it is conceived as a bright light that helps the doctor to see where the disease is located in the patient's body.

The collected material on North American Indian disease ideology and practice shows that the etiology of diseases is the main issue, and that this etiology is primarily oriented from religion. This has placed curing practices in the focus of ritual behavior, as we find among the Ojibway, whose greatest ceremonies are ceremonies for recovery from illness; the Shoshoni, whose Sun Dance today has a medical implication; and the Navajo, whose whole ceremonial system is dominated by ideas that the sick might regain health and strength.

Perhaps this anchoring of curing in religion contributed to devaluate American Indian health service in the eyes of the early anthropologists. In any case, as "primitive medicine" the American Indian contribution to medicine was considered negligible. Even the use of medical herbs was negatively judged. James Mooney, one of the best experts on the Cherokee

Indians and the foremost ethnological authority on their medicine, comments on their medical art that it would be absurd to suppose that the Indian, "a child in intelligence," should have reached a level in science that could compete with that of "civilized man."[1] The particular reliance on supernaturalism has made a well-known later anthropologist, Sol Tax, differentiate between knowledge and ignorance, and between rational thinking and irrational thinking.[2] Thus, the "primitives," although operating logically, are ignorant and apply an irrational thinking. Their supernaturalism is an example of the latter. But what if this supernaturalism operates as a motor in healing? If this "ignorance" paves the way for cure? It is obvious that we have to reconsider our concepts of knowledge and medicine.

THE GENERAL SETTING OF MEDICAL BELIEFS AND PRACTICES

In a larger perspective, Indian medicine encompasses much more than medical beliefs and practices. It is indeed a whole socioreligious complex that takes in many different cultural facets, as is the case in most countries. These facets have been enumerated and discussed in all the volumes of the Park Ridge Center's Health/Medicine and the Faith Traditions series. In an appraisal of the ten themes as they have appeared in aboriginal North America, the following points of view emerge.

1. *Well-being.* The general concern in medical matters is of course the health and well-being of single individuals or groups of individuals. Health is a gift from the supernatural powers, or an outcome of correct living. This is very clearly realized among the Navajo, among whom the supposed principles of the universe are closely adhered to in order to guarantee good health and a long life span. What matters is this life, not so much the life to come; about the latter the Navajo profess to know almost nothing. The Navajo have also a preventive ritual against a possible succumbing to sickness, the Blessingway ceremony. It is very common in certain tribes that people try to harden themselves and thus withstand diseases; there are excellent examples from the Tlingit.

2. *Sexuality.* Sex is everywhere regarded as a normal expression of life. It is only repressed in some ritual connections—for instance, before hunting, in order not to offend the game. Sexual power is namely a great and dangerous power since it is creative. In some ceremonies, particularly among horticulturists, representatives of men and women sleep together in order to stimulate vegetation and general growth.

It is generally understood that sexual coitus is the act through which babies are conceived. Life begins in the womb, but the souls may be preexistent—they come from the sky, and/or they are given by the Supreme Being, as among the Shoshoni. It is common in North America that the breath soul in particular has come from God. It is even said (as among the Delaware) that man is part of God.

3. *Passages.* The human life span is marked by special rites at birth, naming, puberty, disease, and death. We have seen how the birth of a child among Shoshoni and Tlingit has been surrounded by very strict observances, and how the father of the child has undergone particular exercises in order to facilitate the advance of the baby (a custom internationally known as couvade). The naming of the child is in many tribes a protection against bad luck, since the given name, which is often taken from an ancestor or a spirit, incorporates the power associated with this being. (Of course, other names may be meaningless nicknames.)

Life is a dangerous journey and all the different passages need supernatural protection and guidance. The transition from child to adult person at puberty is considered a particularly hazardous period. Athapascan girls in Alaska, western Canada, and the Southwest (Apache) undergo great ceremonies of purification and initiation, the greatest ceremonies performed in the tribe. Death and renewal rituals are known to accompany the coming of age among youths in the Southwest and California. In the Eastern Woodlands, parts of the Plains, and on the Plateau the acquisition of an individual guardian spirit has been connected with a boy's puberty ceremony.

Everywhere the wish for a healthy, happy, and long life was common, although formerly in warrior tribes like those on the Plains the virtue of dying young and forceful in a fight was much praised.

4. *Morality.* It is very difficult to give a general evaluation of what is and has been considered to be right and wrong among North American Indians, since the value patterns shifted with tribes and culture patterns. Still, it is possible to mention as the common denominator what has appeared as being good for the tribe, its outlook on life, its social structure, its traditions, and so on. As we have found, there have been great differences between the tribes in these respects. In particular there are differences in the way individuals and organizations of individuals are valued between collectivistic agriculturists and individualistic hunters and collectors. Morals are always inspired by social consensus and tradition (very often in myths that describe right and wrong behavior).

5. *Dignity.* The sanctity of life is respected as far as it concerns one's own tribe and community, and this may be extended to other groups provided

they are not considered enemies. There are, however, important exceptions. Individuals transgressing tribal norms (thieves, murderers, and the like) are less befitted to lay claim to personal welfare and quality of life. Witches, for instance, have been killed in many places.

There are situations when individuals have committed suicide because their life has lost its meaning and dignity. We know that in the beginning of the nineteenth century proud Plains Indians preferred suicide to having a bad reputation or a physical deformation. There are reports of how young chiefs dressed up in their finest regalia and stabbed themselves to death when facing smallpox rather than continue living disfigured.

In the past twins were often put to death since one of the pair was supposed to have evil powers; at least in some instances the myth of the twin gods (one of whom is good, the other evil) was here prototypical. In wandering societies the aged and infirm were formerly left to die alone, usually at their own request, since they were too powerless to follow the movements of the camp. This was particularly the case in Canada until recent times. Similarly, crippled and hopelessly sick individuals could in ancient days be left by a traveling group, no consideration being given to their suffering: the survival of the group had in strenuous situations a higher priority than the fate of the single individual.

6. *Madness*. There are (and have been) several causes assigned to what has been considered insanity. We have seen examples of two causes: reception in vision of the "wrong" kind of guardian spirit, and intrusion into a person's body of a madness-giving disease spirit, basically sent by a witch. The loss of one's free-soul (the soul that for shorter periods can leave the body, as in a dream, without the person getting hurt), for instance, through its capture by ghosts, may lead to insanity. On the other hand, we rarely hear about insanity due to possession in psychological meaning, that is, to a spirit superseding the person's own ego.

Many aberrations from normal behavior that we would judge to be insane are not so understood by Indians, particularly if the behavior is congruent with what could be expected from certain individuals, for instance shamans or members of contrary-behaved societies whose rules of appearance have been decided by spirits in visionary experiences.

7. *Healing*. Healing has been the main theme in this book, and the concepts, practices, and practitioners have been surveyed in a comparative light above. Most references to Indian indigenous health and medicine in the source literature deal with this matter.

8. *Caring*. From the foregoing account it should be clear that the caring of the sick is a prominent feature of Indian social care. Not only the immedi-

ate family, but more distant kinfolk and friends, indeed, in many cases the whole camp or village, may turn up to show their concern. The exhibition of the medicine man is often surrounded by curious spectators who also take part in nursing if so required. Otherwise people participate in singing, masquerading, drumming, and other similar actions. Doctors rarely refuse to pay attention to the sick unless they consider themselves incompetent for the cure (for instance, if they are not specialized to take care of a particular disease). The patients are as a rule treated and nursed at home.

9. *Suffering*. Life is full of pain and suffering. Different myths try to illuminate why this is so: why childbearing is accompanied by pain, why there is hardship in daily life, why people have to be sick and die and leave their dear ones. Suffering is also the main theme in many relations to the supernatural; the self-torture of the visionary on the Plains in his efforts to create right communication with the supernatural powers is well known. Indians have shown great control in enduring pain, certainly to no little extent due to their harsh training as children. The suffering in illness is mostly taken with equanimity by the patients.

10. *Dying*. American Indians value this life as important, whilst life after death is mostly a shadowy counterpart to this life. To them death is an anomaly that has to be accounted for: myths tell that it was instituted by a council of primeval beings, by the Trickster, or by an oracle. The dying person is mostly surrounded by his or her family, although among northern Athapascans and the Navajo the place of death is quickly shunned and every contact with the dead body is avoided. Many tribes have in the past had circumstantial funerary ceremonies and buried their dead with lavish gifts.

There are plenty of traditions recounting the journey of the dead person to the world of ghosts. Often the deceased person has started to the other world before death enters: that is, the free-soul has left the body, and when it arrives at the land of the dead the body-soul, which gives the body life and motion, also leaves, which is tantamount to death. Sometimes there are four days spent between death and burial, considered to be the time the soul needs to make its way to the land of the dead.

The looks and character of the land of the dead are similar to the surroundings of the living on earth, although it may be more happy ("happy hunting grounds") or less attractive than its counterpart in the world of the living. Its position varies—it may be found somewhere beyond the quarters of the living, in the sky, or in the underworld, behind the mountains, on an island in the sea, and so forth. There is sometimes a social and even an ethical differentiation between different realms of the dead, whereby ways of dying and the degree of a person's adherence to the social code are important measurements. Life after death is vaguely figured, except in personal reminiscences of out-of-body experiences and mythical tales. Reincarnation beliefs exist side by side with ideas of a future life in another existence. Immortality is less often spoken about.

Native medical conceptions presuppose and are surrounded by and integrated with all these ideas and practices. Very often, indeed, they are also the prerequisites for the development of the world of ideas and practices. This is just the mark of American Indian medicine: that it is holistic, bringing both the patient and the world around into a meaningful religious perspective.

Notes

Introduction

1. Medical specialists could be of either sex but they were mainly male so I will use the label "medicine men."

2. Like all religious people North American Indians make, in principle, a clear distinction between what is "natural" in the sense of common, usual, profane, and "supernatural" in the sense of originating in another dimension of reality; see my article "The Concept of the Supernatural in Primal Religion." Scholars sometimes confuse "supernatural" with "transcendent," but the supernatural is often immanent. It is therefore wrong to maintain, as some critics do, that American Natives were not and are not believers in a supernatural world because their spirits appeared in common life and ritual (as for instance Christian spirits and saints do!). It is another matter that in everyday situations and in the narration of myths a person does not always differentiate between natural and supernatural events.

3. This is a general characteristic, and does not necessarily imply any psychological reductionism that attributes cures to psychological processes rather than spiritual agencies.

4. Cf., for instance, Hultkrantz, *Belief and Worship in Native North America*, pp. 28–47.

Chapter 1/The Cultural and Religious Setting

1. The cultural perspective here is historical and should not be confused with cultural evolutionism. Archaeological and historical data are the basis of the reconstruction. Characteristics like "higher" and "simpler" refer to levels of sociocultural integration and sophistication, not to any unilinear evolution.

2. Benedict, *Patterns of Culture*, especially pp. 15–29.

3. This idea of cosmic harmony appears a little everywhere but has been particularly elaborated in the Southwest.

4. For the distinction between different Native categories of medical experts, see Hultkrantz, "The Shaman and the Medicine-Man." Eliade's definition of shaman in his book *Shamanism: Archaic Techniques of Ecstasy*, pp. 3–13, has been criticized in Hultkrantz, "A Definition of Shamanism." See also Hultkrantz, "Ecological and

Phenomenological Aspects of Shamanism," pp. 30f. On shamanism, see also Harner, *Hallucinogens and Shamanism* and *The Way of the Shaman;* Hoppál and von Sadovszky, *Shamanism: Past and Present;* and Leh, "The Shaman in Aboriginal North American Society."

5. Hartmann, *Die Plains- und Prärieindianer Nordamerikas,* p. 186; Wheatley, *The Pivot of the Four Quarters,* p. 414.

Chapter 2/Traditional Medicine in the Northeast

1. See Kenton, *The Jesuit Relations and Allied Documents,* pp. 79ff., and Leacock, "Seventeenth-Century Montagnais Social Relations and Values," pp. 192f.

2. Hultkrantz, "The Problem of Christian Influence on Northern Algonkian Eschatology."

3. Gilfillan, "The Ojibways in Minnesota," p. 59.

4. Teicher, "Windigo Psychosis," pp. 109f.

5. Vecsey, *Traditional Ojibwa Religion and Its Historical Changes,* p. 145.

6. Mandelbaum, "The Plains Cree," p. 254.

7. Hilger, *Chippewa Child Life,* p. 89.

8. Kinietz, *The Indians of the Western Great Lakes,* p. 306.

9. Jenness, *The Ojibwa Indians of Parry Island,* p. 18.

10. Coleman, "The Religion of the Ojibwa of Northern Minnesota," pp. 52f.

11. Jenness, *Ojibwa Indians of Parry Island,* p. 20.

12. Densmore, *Chippewa Customs,* pp. 46f.

13. Jenness, *Ojibwa Indians of Parry Island,* pp. 61, 82ff.; Hilger, *Chippewa Child Life,* pp. 90ff.

14. Hilger, *Chippewa Child Life,* pp. 93f.; Steinbring, "Saulteaux of Lake Winnipeg," p. 249.

15. Jenness, *Ojibwa Indians of Parry Island,* pp. 63ff.; Kinietz, *Chippewa Village,* pp. 167ff.; Grim, *The Shaman,* pp. 140ff.

16. Kinietz, *Chippewa Village,* p. 170.

17. Jenness, *Ojibwa Indians of Parry Island,* pp. 65ff.; Grim, *The Shaman,* pp. 149ff.

18. Jenness, *Ojibwa Indians of Parry Island,* p. 67.

19. Harlan Smith, "Certain Shamanistic Ceremonies among the Ojibwas," p. 283.

20. Hallowell, "The Spirits of the Dead in Saulteaux Life and Thought," p. 33.

21. Jenness, *Ojibwa Indians of Parry Island,* pp. 62f.; Vecsey, *Traditional Ojibwa Religion,* pp. 191f.; Hoffman, "The Midéwiwin or 'Grand Medicine Society' of the Ojibwa," pp. 156f.; Krusche, "The Wabeno Cult as an Adversary of the Midewiwin"; Grim, *The Shaman,* pp. 144ff.

22. On the midewiwin, see Hoffman, "The Midéwiwin," and Vecsey, *Traditional Ojibwa Religion,* pp. 174–90.

23. Ray, "Historic Backgrounds of the Conjuring Complex."

24. Hallowell, *The Role of Conjuring in Saulteaux Society;* John Cooper, "The Shaking Tent Rite among Plains and Forest Algonquians"; Hilger, *Chippewa Child Life,* pp. 75ff.; Brown and Brightman, "*The Orders of the Dreamed,*" pp. 39ff., 61ff., 102ff., 146f.

25. Burgesse, "The Spirit Wigwam as Described by Tommie Moar," p. 51.

26. Kohl, *Kitschi-Gami*, vol. 2, p. 78.

27. Hallowell, "Sin, Sex and Sickness in Saulteaux Belief," pp. 196f.

28. Hoffman, "The Midéwiwin," pp. 187ff.; Densmore, *Chippewa Customs*, pp. 86ff.; Jenness, *Ojibwa Indians of Parry Island*, pp. 69ff.; Kinietz, *Chippewa Village*, pp. 174ff.; Hilger, *Chippewa Child Life*, pp. 69ff.; Landes, *Ojibwa Religion and the Midewiwin*, pp. 71ff.

29. See in particular Dewdney, *The Sacred Scrolls of the Southern Ojibway*.

30. Jenness, *Ojibwa Indians of Parry Island*, p. 75.

Chapter 3/Traditional Medicine on the Northwest Coast

1. Swanton, *Social Condition, Beliefs, and Linguistic Relationship of the Tlingit Indians*, p. 463.

2. Holmberg, *Ethnographische Skizzen*, pp. 37f.

3. See Holmberg, ibid.

4. Aurel and Arthur Krause, *Zur Tschuktschen-Halbinsel und zu den Tlinkit-Indianern*, p. 171.

5. Ibid., p. 134.

6. Cited in Aurel Krause, *The Tlingit Indians*, p. 173.

7. Krause, *The Tlingit Indians*, p. 110.

8. Holmberg, *Ethnographische Skizzen*, p. 42.

9. Krause, *The Tlingit Indians*, p. 103.

10. Aurel and Arthur Krause, *Zur Tschuktschen-Halbinsel*, p. 187.

11. Krause, *The Tlingit Indians*, p. 115.

12. See, for example, de Laguna, *Under Mount Saint Elias*, part 2, pp. 654–59. De Laguna emphasizes that there was apparently no clear line drawn between curative medicines and "magical medicines" that could ward off misfortune or bring good luck. They were all manifestations of supernatural power (p. 654).

13. Swanton, *Social Condition, Beliefs, and Linguistic Relationship of the Tlingit Indians*, p. 446.

14. Ibid.

15. It seems that those who became witches were infected by other witches. Witches were hated because they turned against their own kin. Cf. de Laguna, *Under Mount Saint Elias*, pp. 708ff.

16. Holmberg, *Ethnographische Skizzen*, p. 71.

17. De Laguna, *Under Mount Saint Elias*, p. 670.

18. Krause, *The Tlingit Indians*, p. 194.

19. De Laguna, *Under Mount Saint Elias*, pp. 684, 687ff.; Swanton, *Social Condition, Beliefs, and Linguistic Relationship of the Tlingit Indians*, p. 464.

20. De Laguna, *Under Mount Saint Elias*, p. 678.

21. Ibid., pp. 719f.

22. Ibid., p. 690.

23. Aurel and Arthur Krause, *Zur Tschuktschen-Halbinsel*, p. 146.

24. De Laguna, "Tlingit Shamans."

25. De Laguna, *Under Mount Saint Elias*, p. 702.

26. De Laguna notes that the sick person is usually cured by a shaman from another sib. This may have to do with the possible occurrence of witchcraft: a shaman belonging to the same sib as the patient runs great risks from the relatives of the witch he points out. See de Laguna, *Under Mount Saint Elias,* p. 709.

27. Cf. de Laguna, *Under Mount Saint Elias,* pp. 736f.

28. Krause, *The Tlingit Indians,* p. 203.

29. Cited in de Laguna, *Under Mount Saint Elias,* p. 721.

30. Jilek, *Indian Healing,* p. 10.

31. Eliade, *Shamanism,* pp. 33ff.

32. Jilek, *Indian Healing,* p. 66.

33. Duff, *The Upper Stalo Indians,* p. 113.

34. Marian Smith, *The Puyallup-Nisqually,* pp. 77ff.

35. Haeberlin, "SbEtEtda'q," pp. 249–57.

36. Smith, *The Puyallup-Nisqually,* p. 98.

37. Jilek, *Indian Healing,* pp. 90, 138ff.

38. Jilek, ibid., p. 90.

Chapter 4/Tranditional Medicine on the Plains

1. Hultkrantz, *Native Religions of North America,* pp. 66ff.

2. Hulkrantz, *Belief and Worship in Native North America,* pp. 235ff.

3. Bourke, *On the Border with Crook,* pp. 337f.

4. Cf. Hultkrantz, "The Peril of Visions."

5. See Hultkrantz, "The Origin of Death Myth."

6. Hultkrantz, "The Concept of the Soul held by the Wind River Shoshone," pp. 36f.

7. Cf. Hultkrantz, "The Peril of Visions."

8. Kroeber, *The Arapaho,* p. 451.

9. Ibid., pp. 438, 452.

10. Ibid., p. 20.

11. Cf. Kemnitzer, "Structure, Content, and Cultural Meaning of *yuwipi;*" Powers, *Yuwipi.*

12. For another presentation of this medicine ceremony, see Hultkrantz, *Belief and Worship in Native North America,* pp. 65–72.

13. Parks and Wedel, "Pawnee Geography."

14. Weltfish, *The Lost Universe,* pp. 347ff.

Chapter 5/Traditional Medicine in the Southeast

1. Mooney, "Myths of the Cherokee," pp. 250ff., quotation from p. 252; Mooney, "The Sacred Formulas of the Cherokees," pp. 319ff.

2. Mooney and Olbrechts, *The Swimmer Manuscript,* pp. 27ff.

3. Martin, *Keepers of the Game,* pp. 129f., 144.

Chapter 6/Traditional Medicine in the Southwest

1. Kroeber, *Handbook of the Indians of California*, pp. 754f., 775ff.
2. Parsons, *Hopi and Zuñi Ceremonialism*, p. 71.
3. Parsons, *Pueblo Indian Religion*, vol. 2, p. 708.
4. Parsons, *Pueblo Indian Religion*, vol. 2, p. 879 n.
5. Cushing, *Zuñi*, p. 220.
6. Stevenson, "The Zuñi Indians," p. 552.
7. Ibid., pp. 487–90.
8. Benedict, *Zuni Mythology*, vol. 1, pp. 188f.
9. Cf., for instance, Yazzie, ed., *Navajo History*. There are many versions of this myth.
10. Kluckhohn, "Navaho Morals."
11. Witherspoon, *Language and Art in the Navajo Universe*, pp. 75f.
12. Witherspoon, ibid., pp. 8f., 22, and passim.
13. Ibid., pp. 30ff.
14. Ibid., pp. 23ff.
15. Case, "Blessing Way."
16. See for instance Leighton and Leighton, *Gregorio, the Hand-trembler*.
17. Reichard, *Navajo Medicine Man*; Wyman, *Navaho Indian Painting*.
18. Bahr et al., *Piman Shamanism and Staying Disease*, pp. 19ff.

Chapter 7/Medicine in New Religions

1. Parker, "The Code of Handsome Lake," pp. 113ff.
2. Deardorff, "The Religion of Handsome Lake," p. 101.
3. Bailey, *Wovoka: The Indian Messiah*, pp. 59ff., 67f. It seems that Wovoka's medical talents, like those of Wodziwob, his predecessor as Ghost Dance leader, came to the fore after the end of the Ghost Dance; see Hittman, *Wovoka and the Ghost Dance*, pp. 143ff.
4. La Barre, *The Peyote Cult*; Stewart, *Peyote Religion*.
5. Schultes, "The Appeal of Peyote," pp. 709f.
6. Siskin, *Washo Shamans and Peyotists*; d'Azevedo, "Washoe," pp. 489ff., 496.
7. Merriam and d'Azevedo, "Washo Peyote Songs," p. 618.
8. See Lopatin, "Origin of the Native American Steam Bath," and Paper, "Sweat Lodge."

Chapter 8/Transcultural Medical Relations

1. Landy, "Role Adaptation," pp. 106f.
2. Powers, *Beyond the Vision*, pp. 126ff.
3. Garro, "Resort to Folk Healers," p. 319.
4. Powers, *Beyond the Vision*, pp. 126–46.
5. Jilek, "Native Renaissance," p. 143.
6. Voget, *The Shoshoni-Crow Sun Dance*, p. 318.

7. Handelman, "Transcultural Shamanic Healing," pp. 157, 158.

8. Fogelson, "Change, Persistence, and Accommodation in Cherokee Medicomagical Beliefs," p. 222.

9. Adair, "Physicians, Medicine Men, and Their Navaho Patients," p. 246.

10. Gurt, "Fältnoteringar," p. 24.

11. Black Elk and Lyon, *Black Elk*, pp. 171ff.

12. Young, Ingram, and Swartz, "A Cree Healer Attempts to Improve the Competitive Position of Native Medicine."

13. Kunitz, *Disease, Change, and the Role of Medicine: The Navajo Experience.*

Conclusions

1. Cited in Moses, *The Indian Man*, p. 48.

2. Tax, "Animistic and Rational Thought," pp. 411ff.

Bibliographical Notes

This survey of culture, religion, and medicine in different parts of aboriginal North America is based on a great number of publications, most of which cannot be noted here. The following specification of literature that has been used for this book is therefore only a selection. For complete information on the books and articles mentioned here, the reader is directed to the Bibliography proper.

Introduction

For a general short analysis of American Indian medicine, see Åke Hultkrantz, "Health, Religion, and Medicine in Native North American Traditions."

A survey written for young readers is Evelyn Wolfson, *From the Earth to Beyond the Sky: Native American Medicine.*

There are a few older surveys of North American medicine. Two distinguished papers are Forrest E. Clements, *Primitive Concepts of Disease;* and S. L. Rogers, "Disease Concepts in North America." Two other classic articles should be mentioned: Weston La Barre, "Primitive Psychotherapy in Native American Cultures"; and W. W. Elmendorf, "Soul Loss Illness in Western North America."

Chapter 1 / The Cultural and Religious Setting

The historical North American Indian cultures may be studied in common ethnographical textbooks, such as Robert F. Spencer, Jesse D. Jennings, et al., *The Native Americans.* The religious areas of North America are delineated in Lawrence E. Sullivan, ed., *Native American Religions: North America.*

For the basic medical ideas, see the article by Hultkrantz cited above under "Introduction."

Chapter 2 / Traditional Medicine in the Northeast

A general picture of Ojibway religion is presented in Christopher Vecsey, *Traditional Ojibwa Religion and Its Historical Changes.* There is no monograph on Cree religion in the Woodlands area.

Ideas of disease and shamanism may be found in Diamond Jenness, *The Ojibwa Indians of Parry Island: Their Social and Religious Life;* and in John A. Grim, *The Shaman: Patterns of Siberian and Ojibway Healing.*

There are several good works on the Ojibway medicine society. See, for instance, W. J. Hoffman, "The Midéwiwin or 'Grand Medicine Society' of the Ojibwa"; and Ruth Landes, *Ojibwa Religion and the Midewiwin.*

Chapter 3 / Traditional Medicine on the Northwest Coast

The main sources on the Tlingit are Aurel Krause, *The Tlingit Indians;* John R. Swanton, *Social Condition, Beliefs, and Linguistic Relationship of the Tlingit Indians;* and Frederica de Laguna, *Under Mount Saint Elias: The History and Culture of the Yakutat Tlingit.* An important article on Tlingit doctors is Frederica de Laguna, "Tlingit Shamans."

The Coast Salish Indians are discussed in H. G. Barnett, *The Coast Salish of British Columbia;* Wilson Duff, *The Upper Stalo Indians;* Hermann Haeberlin and Erna Gunther, *The Indians of Puget Sound;* and Marian W. Smith, *The Puyallup-Nisqually.*

Descriptions of the Spirit Canoe ceremony are contained in a classic paper by Herman Haberlin, "SbEtEtda'q: A Shamanistic Performance of the Coast Salish"; and in Wolfgang G. Jilek, *Indian Healing: Shamanic Ceremonialism in the Pacific Northwest Today.*

Chapter 4 / Traditional Medicine on the Plains

The information on Plains Shoshoni culture and religion is based on my field research, 1948–58. My material is, with some few exceptions, not yet published. Some of my published papers can be found in my book *Belief and Worship in Native North America.* A general description of Shoshoni religion is presented in Hultkrantz, *Native Religions of North America,* pp. 36–84.

The standard monograph on the Arapaho is A. L. Kroeber, *The Arapaho.* The Arapaho Spirit Lodge session, observed in my own field research in 1955, has been discussed in a general and psychological setting in Hultkrantz, *Belief and Worship in Native North America,* pp. 61–90. The parent Lakota ceremony is analyzed in Luis S. Kemnitzer, "Structure, Content, and Cultural Meaning of *yuwipi:* A Modern Lakota Healing Ritual."

The Pawnee religious and medical beliefs are accounted for in James E. Murie, *Ceremonies of the Pawnee;* and in Gene Weltfish, *The Lost Universe.*

Chapter 5 / Traditional Medicine of the Southeast

The general cultural and religious background of the Cherokee is given in John R. Swanton, "Aboriginal Culture of the Southeast"; and in W. H. Gilbert, "The

Eastern Cherokees." Cherokee origin myths are contained in James Mooney, "Myths of the Cherokee."

On diseases provoked by animals, see Calvin Martin, *Keepers of the Game: Indian-Animal Relationships and the Fur Trade*, pp. 128ff. Compare, however, the different view in W. C. Sturtevant, "Animals and Disease in Indian Belief."

For the Cherokee doctor and his medicine books, see James Mooney, "The Sacred Formulas of the Cherokees"; James Mooney and F. M. Olbrechts, *The Swimmer Manuscript;* and J. F. and A. G. Kilpatrick, *Notebook of a Cherokee Shaman.*

Chapter 6 / Traditional Medicine in the Southwest

The main monograph on Pueblo religion and medicine is Elsie Clews Parsons, *Pueblo Indian Religion.* The whole southwestern area has been comprehended in Ruth M. Underhill's instructive *Ceremonial Patterns in the Greater Southwest.*

Zuni culture and religion have been described in Matilda Coxe Stevenson, "The Zuñi Indians." Important aspects of F. H. Cushing's writings on the Zuni are found in *Zuñi: Selected Writings of Frank Hamilton Cushing.*

Zuni religion and ceremonialism have been analyzed in three papers by Ruth Bunzel: "Introduction to Zuñi Ceremonialism," "Zuñi Katchinas," and "Zuñi Ritual Poetry." F. H. Cushing is the author of "Zuñi Fetiches." There is an outline of Zuni religion in Hultkrantz, *Native Religions of North America*, pp. 86–124.

The Navajo literature is rich. A good introduction to Navajo religion and medical thinking is Gary Witherspoon, *Language and Art in the Navajo Universe.* Other valuable volumes are Sam D. Gill, *Songs of Life: An Introduction to Navajo Religious Culture;* and Guy H. Cooper, *Development and Stress in Navajo Religion.*

Among works directly concerned with our text should be mentioned Clyde Kluckhohn, "Navaho Morals"; Gladys A. Reichard, *Prayer: The Compulsive Word;* and Sam D. Gill, "Prayer as Person: The Performative Force in Navajo Prayer Acts."

For cosmological healing among the Navajo, see Charles C. Case, "Blessing Way: The Core Ritual of Navajo Ceremony"; Charlotte J. Frisbie and David P. McAllester, eds., *Navajo Blessingway Singer: The Autobiography of Frank Mitchell, 1881–1967;* and Leland C. Wyman and Flora L. Bailey, *Navaho Upward-Reaching Way.*

The Pima and Papago culture and religion are recorded in Frank Russell, *The Pima Indians;* and Ruth M. Underhill, *Papago Indian Religion.*

The disease treatment is accounted for in Donald M. Bahr et al., *Piman Shamanism and Staying Disease;* and in Donald M. Bahr, "Pima and Papago Medicine and Philosophy."

Chapter 7 / Medicine in New Religions

Literature on prophets and movements discussed in the text can be found in M. H. Deardorff, "The Religion of Handsome Lake"; Paul Bailey, *Wovoka: The Indian Messiah;* Weston La Barre, *The Peyote Cult;* and Edgar E. Siskin, *Washo Shamans and Peyotists: Religious Conflict in an American Indian Tribe.* In connection with the sweat lodge movement, see Ivan A. Lopatin, "Origin of the Native American Steam Bath."

Chapter 8 / Transcultural Medical Relations

For a general introduction, see Charles John Erasmus, "Changing Folk Beliefs and the Relativity of Empirical Knowledge"; David Landy, "Role Adaptation: Traditional Curers under the Impact of Western Medicine"; and Wolfgang G. Jilek, "Native Renaissance: The Survival and Revival of Indigenous Therapeutic Ceremonials among North American Indians."

On investigations of different tribes in the modern process, see W. K. Powers, *Beyond the Vision: Essays on American Indian Culture* (pp. 126ff. on the Lakota); Wallace Black Elk and William S. Lyon, *Black Elk: The Sacred Ways of a Lakota;* Don Handelman, "Transcultural Shamanic Healing: A Washo Example"; Raymond D. Fogelson, "Change, Persistence, and Accomodation in Cherokee Medico-magico Beliefs"; D. E. Young et al., "A Cree Healer Attempts to Improve the Competitive Position of Native Medicine"; and Stephen J. Kunitz, *Disease, Change, and the Role of Medicine: The Navajo Experience.*

Conclusions

The following titles may be referred to: L. G. Moses, *The Indian Man: A Biography of James Mooney,* p. 48; and Sol Tax, "Animistic and Rational Thought.

Bibliography

Adair, John. "Physicians, Medicine Men, and Their Navaho Patients," in I. Galdston, ed., *Man's Image in Medicine and Anthropology*, pp. 237–57. New York: International Universities Press, 1963.

Bahr, Donald M. "Pima and Papago Medicine and Philosophy," in *Handbook of North American Indians*, vol. 10, pp. 193–200. Washington, D.C.: Smithsonian Institution, 1983.

Bahr, Donald M., Juan Gregorio, David I. Lopez, and Albert Alvarez. *Piman Shamanism and Staying Disease*. Tucson: University of Arizona Press, 1974.

Bailey, Paul. *Wovoka: The Indian Messiah*. Los Angeles: Westernlore Press, 1957.

Barnett, H. G. *The Coast Salish of British Columbia*. Eugene: University of Oregon Press, 1955.

Benedict, Ruth F. *Patterns of Culture*. London: Routledge, 1946.

———. *Zuni Mythology*. 2 vols. Columbia University Contributions to Anthropology 21. New York: Columbia University Press, 1935.

Black Elk, Wallace, and William S. Lyon. *Black Elk: The Sacred Ways of a Lakota*. San Francisco: Harper & Row, 1990.

Bourke, John G. *On the Border with Crook*. New York: Charles Scribner's Sons, 1891.

Brown, Jennifer S. H., and Robert Brightman. *"The Orders of the Dreamed": George Nelson on Cree and Northern Ojibwa Religion and Myth, 1823*. Winnipeg: University of Manitoba Press, 1988.

Bunzel, Ruth. "Introduction to Zuñi Ceremonialism," *47th Annual Report of the Bureau of American Ethnology*, pp. 467–544. Washington, D.C., 1932.

———. "Zuñi Katcinas," *47th Annual Report of the Bureau of American Ethnology*, pp. 837–1086. Washington, D.C., 1932.

———. "Zuñi Ritual Poetry," *47th Annual Report of the Bureau of American Ethnology*, pp. 611–835. Washington, D.C., 1932.

Burgesse, J. Allan. "The Spirit Wigwam as Described by Tommie Moar, Pointe Bleue," *Primitive Man* 17, nos. 3–4 (1944): 50–53.

Case, Charles C. "Blessing Way: The Core Ritual of Navajo Ceremony," *Plateau* 40–41 (1967–69): 35–42.

Clements, Forrest E. *Primitive Concepts of Disease*. University of California Publications in American Archaeology and Ethnology 32, no. 2. 1932.

Coleman, Sister Bernard. "The Religion of the Ojibwa of Northern Minnesota," *Primitive Man* 10, nos. 3–4 (1937): 33–57.

Cooper, Guy H. *Development and Stress in Navajo Religion.* Stockholm Studies in Comparative Religion 23. Stockholm, 1984.

Cooper, John M. "The Shaking Tent Rite among Plains and Forest Algonquians," *Primitive Man* 17, nos. 3–4 (1944): 60–84.

Cushing, Frank Hamilton. *Zuñi: Selected Writings of Frank Hamilton Cushing.* ed. J. Green. Lincoln: University of Nebraska Press, 1979.

———. "Zuñi Fetiches," *2nd Annual Report of the Bureau of American Ethnology,* pp. 9–45. Washington, D.C., 1883.

d'Azevedo, Warren L. "Washoe," in *Handbook of North American Indians,* vol. 11, pp. 466–98. Washington, D.C.: Smithsonian Institution, 1986.

Deardorff, M. H. "The Religion of Handsome Lake," *Bulletin 149 of the Bureau of American Ethnology,* pp. 77–108. Washington, D.C., 1951.

de Laguna, Frederica. "Tlingit Shamans," in *The Far North: 2000 Years of American Eskimo and Indian Art,* ed. Henry B. Collins, pp. 227–79. Bloomington: Indiana University Press, 1977.

———. *Under Mount Saint Elias: The History and Culture of the Yakutat Tlingit,* part 2. Smithsonian Contributions to Anthropology 7. Washington, D.C.: Smithsonian Institution, 1972.

Densmore, Frances. *Chippewa Customs,* Bulletin 86 of the Bureau of American Ethnology. Washington, D.C.. 1929.

Dewdney, Selwyn. *The Sacred Scrolls of the Southern Ojibway.* Toronto and Buffalo: University of Toronto Press, 1975.

Duff, Wilson. *The Upper Stalo Indians.* Victoria: British Columbia Provincial Museum, 1952.

Eliade, Mircea. *Shamanism: Archaic Techniques of Ecstasy.* New York: Bollingen Foundation, 1964.

Elmendorf, W. W. "Soul Loss Illness in Western North America," *Proceedings of the International Congress of Americanists* 29, no. 3 (1952): 104–14.

Erasmus, Charles John. "Changing Folk Beliefs and the Relativity of Empirical Knowledge," *Southwestern Journal of Anthropology* 8 (1952): 411–28.

Fogelson, Raymond D. "Change, Persistence, and Accommodation in Cherokee Medico-magical Beliefs," in W. N. Fenton and John Gulick, eds., *Symposium on Cherokee and Iroquois Culture,* pp. 215–25. Bulletin 180 of the Bureau of American Ethnology. Washington, D.C., 1961.

Frisbie, Charlotte J., and David P. McAllester, eds. *Navajo Blessingway Singer: The Autobiography of Frank Mitchell, 1881–1967.* Tucson: University of Arizona Press, 1978.

Garro, L. C. "Resort to Folk Healers in a Manitoba Ojibwa Community," *Arctic Medical Research,* 47, suppl. 1 (1988): 317–20.

Gilbert, W. H. "The Eastern Cherokees," *Bulletin 133 of the Bureau of American Ethnology,* pp. 169–414. Washington, D.C., 1943.

Gilfillan, Joseph Alexander. "The Ojibways in Minnesota," *Collections of the Minnesota Historical Society* 9 (1901): 55–128.

Gill, Sam D. "Prayer as Person: The Performative Force in Navajo Prayer Acts," *History of Religions* 17, no. 2 (1977): 143–57.

———. *Songs of Life: An Introduction to Navajo Religious Culture.* Iconography of Religions 10, no. 3. Leiden: E. J. Brill, 1979.

Grim, John A. *The Shaman: Patterns of Siberian and Ojibway Healing*. Norman: University of Oklahoma Press, 1983.

Gurt, Carl Johan. "Fältnoteringar från Nordamerikas nordvästkust," in *Svenska Amerikanistsällskapets Årsskrift* [1989], pp. 18–28. Uppsala: Svenska Amerikanistsällskapet, 1990.

Haeberlin, Herman. "SbEtEtda'q: A Shamanistic Performance of the Coast Salish," *American Anthropologist* 20, no. 3 (1918): 249–57.

Haeberlin, Hermann, and Erna Gunther. *The Indians of Puget Sound*. University of Washington Publications in Anthropology 4, no. 1. Seattle, 1942.

Hallowell, A. Irving. *The Role of Conjuring in Saulteaux Society*. Publications of the Philadelphia Anthropological Society 2. Philadelphia, 1942.

———. "Sin, Sex and Sickness in Saulteaux Belief," *British Journal of Medical Psychology* 18 (1939): 191–97.

———. "The Spirits of the Dead in Saulteaux Life and Thought," *Journal of the Royal Anthropological Institute* 70, no. 1 (1940): 29–51.

Handelman, Don. "Transcultural Shamanic Healing: A Washo Example," *Ethnos* 32 (1967): 149–66.

Harner, Michael J. *The Way of the Shaman*. San Francisco: Harper & Row, 1980.

———, ed. *Hallucinogens and Shamanism*. New York: Oxford University Press, 1973.

Hartmann, Horst. *Die Plains- und Prärieindianer Nordamerikas*. Berlin: Museum für Völkerkunde, 1973.

Hilger, Sister M. Inez. *Chippewa Child Life and Its Cultural Background*. Bulletin 146 of the Bureau of American Ethnology. Washington, D.C. 1951.

Hittman, Michael. *Wovoka and the Ghost Dance*. Carson City, Nev.: Grace Dangberg Foundation, 1990.

Hoffman, W. J. "The Midéwiwin or 'Grand Medicine Society' of the Ojibwa," *7th Annual Report of the Bureau of American Ethnology*, pp. 145–300. Washington, D.C.: Smithsonian Institution, 1891.

Holmberg, H. J. *Ethnographische Skizzen über die Völker des russischen Amerika*. Helsingfors: Finnish Society of Sciences, 1855.

Hoppál, Mihály, and Otto von Sadovszky, eds. *Shamanism: Past and Present*. 2 vols. Istor Books 1. Budapest: Ethnographic Institute, 1989.

Hultkrantz, Åke. *Belief and Worship in Native North America*. Syracuse: University of Syracuse Press, 1981.

———. "The Concept of the Soul Held by the Wind River Shoshone," *Ethnos* 16, nos. 1–2 (1951): 18–44.

———. "The Concept of the Supernatural in Primal Religion," *History of Religions* 22, no. 3 (1983): 231–53.

———. "A Definition of Shamanism," *Temenos* 9 (1973): 25–37.

———. "Ecological and Phenomenological Aspects of Shamanism," in V. Diószegi and M. Hoppál, eds., *Shamanism in Siberia*, pp. 27–58. Budapest, 1978.

———. "Health, Religion, and Medicine in Native North American Traditions," in Lawrence E. Sullivan, ed., *Healing and Restoring: Health and Medicine in the World's Religious Traditions*, pp. 327–58. New York: Macmillan, 1989.

———. *Native Religions of North America*. San Francisco: Harper & Row, 1987.

———. "The Origin of Death Myth as Found among the Wind River Shoshoni Indians," *Ethnos* 20, nos. 2–3 (1955): 127–36.

————. "The Peril of Visions: Changes of Vision Patterns among the Wind River Shoshoni," *History of Religions* 26, no. 1 (1986): 34–46.

————. "The Problem of Christian Influence on Northern Algonkian Eschatology," *Studies in Religion* 9, no. 2 (1980): 161–83.

————. "The Shaman and the Medicine-Man," *Social Science & Medicine* 20, no. 5 (1985): 511–15.

Jenness, Diamond. *The Ojibwa Indians of Parry Island: Their Social and Religious Life.* Bulletin 78 of the Canada Department of Mines. Ottawa, 1935.

Jilek, Wolfgang G. *Indian Healing: Shamanic Ceremonialism in the Pacific Northwest Today.* Surrey, B.C.: Hancock House Publications, 1982.

————. "Native Renaissance: The Survival and Revival of Indigenous Therapeutic Ceremonials among North American Indians," *Transcultural Psychiatric Research Review* 15 (1978): 117–47.

Kemnitzer, Luis S. "Structure, Content, and Cultural Meaning of *yuwipi*: A Modern Lakota Healing Ritual," *American Ethnologist* 3, no. 2 (1976): 261–80.

Kenton, Edna, ed. *The Jesuit Relations and Allied Documents.* New York: Vanguard press, 1954.

Kilpatrick, A. G. *Notebook of a Cherokee Shaman.* Smithsonian Contributions to Anthropology 2, no. 6. Washington, D.C. 1970.

Kinietz, W. Vernon. *Chippewa Village.* Bulletin 25 of the Cranbrook Institute of Science. Bloomfield Hills, Mich., 1947.

————. *The Indians of the Western Great Lakes, 1615–1760.* Occasional Contributions from the Musuem of Anthropology of the University of Michigan 10. Ann Arbor, 1940.

Kluckhohn, Clyde. "Navaho Morals," in Vergilius Ferm, ed., *Encyclopedia of Morals*, pp. 383–90. New York: Philosophical Library, 1956.

Kohl, J. G. *Kitschi-Gami oder Erzählungen vom Obern See.* 2 parts. 1859. Reprint. Graz: Akademische Druck- und Verlagsanstalt, 1970.

Krause, Aurel. *The Tlingit Indians.* German original 1885. Trans. Erna Gunther. Seattle: University of Washington Press, 1956.

Krause, Aurel, and Arthur Krause. *Zur Tschuktschen-Halbinsel und zu den Tlinkit-Indianern 1881/82.* Berlin: Dietrich Reimer, 1984.

Kroeber, Alfred L. *The Arapaho.* 1902–7. Reprint. Lincoln: University of Nebraska Press, 1983.

————. *Handbook of the Indians of California.* Bulletin 78 of the Bureau of American Ethnology. Washington, D.C., 1925.

Krusche, Rolf. "The Wabeno Cult as an Adversary of the Midewiwin," in Pieter Hovens, ed., *North American Indian Studies: European Contributions*, pp. 77–98. Göttingen: Edition Herodot, 1981.

Kunitz, Stephen J. *Disease, Change, and the Role of Medicine: The Navajo Experience.* Berkeley and Los Angeles: University of California Press, 1983.

La Barre, Weston. *The Peyote Cult.* 4th ed. Hamden, Conn.: Archon Books, 1975.

————. "Primitive Psychotherapy in Native American Cultures," *Journal of Abnormal and Social Psychology* 24 (1947): 294–309.

Landes, Ruth. *Ojibwa Religion and the Midewiwin.* Madison: University of Wisconsin Press, 1968.

Landy, David. "Role Adaptation: Traditional Curers under the Impact of Western Medicine," *American Ethnologist* 1, no. 1 (1974): 103–27.

Leacock, Eleanor. "Seventeenth-Century Montagnais Social Relations and Values," in *Handbook of North American Indians,* vol. 6, pp. 190–95. Washington, D.C.: Smithsonian Institution, 1981.

Leh, Leonard L. "The Shaman in Aboriginal North American Society," *University of Colorado Studies* 21 (1934): 199–263.

Leighton, A. H., and D. C. Leighton. *Gregorio, the Hand-trembler: A Psycho-Biological Study of a Navaho Indian.* Papers of the Peabody Museum of American Archaeology and Ethnology 40. Cambridge, Mass.: Harvard University Press, 1949.

Lopatin, Ivan A. "Origin of the Native American Steam Bath," *American Anthropologist* 62 (1960): 977–93.

Mandelbaum, David G. "The Plains Cree," *Anthropological Papers of the American Musuem of Natural History* 37, part 2. New York, 1940.

Martin, Calvin. *Keepers of the Game: Indian-Animal Relationships and the Fur Trade.* Berkeley and Los Angeles: University of California Press, 1978.

Merriam, Alan P., and W. L. d'Azevedo. "Washo Peyote Songs," *American Anthropologist* 59, no. 4 (1957): 615–41.

Mooney, James. "Myths of the Cherokee," *19th Annual Report of the Bureau of American Ethnology,* part 1, pp. 3–548. Washington, D.C., 1900.

———. "The Sacred Formulas of the Cherokees," *7th Annual Report of the Bureau of American Ethnology,* pp. 301–97. Washington, D.C., 1891.

Mooney, James, and F. M. Olbrechts. *The Swimmer Manuscript.* Bulletin 99 of the Bureau of American Ethnology. Washington, D.C., 1932.

Moses, L. G. *The Indian Man: A Biography of James Mooney.* Urbana: University of Illinois Press, 1984.

Murie, James E. *Ceremonies of the Pawnee.* 2 vols. Ed. Douglas R. Parks. Smithsonian Contributions to Anthropology 27. Washington, D.C., 1981.

Paper, Jordan. "'Sweat Lodge': A Northern Native American Ritual for Communal Shamanic Trance," *Temenos* 26 (1990): 85–94.

Parker, Arthur C. "The Code of Handsome Lake," in William N. Fenton, ed., *Parker on the Iroquois.* Syracuse: Syracuse University Press, 1968.

Parks, Douglas R., and Waldo R. Wedel. "Pawnee Geography, Historical and Sacred," *Great Plains Quarterly* 5, no. 3 (1985): 143–76.

Parsons, Elsie Clews. *Hopi and Zuñi Ceremonialism.* Memoir 39 of the American Anthropological Association. Menasha, Wis., 1933.

———. *Pueblo Indian Religion.* 2 vols. Chicago: University of Chicago Press, 1939.

Powers, William K. *Beyond the Vision: Essays on American Indian Culture.* Norman: University of Oklahoma Press, 1987.

———. *Yuwipi: Vision and Experience in Oglala Ritual.* Lincoln: University of Nebraska Press, 1982.

Ray, Verne F. "Historic Backgrounds of the Conjuring Complex in the Plateau and the Plains," in Leslie Spier, A. I. Hallowell, and S. S. Newman, eds., *Language, Culture, and Personality: Essays in Memory of Edward Sapir,* pp. 204–16. Menasha, Wis.: Sapir Memorial Publication Fund, 1941.

Reichard, Gladys A. *Navajo Medicine Man.* New York: J. J. Augustin, 1939.

———. *Prayer: The Compulsive Word.* Monographs of the American Ethnological Society 7. New York, 1944.

Rogers, S. L. "Disease Concepts in North America," *American Anthropologist* 46 (1944): 558–64.

Russell, Frank. *The Pima Indians.* 1908: Reprint. Tucson: University of Arizona Press, 1975.

Schultes, Richard E. "The Appeal of Peyote *(Lophophora Williamsii)* as a Medicine," *American Anthropologist* 40 (1938): 698–715.

Siskin, Edgar E. *Washo Shamans and Peyotists: Religious Conflict in an American Indian Tribe.* Salt Lake City: University of Utah Press, 1983.

Smith, Harlan I. "Certain Shamanistic Ceremonies among the Ojibwas," *American Antiquarian and Oriental Journal* 18 (1896): 282–84.

Smith, Marian W. *The Puyallup-Nisqually.* New York: Columbia University Press, 1940.

Spencer, Robert F., Jesse D. Jennings, et al. *The Native Americans.* New York: Harper & Row, 1965.

Steinbring, Jack H. "Saulteaux of Lake Winnipeg," in *Handbook of North American Indians,* vol. 6, pp. 244–55. Washington, D.C.: Smithsonian Institution, 1981.

Stevenson, Matilda Coxe. "The Zuñi Indians," *23rd Annual Report of the Bureau of American Ethnology,* pp. 13–608. Washington, D.C., 1904.

Stewart, Omer C. *Peyote Religion: A History.* Norman: University of Oklahoma Press, 1987.

Sturtevant, William C. "Animals and Disease in Indian Belief," in Shepard Krech III, ed., *Indians, Animals, and the Fur Trade,* pp. 177–88. Athens: University of Georgia Press, 1981.

Sullivan, Lawrence E., ed. *Native American Religions: North America.* New York: Macmillan, 1989.

Swanton, John R. "Aboriginal Culture of the Southeast," *42nd Annual Report of the Bureau of American Ethnology,* pp. 673–726. Washington, D.C., 1928.

———. *Social Condition, Beliefs, and Linguistic Relationship of the Tlingit Indians.* 1908. Reprint. New York: Johnson Reprint Corporation, 1970.

Tax, Sol. "Animistic and Rational Thought," *Kroeber Anthropological Society Papers* 2 (1950): 1–5.

Teicher, Morton I. "Windigo Psychosis," *Proceedings of the American Ethnological Society,* pp. 1–129. Seattle: University of Washington Press, 1960.

Underhill, Ruth M. *Ceremonial Patterns in the Greater Southwest.* Monographs of the American Ethnological Society 13. New York, 1948.

———. *Papago Indian Religion.* New York: Columbia University Press, 1946.

Vecsey, Christopher. *Traditional Ojibwa Religion and Its Historical Changes.* Philadelphia: American Philosophical Society, 1983.

Voget, Fred. *The Shoshoni-Crow Sun Dance.* Norman: University of Oklahoma Press, 1984.

Weltfish, Gene. *The Lost Universe.* New York: Basic Books, 1965.

Wheatley, Paul. *The Pivot of the Four Quarters.* Chicago: Aldine Publishing, 1971.

Witherspoon, Gary. *Language and Art in the Navajo Universe.* Ann Arbor: University of Michigan Press, 1977.

Wolfson, Evelyn. *From the Earth to Beyond the Sky: Native American Medicine.* Boston: Houghton Mifflin, 1992.

Wyman, Leland C. *Navaho Indian Painting: Symbolism, Artistry, and Psychology.* Boston: Boston University Press, 1959.

Wyman, Leland C., and Flora L. Bailey. *Navaho Upward-Reaching Way.* University of New Mexico Bulletin. Albuquerque, 1943.

Yazzie, Ethelou, ed. *Navajo History,* vol. 1. Tsaile, Ariz.: Navajo Community College Press, 1971.

Young, D. E., G. Ingram, and L. Swartz. "A Cree Healer Attempts to Improve the Competitive Position of Native Medicine," *Arctic Medical Research* 47, suppl. 1 (1988): 313–16.

Index

Health/Medicine and the Faith Traditions